# JAPAN'S
# POSTWAR
# HISTORY

Also by Gary D. Allinson

*Japanese Urbanism: Industry and Politics in Kariya, 1872–1972*

*Political Dynamics in Contemporary Japan*
(coeditor with Yasunori Sone)

*Suburban Tokyo: A Comparative Study in Politics and Social Change*

*The Columbia Guide to Modern Japanese History*

# JAPAN'S
# POSTWAR
# HISTORY

### SECOND EDITION

## GARY D. ALLINSON

CORNELL UNIVERSITY PRESS
ITHACA, NEW YORK

First published 2004 by Cornell University Press
First printing, Cornell Paperbacks, 2004

*Library of Congress Cataloging-in-Publication Data*
Allinson Gary D.
Japan's postwar history / Gary D. Allinson.
p.   cm.
Includes index.
ISBN 978-0-8014-8912-9
(pbk: alk. paper)
1. Japan—History—1945–   I. Title.
DS889.A59   1997
952.04—dc20
96-38163

Printed in the United States of America

Cornell University Press strives to use environmentally responsible suppliers and materials to the fullest extent possible in the publishing of its
books. Such materials include vegetable-based, low-VOC inks and acid-
free papers that are recycled, totally chlorine-free, or partly composed of
nonwood fibers. For further information, visit our website at www
.cornellpress.cornell.edu.

3   5   7   9   Paperback printing   10   8   6   4

# Contents

# Acknowledgments

I EXPRESS MY THANKS PUBLICLY TO four individuals and one funding source whose assistance has been indispensable to the completion of this book. Edward Partt, a historian of modern Japan at the College of William and Mary, provided detailed, perceptive commentary and criticism on the whole of the manuscript. Katy Strzepek, a recent graduate of Kenyon College, gave me an incisive and extremely helpful response to several key chapters. Roger Haydon, acquistions editor at Cornell University Press, offered professionally deft and personally enthusiastic support from beginning to end. And my wife, Pat, read and discussed the manuscript with me at what must have seemed to her endless lengths. The Northeast Asia Council of the Association for Asian Studies granted me an essential Professional Travel Award underwritten with funds from the Japan-U.S. Friendship Commission. To all these individuals and groups, I express my sincere and heartfelt appreciation.

For their generous assistance in providing illustrations, I am extremely grateful to my wife, Pat, and to Gail Lee Bernstein of the University of Arizona, Irving I. Gottesman and Pat Schnatterly of the University of Virginia, Robert J. Smith of Cornell University, and James Zobel of the MacArthur Memorial.

Names of Japanese personalities appear in the text according to Japanese style, with family names first, followed by given names.

G.D.A.

## ACKNOWLEDGMENTS TO SECOND EDITION

I express my continued appreciation to Roger Haydon at Cornell University Press, for his gentle prodding and his unflagging enthusiasm; to my wife Pat, for her calm support and diplomatic criticism; and to an anonymous reader at the press, for shrewd evaluations and incisive recommendations.

# Chronology

1932    Right-wing terrorists assassinate finance minister, head of Mitsui combine. Japan establishes puppet state in Manchuria. Young military officers assassinate prime minister in coup attempt. Political parties yield prime ministership to military leaders.

1933    Japan secedes from League of Nations. Expansion of heavy and military industries spurs economic recovery.

1934    Poor harvests; rural social problems deepen.

1935    Population: 69 million. Average life expectancy (men): 47 years. Right-wing groups intensify ideological attacks on opponents.

1936    Young military officers assassinate Finance Minister Takahashi and others in coup attempt. Japan concludes defense accord with Germany and Italy.

1937    Japan begins invasion of China; captures Nanking. Establishes Cabinet Planning Board.

1938    National Mobilization Act passes. General Araki becomes minister of education. Japanese forces occupy Wuhan cities and Canton.

1939    Japanese military advances to Hainan Island. Japanese army engages Russian forces in Nomonhan Incident. First price control laws go into effect.

1940    Patriotic organizations spring up. Japan concludes Tripartite (Axis) Pact with Germany and Italy; invades French Indochina.

1941    Japan signs neutrality agreement with USSR. General Tojo forms first cabinet. Japanese military land on Malay Peninsula.

Japan draws United States into Pacific War with attack on Pearl Harbor.

1942      Japan's economic production begins to falter; industrial control associations are formed. Japan's southern expansion is arrested with Allied victory in Battle of Midway. Many city dwellers leave for rural areas after first bombing attacks.

1943      Domestic consumption levels decline steadily. Ministry of Munitions is established. Schoolchildren are conscripted for wartime production.

1944      Allied forces recapture Philippines. United States begins incendiary bombing raids on Japanese cities. Allies initiate postwar planning; Bretton Woods agreement is signed.

1945      Population: 72 million. U.S. bombing campaign intensifies; millions flee Japanese cities. Japanese military puts up suicidal defense of Pacific Islands. United States drops A-bombs on Hiroshima and Nagasaki. Emperor Hirohito announces surrender. Allied Occupation begins; first reforms are implemented.

1946      Political purge is initiated. Ministries of Army and Navy are abolished. Land reforms begin. Emperor Hirohito renounces divine status. New constitution is promulgated.

1947      General Strike is prohibited. First Socialist-led government is formed. New constitution is implemented. United States announces Truman Doctrine and Marshall Plan for Europe. Ministry of Labor is established. Local Autonomy Law is enacted.

1948      Reverse course begins in earnest. National Civil Service Law is passed; abolishes right of public workers to strike.

1949      Dodge Line is implemented. Ministry of Commerce and Industry becomes Ministry of International Trade and Industry (MITI). Financial reforms are implemented under Shoup Plan. Yen stabilized at 360 to 1 dollar.

1950      New labor federation (Sohyo) is formed. Korean War begins, stimulating economic revival. "Reds" are purged. Local Civil Service Law is enacted.

1951      San Francisco Peace Treaty and U.S.-Japan Security Pact are signed.

1952      Allied Occupation officially ends.

1953     Government eases restrictions imposed by Occupation authorities.

1954     Self-Defense Forces are established under law.

1955     Population: 89 million. Economic Planning Agency is established. Japan enters the General Agreement on Tariffs and Trade (GATT). Period of high-speed growth begins in earnest. Japan Housing Corporation is created. Liberal Democratic Party (LDP) is formed.

1956     Japan restores diplomatic relations with USSR; also, enters United Nations.

1957     Kishi Nobusuke becomes prime minister; pursues conservative policy agenda, including discussions about revising constitution.

1958     Sharp partisan conflict over revision of National Police Law.

1959     Democratic Socialist Party (DSP) forms in split from Japan Socialist Party (JSP).

1960     Massive demonstrations against renewal of Security Pact. Kishi cabinet falls; Ikeda Hayato forms new government. Miike Mines strike, longest in postwar era, is settled. Income-Doubling Plan is announced.

1961     Agricultural labor force drops to 29 percent of all workers. Basic Agricultural Law is passed.

1962     Japan signs commercial agreement with People's Republic of China. Exports of industrial machinery surpass textile exports.

1963     Urban overcrowding, traffic congestion, and environmental problems all worsen. Basic Law for Small and Medium Enterprises is passed.

1964     International Olympics are held in Tokyo. Three major firms consolidate as Mitsubishi Heavy Industries. Japan enters International Monetary Fund (IMF) and Organization for Economic Cooperation and Development.

1965     Population: 98 million. Average life expectancy (men): 68 years.

1966     Japan's major auto firms consolidate to compete internationally.

1967     Japan implements capital liberalization. Agricultural employment drops to 19 percent of total. Clean Government Party (CGP) wins first seats in the House of Representatives (HOR).

1968    Japan's GNP rises to second after United States. Japan incurs surplus in trade with United States; long period of trade conflict ensues. Era of the Three Cs: car, air-conditioner, and color television.

1969    Japan becomes top TV maker in the world. Urban Redevelopment Law is passed. Japan struggles with rice surpluses.

1970    World Exposition is held in Osaka.

1971    United States agrees to return Okinawa to Japan.

1972    Yen appreciates to 272: $1 in wake of Nixon Shock. Prime Minister Tanaka Kakuei normalizes relations with People's Republic of China.

1973    Oil prices rise sharply; worldwide economic slowdown ensues. Large-Scale Retail Stores Law is passed.

1974    Acute inflation. LDP slips in House of Councillors (HOC) election; period of conservative-progressive parity ensues. National Land Agency is established. Growth in real GNP declines slightly.

1975    Population: 112 million. Textile and shipbuilding industries are cut back. Unemployment rises. Progressive governors are returned in Tokyo, Osaka, and Kanagawa. Public-sector labor unions conduct eight-day, right-to-strike work action.

1976    Lockheed scandal is unveiled; former Prime Minister Tanaka is arrested. LDP retains narrow majority after HOR election. People born since 1945 exceed half of Japan's population.

1977    Trade disputes with United States over TV exports. LDP rebounds in HOC election. Unemployed exceed one million. Record trade surpluses with the European Community. Japan's average life expectancy (men: 73 years) surpasses Sweden's to become longest in world.

1978    MITI sets voluntary restraints on auto exports. Yen rises to 185: $1. Structurally Depressed Industries Law is passed.

1979    Controversies over compensation of local government officials. Ohira Masayoshi presides over close LDP victory in HOR election. Japan settles textile trade dispute with United States.

1980    Ohira dies ten days before HOR election; LDP wins with sympathy vote.

1981    Commission on Administrative Reform is established; privatization agenda is pursued; Special Administrative Reform Law is passed. Japan concludes voluntary auto export restraint agreement with United States.

1982    Health Law for the Elderly is passed. Commission on Administrative Reform recommends privatization of three public corporations. Nakasone Yasuhiro begins five-year term as prime minister; era of conservative policy initiatives ensues.

1983    LDP bargains to retain slim majority in HOR. Structural Reform Law for Specified Industries is passed.

1984    Nissan announces plans to build factory in England. Japan concludes agreements on citrus and meat imports with United States. Elderly people (over age 65) reach 10 percent of population.

1985    Population: 121 million. Toyota announces plans to build factories in United States and Canada. Equal Employment Opportunity Act is passed. Japan concludes agreement with United States on steel exports. National Pension Law is revised. Telecommunications and tobacco monopolies are privatized.

1986    New head of JSP, Doi Takako, becomes first woman to lead a political party in Japanese history. LDP wins large majorities in HOR and HOC elections. Japan reaches semiconductor trade agreement with United States.

1987    New union federation (Rengo) is formed. Japan National Railway is broken up and privatized. Defense expenditures surpass symbolic 1 percent of GNP. Unemployment rate exceeds 3 percent.

1988    Japan has record trade surplus with United States. Japan's foreign direct investment is highest in world for third consecutive year. Japan reaches agreement with United States on construction industry disputes.

1989    Emperor Hirohito dies. Showa Era ends; Heisei Era begins. Recruit scandal tarnishes many politicians. Consumption tax is implemented. Political instability increases: three LDP prime ministers serve in just one year, and LDP loses HOC election.

1990    Speculative bubble bursts. Japan retreats from overseas investments. LDP wins narrow majority in HOC election.

1991　Japan becomes embroiled in disputes over Gulf War, at home and abroad.

1992　Longest postwar economic downturn begins in earnest. Japan New Party (JNP) is formed; runs candidates in HOC election.

1993　Shinseito and Sakigake parties are created. LDP loses majority in HOR election. Non-LDP coalition government takes office. Japanese units participate in U.N. peace-keeping effort in Cambodia.

1994　Major political reform bill passes. Two non-LDP coalition governments fall. LDP returns to power in a Socialist-led coalition government. DSP, CGP, JNP, and Shinseito are dissolved; merge to create Shinshinto. Japan drops voluntary auto export restraints.

1995　Population: 126 million. Average life expectancy (males): 76 years. Recession persists; real per capita income stagnates; yen reaches temporary postwar high of 79: $1. LDP falls well short of majority in HOC election.

1996　LDP forms a new government after winning near majority in HOR election.

1997　Broad economic crisis strikes East and Southeast Asia; Japan's economic problems worsen. Consumption tax rises to 5 percent.

1998　Japan's economic problems deepen further; Diet passes legislation to stimulate economy. LDP falls short of majority in HOC election. Democratic Party of Japan forms.

1999　Diet reinstates "Hinomaru" as national flag and "Kimigayo" as national anthem.

2000　LDP forms new, coalition government after falling short of clear majority in HOR election.

2001　Prime Minister Koizumi Jun'ichiro begins tenure with approval ratings near 80 percent.

2002　Average land prices fall for eleventh consecutive year.

# JAPAN'S
# POSTWAR
# HISTORY

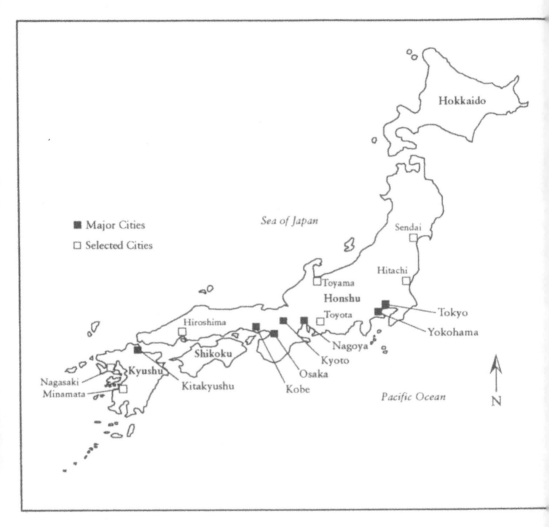

# Introduction

IMAGES OF CONTEMPORARY JAPAN grow daily more familiar. The high-speed Bullet Train has become a standard symbol of Japan's fast-moving society. We think of Japanese families as toting expensive cameras and driving luxury Toyotas. The crowded subways of central Tokyo appear on the evening news, swallowing up commuters rushing home from high-paying jobs in sleek skyscrapers. Magazines depict flocks of adolescents in designer clothing strolling the fashionable shopping districts of Harajuku and the Ginza.

If we were to step back just a bit into the Japanese past, however, we would encounter a significantly different set of images. In the early 1930s, Japan was a relatively poor agrarian society with most people residing in farming villages. A typical family, which we will call the Satos, had six members and spanned three generations. At age sixty-five, Grandfather was the sole member of the oldest generation in the Sato household. His forty-year-old son and his son's thirty-eight-year-old wife made up the second generation, and their three children, at ages fourteen, twelve, and ten, formed the third and youngest.

The Sato family had been farmers in the same village for more than a century. Their origins were hazy, but it was known for certain that the grandfather had inherited two acres of land from his father when he died in 1895. Working hard to manage the trust bestowed by his ancestors, Grandfather expanded the family holdings gradually over the following three decades. When he withdrew from the house headship in 1925 and passed the family lands on to his son, they included three paddy fields producing rice and four dryland plots given over to vegetable cultivation and mulberry trees. As the new head of the household, the younger Sato had to strive diligently just to preserve the holding in the face of a severe agricultural depression that had driven prices down and debt up.

To maintain the farm and to sustain the six-member family, the father and mother put in exceptionally long days throughout the year. Mother commonly arose at 4 A.M. to glean firewood from the forested hillsides nearby and to pick the wild mushrooms that she sold to earn extra money. Father waited until 5:30 to get up, finding the extra sleep necessary after spending eleven-hour days doing backbreaking labor in the fields. When they were not working to produce the annual crop of rice or to cultivate their dryland plots, they wove reed mats that also brought in a little cash income.

Leisure time was scarce. It coincided mainly with two holidays, the Festival of the Dead (*obon*) during the late summer and the New Year's observations in early January. During each of these periods, most farm families took a few days off from their demanding labors. Once in a rare while, the family stole a day or two to participate in a village festival or to visit a shrine in a nearby town. They visited the shrine not as devoted parishioners on a regular basis, but as supplicants who occasionally sought the blessings of the gods or as participants in seasonal rituals.

The Sato family lived in a home built by Grandfather's father in the late nineteenth century. Like most thatch-roofed farmhouses constructed in that period, it covered about eleven hundred square feet and was divided into six different spaces by thin, sliding paper doors. Each person had only one or two changes of clothing and almost no possessions, so most rooms were sparsely furnished. During the cold winter months, the family either huddled around the open fire in the kitchen area or wrapped themselves in blankets and used small charcoal braziers to keep their toes and fingers warm. They drew their water from the village well, used a privy behind the house, and read at night under the two electric lights they had recently installed when a local firm ran a power line into the village.

Electricity had also made radio reception possible for the first time, but the only receiver in the village sat proudly in the home of the largest landowner. He was kind enough to invite his closest neighbors over to hear a major broadcast now and then, although he seldom gave anyone a ride in his new car, the only one in the village. The locals preferred to walk or to ride their bikes, or so they said; by comparison with pulling their rice bales to market on hand-drawn carts, strolling and biking seemed easy.

Rice and other cereal grains were the staples of the Sato family's diet. They each consumed about twenty-two hundred calories a day in 1932, about three-fourths of them from carbohydrates. Protein intake was very low and came mainly in the form of soybean products and an occasional piece of fish. Beef, pork, and poultry were luxuries, milk and cheese nonexistent. The Satos grew vegetables for themselves, and there were a few apple and peach trees that provided fruit in season. A diet so limited in quality, quantity, and variety left everyone in the family susceptible to health problems, and pulmonary and intestinal disorders were common. The diet also had its effects on bodily stature. Like most men his age, the younger Mr. Sato was five feet, two inches tall, and he weighed 120 pounds.

When health problems arose, the family panicked, with good reason. The nearest trained physician practiced in a town forty-five minutes away by bike, bus, and train. The family carried no health insurance, and the government provided no public health services in their rural district. Constantly in debt, the Satos had to borrow money if someone needed medical care. In fact, they still owed money for bills incurred when a fourth child had contracted tuberculosis and died in infancy.

Nor could the family count on public programs to provide an income in retirement. Everyone understood that families themselves were Japan's social security system in old age. That is why Father had dissuaded his oldest son from going on to middle school after he had completed his elementary education. The son, like his father and grandfather before him, was expected to assume the headship of the Sato house, manage the family property, and care for his mother and father in their old age. Savings and retirement annuities were essentially unknown in this agrarian economy. The ongoing operations of the household as a socioeconomic unit provided whatever resources there were to keep young and old alive and well.

One aim of this book is to offer a vivid portrait of Japan's recent past and its effects on families, groups, and communities. The hypothetical Sato family conveys a sense of history as it was lived and experienced. Similar vignettes appear in subsequent chapters, to illustrate how the sweeping changes that Japan has undergone during the postwar era have affected families in various walks of life. These vignettes lend immediacy and tangibility to the complex forces—international as well as national—that have shaped recent developments in Japan.

The overall purpose of this book is to provide a comprehensive synthesis of the first half-century of Japan's postwar history, one that integrates analysis of political, economic, and social topics. This is not primarily a political narrative of the years since 1945. The volume does contain such a narrative, but it also analyzes political relationships, institutions, and behavior by addressing local politics as well as national and by treating both the citizenry and political elites. The book examines policy making and interest-group behavior and, when events require and when documentation permits, military affairs and civil administration.

Economic aspects of Japan's recent history receive equal attention, because they have been so instrumental in shaping Japan's evolution. This book discusses the often dramatic changes that have taken place in Japan's agricultural, manufacturing, and service sectors; it also depicts those changes in the context of a sometimes turbulent international economy. It devotes ample attention to large, well-known enterprises, such as Toyota and Hitachi, that have led postwar developments. It also examines the small and medium-sized enterprises that have played an important role in providing jobs, promoting production, and stimulating demand. In addition, the book discusses Japan's constantly changing economic policies and its role as an international trading power.

Families, groups, and communities are just three topics germane to social history which are examined here. Given the overriding importance of economic growth in Japan's recent past, I assess the gradual changes in the material standard of living and in the behavior of Japanese as consumers. The chapters analyze how these changes have brought higher incomes, improved diets, better health and housing, and longer life expectancies to a large share of the Japanese populace. These chapters also describe the gradual shifts in the roles of women in

Japanese society and the enduring importance of education as a social institution. Two changes of more recent vintage, a growth in the numbers of the elderly and in the amount of leisure activity, come under discussion in concluding chapters.

The intentional brevity of this book prevents treatment of some topics, such as religion, high culture (figurative arts, drama, music, and poetry), intellectual history, and diplomatic affairs. Few of these topics have been studied in detail for the postwar era. When they have been, the Suggested Readings identify major works that rectify omissions. The book does, however, make a slight bow toward one product of high culture, prose literature in the form of novels, novellas, and short stories. I sometimes rely on such works to convey the mood of the times or to provide a more vivid commentary on human affairs than is otherwise available in conventional sources. Using literature as a substitute for other forms of empirical data is controversial, because literature is not "truthful" in the way that history is alleged to be truthful or factual. Literature does, however, possess a verisimilitude, or truthful*ness*, that is valuable for purposes of historical description. This attribute justifies its use here.

Literature receives attention in this book for a second reason: to encourage readers to examine in more detail works treated only briefly below. A large body of Japanese writing is now available in English translation, and it deserves a greater audience than it has attracted. Thus the section on literature in the Suggested Readings cites not only the more realistic works mentioned but also other translations. Together they encompass a range of aesthetic, quasi-autobiographical, and imaginative prose forms which only hints at the versatility of postwar Japanese authors.

This book treats the political, economic, social, and, to a lesser extent, cultural history of Japan not only during the postwar period's first half century. It examines the thirteen years before 1945 as well, owing to the widespread and deep-seated continuities that link prewar and postwar Japan. Continuities were carried by individuals and embedded in institutions. Japanese men and women who lived through World War II, the bombing campaigns on the home front, and the slow postwar recovery found their lives permanently altered by their experiences. Their ideas, affiliations, occupations, status, and life chances were thereafter strongly influenced by what happened to them during the 1930s and 1940s. For a majority of the Japanese people, these experiences had a powerful bearing on how they responded to the political changes and economic opportunities that appeared in the 1950s and after. For elites, wartime and early postwar experience often determined which policies they promoted, how they exercised their influence, and for whom they pursued power.

Continuities were also embedded in institutions. Japanese society had assumed a certain form before the war began in earnest, and even in the face of massive devastation and vigorous reform efforts, it was obliged almost by necessity to revert to that form once recovery began. A strong national bureaucracy; political parties; interest groups; elite universities; sexual roles; major industrial, financial, and commercial firms; and patterns of business relationships that throve before and during the war often endured after it in remarkably similar forms. Consequently, the personal experiences and institutional developments of the 1930s had lasting effects on many changes that occurred in the postwar era.

Owing in part to these facts, this history of postwar Japan begins in 1932. That year marked the inauguration of high imperialism for Japan with the imposition of control over the puppet state of Manchuria. In the same year, the political parties that had once presided over parliamentary governments went into a long retreat, and the government steadily fell under the influence of the military and its collaborators. These are the kinds of political events that often define historical periods, and they contribute to that purpose here.

The crucial reasons for beginning this book in 1932, however, rest on economic considerations. A long agricultural depression and a nagging industrial depression drew to an end around 1932. In the following year, a brief but significant period of economic expansion began under the stimulus of new policies advocated by the minister of finance. His policies provoked broad social changes and structured developments in the industrial economy until the 1970s. Unfortunately, they also underwrote militarization and eased Japan toward war. The years between 1932 and 1945 thus conferred opportunities, imposed burdens, and imparted legacies that profoundly influenced Japan's postwar history, as Chapter 1 demonstrates.

There is a final reason for beginning a history of postwar Japan in

1932, and that is to situate the Allied Occupation in a properly historical context. Noon, August 15, 1945, when Emperor Hirohito announced Japan's surrender, is often taken as the zero hour in Japan's postwar era. That moment allegedly marks a sharp disjunction between what happened before (war and defeat) and what transpired after (democracy and development). In the eyes of many, both Japanese and American, what came after was decisively shaped by the victors and the events of the Allied Occupation, which lasted until 1952. The foreignness of the Occupation and its emphasis on demilitarizing and democratizing Japan all reinforce the sense of disjunction.

There is no denying the influence of the Allied Occupation. As Chapter 2 illustrates, its reforms were broad and deep. Yet some of those reforms had prewar antecedents and Japanese advocates. Moreover, many reforms were carried out with the support and participation of Japanese citizens, and a few were obstructed by them. The Japanese themselves—whether acting as adroit politicians, struggling workers, or landless farmers—played a significant role in determining just how Japan evolved during the Occupation, not to mention thereafter. Given the perspective and knowledge available to us now, we are obliged to concede the limits of Occupation authority and to highlight the significance of Japanese participation. Failure to strike a proper balance in our assessment will only magnify the misunderstandings that seem to plague American perceptions of Japan and thus, also, U.S.-Japanese relations.

In addition to presenting a synthetic analysis of Japan's postwar history which begins in 1932, this volume sets forth a personal interpretation of midcentury Japan. Based on nearly four decades of experience in visiting Japan periodically and in reading, teaching, writing, and conducting research about Japan regularly, my interpretation rests on three crucial assumptions. They support the conceptual architecture of the book as a whole and the organization and arguments of individual chapters. It will be useful, however, to state them explicitly at the outset and to highlight their interpretive implications.

The first assumption is that a proper understanding of Japan's postwar history must be situated in a context that is both cross-national and international. Specialists in the field of Japanese studies often treat Japan as distinctive, if not unique. There are good reasons for this approach, but it can inhibit understanding. We might, in contrast, approach the study of Japan comparatively. For example, by recognizing the many parallels between Japan's postwar experiences and those of Germany, we can enhance our appreciation of the histories of both nations. Those parallels exist owing to the international context in which Japan and Germany, as well as other nations, have evolved. Although both countries clung to many earlier customs and traversed the course of postwar history in different ways, they were also subject to powerful international forces that shaped their evolutions in a similar manner. The influence of American economic policies and middle-class lifestyles and the opportunities and constraints of an interdependent global economy were just a few of such forces.

The international context of postwar history has strongly influenced my interpretation of Japan's high-speed growth between 1955 and 1974. Observers have stressed various single causes for Japan's successes during that era. Some have advocated a Confucian affection for harmony and consensus as the principal cause. Others have asserted the political significance of the developmental state, and still others have pointed to the Japanese system of labor-management relations. In contrast, I have explained Japan's rapid economic growth as the product of a complex set of factors—historical and contemporary, domestic and international—that conjoined momentarily in a manner that Japan was able to exploit effectively. Knowing that Germany, and other nations too, made similar advances during the same era in a somewhat different manner enables us to highlight the distinctiveness of the Japanese achievement. Chapter 3 strives to do just that, although without making explicit and systematic cross-national comparisons.

The second assumption shaping my approach is that monocausal explanations, or interpretations that rely on one cause, cannot do justice to the dynamism and complexity of Japan's postwar history. Monocausal explanations lead to understanding that is partial in two senses of the word. They illuminate only part of the whole, and they are heavily partisan. To cite but one example, theories about the developmental state based on studies of the Ministry of International Trade and Industry (MITI) have served a useful purpose in advancing knowledge about bureaucratic politics and economic growth. Yet when carried to an extreme, such theories neglect the influence of economic and legislative power holders and ignore or diminish the significance of additional factors that promoted development. Moreover, those theories explain the events of some periods better than others.

The only antidote to monocausal explanation in a work of synthetic history is multicausal explanation. This book presents an integrated analysis of political, social, and economic phenomena. On occasion it may seem to emphasize the importance of economic issues and thus to embrace a kind of economic determinism. If so, I readily concede that we cannot understand postwar Japan without appreciating the importance of the economic changes it has experienced. Nonetheless, the book does aim to depict the interdependence of social, political and economic factors in Japan's postwar history. The text illustrates how political decisions—especially in the 1930s, the 1950s, and the 1980s—caused economic changes that transformed Japanese society. It also indicates how anxiety over social conditions, such as material deprivation after the 1920s and population changes after the 1970s, seized the attention of the populace and forced politicians and bureaucrats to concentrate on economic issues when making policies. And of course the book demonstrates in many ways how both economic growth and economic recession have caused social dilemmas that power holders have been obliged to address politically.

My third and final assumption it that static and superficial stereotypes of Japan, so common in the United States today, stigmatize the Japanese people and jeopardize our understanding of Japan's history. Superficial stereotypes depict the Japanese as militant aggressors in the 1930s, as economic animals after the 1960s, and as "poor" Japanese in the 1990s. There is perhaps a grain of truth in each of these characterizations, but they seriously distort the complex realities of these periods and the diversity of the Japanese responses to them. Static stereotypes consign the Japanese to one simplistic mold, condemn Japan as an immutably traditional society, and deny the persistent dynamism inherent in Japan's history.

In an often understated and implicit manner, my interpretation confronts and revises stereotypes like these. It rejects the adage that all Japanese are alike. It repudiates the claim that Japanese are conformist and imitative by nature. It impugns the notion of a rich Japan with poor Japanese. And it demonstrates that Japanese history is constantly subject to a dynamic tension. Japan is always changing, often in contradictory directions. My interpretation strives to convey a sense of this dynamic tension by contrasting the euphoric period of high-speed growth (discussed in Chapter 3) with the following decades of difficult readjustment (examined in Chapters 4 and 5).

The rapid, complex, and sometimes contradictory evolution of Japan's postwar history defies easy generalization. Nonetheless, a synthetic analysis of the political, economic, and social history of the postwar era suggests one overarching claim: a steady expansion and diffusion of wealth has undermined older forms of status and fragmented political power. War and the Occupation played their roles in eliminating the rigidly hierarchical society that prevailed in Japan before 1945, but rising affluence has contributed to a steady blurring of the status attributes that once divided Japan's social strata. Wealth, along with more widespread education, has also contributed to an expansion of the political resources which enables more individuals and groups to exercise greater influence than ever before. This expansion of political resources seems to have gradually undermined the hegemony of the Liberal Democratic Party and left Japan with no clear political direction or partisan authority.

Far from creating a homogeneous society that moves in lock step according to the whims of "Japan, Inc.," the first sixty years of Japan's postwar history produced a volatile society subtly unraveling under the impact of affluence and the individual freedoms, self-indulgence, and political resources that it conferred. To understand the processes that brought Japan's postwar history to that point, we begin Chapter 1 by returning to the year 1932.

# CHAPTER ONE

# Antecedents, 1932–1945

MORE THAN TWO GENERATIONS HAD passed since Japan's modern revolution, the Meiji Restoration of 1868, but many residues of old regimes still lingered in 1932. They included an imperial court, which traced its mythical origins to 660 B.C.; an aristocracy dating from the eighth century; and a military led by descendants of the *samurai*, warriors who first appeared in the twelfth century. In addition, agrarian customs of earlier centuries shaped the behavior of at least half of the nation's people—those who resided in small villages and country towns. Even in the cities some neighborhoods reflected the urban lifestyles, or *chonin bunka*, of the Tokugawa period (1600–1868).

These residues of the past survived amid a society bustling with change in the name of progress. The imperial household invested in the latest financial schemes. Aristocratic courtiers competed for status against industrialists and financiers. Samurai descendants studied the latest military technology through postings to London, Washington, and Berlin. Farmers used techniques that dated from the fifteenth century but faced price competition caused by changes in international markets. And however many pockets of chonin-like culture survived in metropolitan areas, they were overshadowed by new industrial quarters, thriving commercial districts, and growing residential suburbs.

The new and the old meshed uncomfortably in 1932 within a society marked by inequality. During the next few years, a brief economic boom propelled the growth of cities, industries, and middle-class habits, while ancient institutions won a new lease on life and the agrarian populace receded. By the late 1930s, however, many people struggled to sustain a livelihood in an unstable political and economic environment. The strongest forces in Japan, the military and their supporters, had by then set the nation on a course toward war. The conflicts and tensions that grew under the influence of military adventurism guaranteed insecurity at home as well as abroad.

## INEQUALITY

Inequality was pervasive in prewar Japan. A hereditary aristocracy ensured a sense of hierarchy reinforced throughout society by differences in status, wealth, and power. Hierarchy was reflected in the political arena as well. Inherited power still weighed heavily in a country where parliamentary institutions were both young and fragile. Economic institutions, too, were unequal in their influence, owing to pronounced differences in size, resources, and profits. We begin this account of late prewar Japan by examining snapshots of the many facets of inequality in social, political, and economic institutions. Only then can we assess how they changed under the impact of economic recovery and military expansion.

### Social Hierarchy

The imperial household occupied the apex of the social hierarchy in prewar Japan. Before 1868 the status of the Japanese monarch had waxed and waned according to his relations with other ruling groups. The Restoration of 1868 was conducted in the name of the emperor, and it established an imperial government that vested supreme power in the imperial institution. Between 1868 and 1945, therefore, the imperial household was given a formal political standing and a quasi-religious aura that set it above all other institutions in Japanese society. The Japanese government also bestowed vast landholdings on the emperor and managed his financial affairs so that his household possessed an investment portfolio that was one of the largest in the country and oriented toward lucrative firms in Japan's Asian colonies.

Immediately below the imperial institution in the hierarchy of social status was the aristocracy. Initially formed in 1884, this body consisted of three subgroups. Members of a hereditary court aristocracy traced their origins to the Heian period (794–1185). For centuries they had held positions at court, intermarried with imperial and courtly families, and preserved the customs of Japan's aristocratic culture. A second subgroup consisted of descendants of the regional lords, or *daimyo*, of the Tokugawa era. Approximately 260 daimyo had shared political authority until 1868 with the preeminent military house, the Tokugawa. They had been displaced by events following the Restoration. When the government conferred aristocratic titles on them in 1884, it restored them to a position of status and power and also purchased their political support. The third subgroup consisted of men who had demonstrated their merit during and after the Restoration. Some of them were descendants of the samurai class; others were sons of merchant households or farm families. They won noble status by distinguished performance in government, the military, business, and universities.

The roughly one thousand families in the new aristocracy derived their high social status from patents of nobility and proximity to the imperial household. In addition, they enjoyed some assurance of wealth by virtue of their noble rank and guarantees of educational privilege through attendance at the Peers School. The male heads of aristocratic households were also eligible to serve in the upper house of the national legislature, the House of Peers. This aristocracy exercised a near monopoly over status, wealth, and power.

Below the aristocracy, status was conferred in a descending hierarchy of subtle gradations. The marks of social status were far clearer in rural than in urban Japan. In the countryside, the most prominent families controlled large landholdings and other investments. Resident for generations, they had long participated in local affairs. New arrivals to a rural village or a provincial town who possessed greater wealth and better educations might challenge them for preeminence, but longevity and family standing outweighed such claims.

A substantial group of respectable, small-holding farm families formed a middle stratum in the countryside. They, too, might have been resident in their villages for generations, but they differed from the old-line elite in having smaller farms, few if any outside investments, lower levels of education, and modest prestige. Families like our hypothetical Sato family were representative of households in this stratum.

At the base of rural society was a large body of landless or nearly landless tenants. Some of them organized sporadically in the 1920s and

**1. Plowing a field, 1936.** *Tilling a small plot with horse-drawn wooden implements, a farmer wears a hat and back protector made from reeds to shield himself from rain.* (Courtesy of Robert J. Smith.)

1930s to express their demands for more equality and better treatment, with occasional success. Most of them, however, struggled to earn a living under conditions of pronounced deference and dependence. Their betters regarded them with a mixture of emotions that ranged from understanding generosity to contemptuous pity.

In urban Japan, status was more fluid and ambiguous. Old wealth sustained the high status of families that had lived for generations in downtown districts. But new wealth counted for more in the cities than in the countryside. Families that had made fortunes in banking, cotton spinning, coal mining, and food processing enjoyed high status. So did those in the growing ranks of white-collar professionals. The most prestigious white-collar workers were university graduates who staffed the national civil service, the nation's new banks and insurance companies, its international trading firms, and its hospitals and universities. These individuals were laying the foundation for a "middle class" whose membership would explode after the 1960s. In the early 1930s, however, they were a thin urban stratum that occupied a narrow band just below the upper reaches of the social pyramid.

In addition to the aristocracy and these economically favored groups, a large body of people in a middling status populated the cities. The owners of small retail shops and craft establishments were numerous. So were families that owned small manufacturing firms and wholesale enterprises. White-collar workers in menial clerical positions were members of this group as well. Diligence, frugality, and upward striving characterized the behavior of many in these callings. Some had the talent and luck that produced success and upward mobility, but the odds were against most of them.

At the bottom of urban society was an even larger mass of persons whose status was often so low that society almost failed to mark it. Many were young people. They included women who worked for short tenures as household servants and men who held jobs in retail shops, wholesale firms, or factories. Others were recent migrants from rural Japan employed in factories, transport companies, and construction firms. Still others were members of a social group known as *burakumin*. Treated as outcasts, they worked in such low-status occupations as tanning and street cleaning. The big cities also attracted many people who survived by using their wits, their bodies, or both in the large entertainment districts that catered to a male clientele.

There were clear differences in income among urban residents. Laborers earned about ¥ 80 per month and salaried workers about ¥ 90, but the poorest urban families had to survive on much less. White-collar workers with secure jobs as teachers and government employees made around ¥ 140 per month, and upper-level managers in major firms earned more than ¥ 200. Finally, there were those who earned ¥ 1,000 per month, or more. They included some members of the aristocracy, leaders of major business enterprises, high-ranking officers in the army and navy, and successful private investors. The most privileged thus enjoyed monthly incomes that were twenty times, or more, larger than those of poor urban families.

Expenditures offer another perspective on wealth differences among urban households. The share of income spent on food is one index of economic well-being. Contemporary middle-class American families commonly spend less than 20 percent of their monthly outlays on food. Japanese laborers in 1932, with incomes of ¥ 80 per month, spent one-third or more on food, whereas salaried workers spent around 25–30 percent. Both groups spent an additional 25 percent on clothing and shelter, so neither could purchase much beyond necessities. Secure white-collar workers and upper-level managers had enough disposable income to make discretionary purchases. And the wealthiest families lived in a world apart. They owned manicured estates staffed with hired servants, and their sons studied at Oxford, vacationed in Europe, and yachted on the Mediterranean.

Poverty was visible and widespread in some sections of every city, but it was endemic in the countryside. Farm families had an average monthly cash income of only ¥ 60 in 1932. In addition, a typical farm family had two more mouths to feed—six instead of four. Farm families consumed directly some of what they produced, so they did not have to buy everything they ate; but they did have to buy processed foods and fish. An average farm family had to devote 60 percent of its income— or more—to food, clothing, and shelter. These averages, of course, obscure differences among farm families. Most landlords lived well and some middling farm families lived comfortably, but the poorest tenant households lived in misery.

Many families in rural Japan lived at or below the edge of poverty in the early 1930s. High levels of household debt, the sale of daughters into prostitution, widespread malnutrition and disease, high rates of infant mortality, the small stature of army recruits from rural areas, and the very low level of discretionary purchases all underscore the deprivation that plagued millions of poor, rural families. It is not surprising that the average life expectancy at birth for males during the early 1930s was about forty-six. Japan was a relatively poor country in 1932, and its rural tenantry was especially poor.

A poignant illustration of the lives of poor tenants appears in Nagatsuka Takashi's novel *The Soil*. Nagatsuka was a landowner who based his work on personal observations of life in a village north of Tokyo during the early twentieth century. *The Soil* depicts how the death of a wife, mother, and crucial income earner drastically undermines the social and economic well-being of her surviving husband and two children. The husband is obliged to exploit his young daughter

**2. Pulling a cart, 1936.** *A hand-drawn cart, like this one being used to deliver rice bales, was the principal vehicle used for short haulage in both rural and urban areas until well into the 1950s.* (Courtesy of Robert J. Smith.)

unmercifully, preventing her from leading her own life. He is also forced into petty theft, but to no avail. Despite continual backbreaking labor, conditions so worsen that members of the family are barely able to keep the clothes on their backs.

The collective memory of this rural experience of poverty exerted a powerful influence on political policy and human behavior in the post-war era. Among the poor who suffered deprivation directly, the experience accustomed them to an ethic of sacrifice. At the same time, it fed a desire for the material comforts that economic growth provided. Future leaders who witnessed this distress drew another lesson from it. They determined to pursue government policies after the war which would diminish agrarian poverty and cushion the ill effects of city growth on rural Japan.

### Political Inequalities

Poverty accompanied low status and wealth attended high, so social standing and material well-being often correlated in prewar Japan. The same was not always true of power, at least in national politics. Many wealthy, high-status individuals did influence the nation's affairs, but so did some individuals of modest status and minimal wealth. The latter were often lifelong party politicians who represented rural districts in the lower house of the national legislature. They had enjoyed a brief heyday of parliamentary influence under cabinet governments during the 1920s. By the early 1930s, however, they were waging a losing contest for power with competitors who represented the interests of the aristocracy, the bureaucracy, the military, and big business.

The contest for political power during the 1930s took place within a complex structure of formal and informal institutions. Under the Meiji Constitution of 1889, the emperor exercised all legislative, executive, and judicial powers. Theoretically, his authority was supreme. In practice, he had to delegate his powers to loyal public servants whom he appointed to carry out his will. The formal structure of national government laid out in the constitution consisted of an advisory privy council, a cabinet and a prime minister, a bicameral legislature, a judiciary with limited powers of constitutional review, and a military with substantial autonomy. In addition, a carefully selected body of national civil servants—the bureaucracy—emerged to administer the day-to-day affairs of state.

In addition to these formal structures of state authority, informal bodies arose to exercise significant powers. One of these was the *genro*, or elder statesmen. Originating in the 1890s, the genro helped to integrate a potentially fragmented government. Composed of high-ranking state officials who had served during the two decades that preceded 1900, the elder statesmen relied primarily on their experience, stature, and connections for their influence. For nearly forty years they selected prime ministers, determined cabinet ministers, and provided essential advice to the emperor. Only one genro was alive in the early 1930s, however, and his powers were waning. Inheriting some of the influence of the elder statesmen was another informal body called the *jushin*. With a shifting, indeterminate membership, this group functioned during the 1930s to advise the emperor and to nominate candidates for prime minister.

Political power at the national level was fragmented and diffuse. No single element within the constitutional order, either formal or informal, exercised a decisive influence in 1932. Rather, the occupants of the various sites of power struggled among themselves for ascendancy. The aristocracy pursued its interests through one body of the legislature, the House of Peers, and, on occasion, through direct service in the cabinet or on advisory bodies. The military exercised its influence within the government through two seats on the cabinet and through private audiences with the emperor conducted by the leaders of its general staff. Elected politicians relied on the other body of the legislature, the House of Representatives, and on the cabinet as their forums of influence, as did members of big business. And the national civil servants in the bureaucracy, although often competing among themselves, strove to impose some measure of coherence and integration on national policy.

Inequality was an inherent characteristic of national politics because it was an almost exclusively elite preserve. Aristocrats, generals, admirals, bureaucrats, prominent businessmen, and scions of powerful provincial families dominated political competition at the center. This structure of power provided few if any places for members of the urban middle class, farmers of middling status, industrial laborers, or tenant farmers—and no place at all for women. Some of these groups were effectively disfranchised by election laws that awarded the vote only to male citizens over the age of twenty-five. Others took little interest in national politics. And still others operated within systems of patron-client relations, whereby tenants bowed to the wishes of their landlords and workers followed the lead of their managers.

At lower levels of the political system, inequality was a characteristic feature, too. Japan was subdivided into forty-six prefectures, or *ken*, subnational administrative divisions that were like American states in some ways. Prefectures did not enjoy the rights and autonomy of American states, however; instead, they operated as an arm of a centralized national government. Their governors were appointed civil servants doing a tour of duty as members of the Ministry of Home Affairs. Other high-ranking prefectural administrators, such as department heads, were also Home Ministry officials on temporary assignment. The ministry's reach extended deeply into the administrative affairs of many cities, towns, and villages as well. The carefully regulated elective politics that did emerge in Japan's municipalities was ordinarily the preserve of local elites, usually prominent landlords or merchants, who exercised a long-standing, almost hereditary claim on local office.

Reflecting and reinforcing these inequalities in power was a national system of public education. The nation's schools had taken shape during the late nineteenth century through a process of trial and error overseen by the Ministry of Education. By the 1930s the schools provided a diversity of training that effectively served the needs of a rapidly industrializing society. The system guaranteed almost everyone a minimum level of education. It also provided a smaller portion of the populace with some additional training, often of a vocational sort, and it offered a tiny segment of the populace a highly advanced education.

By the 1930s nearly everyone of school age got at least six, sometimes eight, years of elementary education. The purpose of this training was to impart a basic literacy in language and numbers and to inculcate the terms of citizenship as they were defined in prewar Japan. Citizenship entailed loyalty to the emperor and nation; duty to family, parents, and community; and sincerity in all one did. Most elementary school leavers went directly into the labor force, as mill hands, household servants, urban laborers, or farm workers.

Upon finishing eight years of schooling, a small portion of each cohort pursued additional training. There were numerous options. For those wanting advanced academic training, the next step was a middle school education that ran for five years. For those with vocational interests, special schools provided further training in agricultural, commercial, and industrial skills. Normal schools and technical institutes were venues for training teachers and engineers, respectively. And private colleges prepared students for careers in business, journalism, and law.

The most advanced course of education was reserved for a talented few. It carried middle school graduates into higher schools and universities. Until 1918 a mere eight public higher schools operated much like exclusive private preparatory schools in the United States do today, to prepare their students for an elite university education. (By 1940 the eight had grown to thirty-two.) Higher school graduates completed their formal education at one of nine imperial universities when they were in their early twenties. The imperial universities in Tokyo and Kyoto were the oldest and most prestigious among these, and a degree from either school almost ensured success in later life. Success was attributable both to the quality and stature of these universities and to the rarity of their degrees.

Although this system of education offered some people of modest origins an opportunity for upward mobility, it essentially reinforced existing patterns of status. The middle schools were the bottleneck to an advanced education for those of modest means. They were often private institutions located in cities and towns, so a combination of tuition and boarding fees put their costs out of reach for many. Sometimes, however, an indulgent uncle, an enthusiastic village council, or an opportune scholarship financed a talented student at middle school. Having completed this stage, students could count on government support to underwrite their years in higher school and university. In these ways some members of poor, low-status groups did win degrees from Tokyo and Kyoto and go on to distinguished careers in business, education, and public service. They were relatively rare, however, among the descendants of samurai families, prominent merchants, large landlords, and newly rich urbanites who dominated the graduating classes at imperial universities.

The education system functioned in a different manner to reinforce yet another inequality within Japanese society, sexual inequality. The prestige tracks in Japanese education were reserved almost exclusively for male students. The higher schools and universities were solely male bastions. So were the technical institutes. The normal schools accepted women, but men predominated. Women enjoyed some opportunities for advanced education beyond higher elementary school. They could attend more advanced schools for women, and there were a few women's colleges. But the curriculum at those institutions emphasized domestic skills and allegedly more feminine callings, such as literature, in contrast to law and engineering.

In all of these respects, the school system was shaping women's lives according to prevailing gender norms. The phrase *ryosai kenbo* encapsulated the standard expectations for women. First articulated in the late nineteenth century by the male leaders of the new state, ryosai kenbo prescribed a dual role for women as "good wives" and "wise mothers." Most men and many women thought that a woman's place was in the home and that her primary obligations were to her husband and children. While she put her feminine, managerial skills to work in the domestic sphere, her husband could pursue his obligations in the public spheres where labor was paid and politics played out.

However deep and extensive these gender norms were, even in prewar Japan there were women and men who contested them. They did so by writing about alternatives and by organizing to change norms, in women's suffrage movements, for example. Nothing undermined norms more, however, than the realities of daily life. Farm women had long shared the burden of work with their husbands. So, too, had the wives of urban merchants and craftsmen. In the twentieth century, more women entered the work force in other roles. Many took low-paying jobs in textile mills, but others assumed higher-status positions in commerce, finance, and publishing. Though the good-wife, wise-mother ideal still held sway in the 1930s, it faced discomfiting challenges in the form of new ideas, organized resistance, and changing economic opportunities.

### Economic Diversity

Like the political structure in the early 1930s, the economic structure also was beset with inequality. In this realm, inequality arose owing to differences in the scale of enterprises (determined both by the size of a firm's physical plant and the number of workers it employed). Economic inequality was also a function of differences in access to capital, in up-to-date equipment, in wage practices, and in the skills of workers and managers. Observers have often employed these categories—scale, capital, equipment, pay, and skills—to assert that Japan's prewar economy was characterized by its dualism. There were, according to this view, some rich enterprises with large, well-paid work forces in big factories utilizing the latest equipment under the supervision of university-trained managers. They operated in a sea of tiny firms that relied on low-skilled, poorly paid workers using simple tools under the direction of self-trained owner-managers.

Although there is some truth to the image of duality, it is more accurate to envision the structure of Japan's industrial economy in 1932 in terms of a gradation of difference. There were indeed some very large firms and a great many small ones that fit the categories above. There were also, however, many firms in between that combined features of both the large and small firms. Some used advanced technology in small plants employing a few hundred workers to make specialized components for a final producer. This kind of subcontractor was especially common in new industries making aircraft, machine tools, and electric products. There were other small firms with a few score workers who used simple, manual techniques to make low-cost items for domestic or external markets. And there were literally thousands of tiny establishments with only two or three workers. They provided craft items and processed foods that consumers needed on a regular basis, such as pots and pans, door panels and floor mats, and bean curd and condiments. The small and the medium-sized firms dominated the Japanese economy numerically in 1932, and they satisfied almost all domestic demand for household goods, food products, and most other daily necessities.

The large firms enjoyed a prestige out of proportion to their numbers. There were just a few thousand large-scale enterprises, but they employed more than one-tenth of the labor force, and they accounted for an even larger share of the gross domestic product. They were also highly visible because they were often new, large, and different. Many had appeared in the late nineteenth century or during the early twentieth. Some employed tens of thousands of workers in factories that dwarfed rural towns or urban neighborhoods. Many produced modern goods for sale abroad in competition with Great Britain, Germany, and the United States. This large industrial sector consisted of three

subgroups: government enterprises, independent firms, and the
*zaibatsu.*

The national government owned and operated large industrial enterprises, in addition to a national railway system and the country's
telephone and telegraph systems. The most important government-
owned industrial enterprise was Yahata Steel. Built at the end of the
nineteenth century at a site in northern Kyushu, Yahata was among the
top three steel firms in 1932. The government also operated arsenals
and naval shipyards.

Independent firms operated in a wide range of industries, but many
of the largest were textile makers. Most workers in Japan's modern
industrial sector toiled in the humid, noisome factories of the textile
industry in 1932. Centered on the city of Osaka, the industry was noted
for its independent-minded entrepreneurs and for its high profits and
sheer size. Nearly a dozen large textile firms, such as Kanegafuchi
Spinning and Toyo Spinning, each employed tens of thousands of
young women in large mills. They spun yarns and wove fabrics, mainly
from cotton and wool, and a large share of their output was exported
abroad.

The other independent firms specialized in a single product or
product line. Some of these firms were former government enterprises
established after the Meiji Restoration and sold to private buyers in the
1880s. Others were private enterprises established during the twentieth
century by hard-driving businessmen. The largest among them brewed
beer, made steel, manufactured paper, pressed glass, and refined sugar.
They catered to the needs of a modernizing domestic economy and a
growing export trade.

The most prominent and conspicuous large-scale enterprises were
the zaibatsu. This term originated in the early 1900s to describe a
distinctive organization emerging under special legal and economic
circumstances. The zaibatsu were all owned by a family or a family
group that exercised its financial control through a holding company. A
zaibatsu usually consisted of about ten interlinked firms that ordinarily
included a bank, an international trading firm, a real estate entity, an
insurance company, several manufacturing firms, and a mining company. Ownership by the holding company, interlocking directorships,
and cross-holding of shares provided the means for coordinating these
diverse enterprises under the managerial supervision of the holding

company. Zaibatsu formed in part to insulate themselves from the volatility of prewar Japanese capital markets by generating their capital internally. In this way the zaibatsu achieved a high degree of autonomy, which they used to pursue a coordinated strategy of expansion and innovation.

The four most important zaibatsu in 1932 were Mitsui, Mitsubishi, Sumitomo, and Yasuda. Each had a somewhat different history and organization. Mitsui traced its origins to the seventeenth century and the dry goods industry. It was especially strong in finance, trade, and coal mining. The Iwasaki family had formed the Mitsubishi zaibatsu in the 1870s. Mining, shipbuilding, and heavy industry were the mainstays of this enterprise. Like Mitsui, Sumitomo also dated from the Tokugawa era. Its origins as a copper refiner contributed to its stature as a specialist in the metals trades. Yasuda was a product of the late Tokugawa period, when Yasuda Zenjiro laid the foundations for his financial conglomerate as a money lender and banker. There were also a few smaller, less diversified zaibatsu, such as the Asano and Furukawa combines, which had first appeared during the late nineteenth century. During the twentieth century, even newer zaibatsu arose. Often centered on a major firm in a single industry, they included Nippon Chisso in chemicals and Nissan in vehicle manufacturing.

Thus we have an essentially static image of widespread inequality in the Japan of 1932. The distribution of status, wealth, and power fostered clear distinctions within the populace. Educational access and achievement reinforced these distinctions, both among social groups and between the sexes. A polity dominated by elites at both national and local levels further reinforced an inequality that was underpinned by the structure of the economy itself. During the tumultuous 1930s, this society changed dramatically, although it was neither reformed nor revolutionized.

## INSTABILITY

Conventional accounts of Japanese history in the 1930s grant center stage to domestic politics and imperial conquest. These were important matters, but political events and imperial ventures were not the only forces shaping Japanese history during that decade. Economic, social, and ideological changes were also important in determining both short-term events that ended in 1945 and long-term developments extending into the postwar era. From this perspective, the policies adopted to pull Japan out of depression decisively shaped the course of Japanese history after 1932. Indeed, along with an increasingly more bellicose nationalism, economic recovery and its benefits eased the Japanese populace toward acquiescence in imperial expansion in Asia and, eventually, war in the Pacific.

### Economic Recovery

Japan entered the 1930s under the shadow of an extended economic depression. In the modern industrial sector, the depression was a continuation of an economic downturn that had followed World War I. Many Japanese firms had expanded rapidly to meet wartime demand in markets that European combatants were no longer serving. For a brief moment, they reaped high profits. But when the war ended and European suppliers returned, Japanese firms had to undertake deep cutbacks. Some industries needed almost a decade to restore employment to the levels reached by the end of World War I.

In the agricultural sector, the depression arose from a combination of domestic and international causes. Farm prices had begun to fall in Japan as early as the mid-1920s, owing in part to increased imports of rice from Japan's Asian colonies. Farm prices took another plunge in the late 1920s with the onset of a worldwide depression. The sharp drop in silk prices after 1929 was especially damaging to Japan's rural economy, because many families participated in the silk industry as a way to make extra cash. While farm prices fell, so did the prices for products that farmers bought. But farm prices always fell faster and farther. This left many farm families with no recourse but debt.

Under these circumstances, real and disguised unemployment were widespread during the 1920s and early 1930s. Urban workers laid off from their jobs sometimes stayed in the cities and found whatever work they could during the 1920s. For many this meant low-paying jobs in wholesale and retail concerns, where they did what looked suspiciously like make-work. Other redundant workers, however, returned to their home villages, where they traded their labor for food and shelter. But even with an extra hand or two, farm families were hard pressed to feed additional mouths. Many rural households were thus severely stressed.

3. **Carrying mulberry leaves, late 1930s.** *A woman in a Kyushu village uses mulberry leaves to feed silk worms for extra income.* (Courtesy of Robert J. Smith.)

Credit for the policies that finally brought an end to the depression must go in large measure to Finance Minister Takahashi Korekiyo. Several years before John Maynard Keynes articulated the virtues of countercyclical government spending in his famous treatise of 1936, Takahashi adopted such spending in Japan. He persuaded the government to increase public debt in order to boost investment that would stimulate the economy. Beginning in 1933 his policies produced quick results, and Japan emerged from the worldwide depression as early as any nation.

Subsequent budgets called for increased public borrowing to finance further expansion. Because the military was successful in winning control over the lion's share of the increases, much new investment underwrote expansion of heavy industry. Government arsenals absorbed some of these funds, but the private sector also attracted substantial revenues. In 1933 alone, private investment was three times the size of the preceding year, and the modern sector of the Japanese economy embarked on a short period of frenetic growth.

Old zaibatsu, new zaibatsu, independent firms, and a widening range of small and medium-sized enterprises all benefited from Takahashi's policies. The Mitsui enterprise reaped profits by exploiting its strong trading position in Manchuria and by creating new firms in such fields as chemical production. Mitsubishi was already a major shipbuilder; it expanded into the production of aircraft and other commodities purchased by the military. Sumitomo took advantage of its long-standing expertise in metals production to meet surging demand in heavy industry. Yasuda, as a financial combine, played a major role in underwriting such new entities as Hitachi and Nissan, which both benefited from military contracts.

Hitachi and Nissan were just two of many subsequently prominent postwar firms that assumed their corporate shape during this era. Hitachi was founded in 1920 to make mining and electrical equipment. Nissan began in 1928 as a multifaceted venture in heavy industry and vehicle manufacturing. The Toyota auto firm was incorporated in 1937, when it split off from a loom manufacturing company to assume independent form as another vehicle manufacturer. Both Nissan and Toyota became important military suppliers. Two giants of the postwar consumer electric industry also assumed corporate form in the 1930s. Matsushita had been making small electrical items since 1918; in 1935 it incorporated to better manage its growing production in the suburbs north of Osaka. Toshiba assumed its present form in 1939, when two manufacturers of electrical equipment in the Tokyo area combined their operations to serve both a growing consumer market and a thriving military demand. The emergence and expansion of firms like these spurred the transition from an economy based on light industry (textiles and food processing) to one reliant on heavy industry (steel, ships, vehicles, and machines).

Many of the new zaibatsu and independent firms produced large, complex products with numerous components, such as trucks, aircraft, and ships. Rather than make all components under a single enterprise, Japanese managers preferred to subcontract a large share of component manufacturing to smaller firms. This strategy reduced investment costs and increased flexibility. Consequently, small-scale parts suppliers grew in tandem with large-scale final producers. Many smaller firms arose in bustling new industrial zones in the Osaka, Nagoya, and Tokyo regions. Some of them were well integrated into the production processes of the large firms they supplied, through managerial supervision, financial support, and engineering assistance. In other cases, small subcontracting firms sprang up through the initiative of individuals with limited skills and capital but with some contacts and competitive drive.

This sector of the industrial economy was unusually volatile. As it grew rapidly as a whole, many small firms faced high risks of bankruptcy. During the 1930s and early 1940s, the national government came to recognize the significance of this branch of industry. Through the Ministry of Commerce and Industry, the prewar predecessor of the Ministry of International Trade and Industry (MITI), the government adopted policies that assisted small enterprises with financing, acquisition, and marketing. The government's wartime interest in these smaller firms lent them a collective political influence they had seldom enjoyed before and did not hesitate to exploit after the war.

The boom in heavy industry during the 1930s promoted dramatic expansion in some industries that played a major role in the postwar era. To better understand their prewar point of departure, and to situate Japanese industry in the international context of the 1930s, a closer look at the steel industry will prove illuminating. In 1930, Japan produced 2.3 million tons of raw steel. The world's leading producer in that year, the United States, turned out 41.4 million tons. Germany produced 28 percent of the American output; England, 18 percent. Japan's steel output was only 6 percent of American production. In the next decade, Japan built many steel factories and more than tripled its raw steel production. Leading the way was Japan Steel, a private-sector giant created in 1934 when Fuji Steel and some other private firms merged with the government's Yahata Steel. Nonetheless, in 1940 the indices of production for these countries were: United States, 100 (at 60.8 million tons); Germany, 31; England, 22; and Japan, 11.

These figures illustrate two facts about the prewar Japanese economy that demand emphasis. Although Japan had been experiencing discernible economic growth since the late nineteenth century, its modern industrial sector (exemplified by the steel industry) was still significantly smaller in 1940 than the industrial sectors of the United States, Germany, and England. Moreover, with such a small steel-making capacity, Japan was in an exceedingly weak position to challenge the United States in a modern war fought on land and sea and in the air.

Expanding domestic production spurred growth in exports, especially in the textile trades. In 1935, Japan achieved a record level of cotton cloth exports. In the following year it became the world's largest producer of synthetic fibers. As Japan exported more of its goods abroad, however, it encountered increasing opposition from other powers, especially Great Britain and the United States. The world was already dividing itself into a series of autonomous trading blocs, and opposition to its exports encouraged Japan to carve out its own bloc. Its trade sphere in Asia focused initially on its colonies in Korea, Manchuria, and Taiwan. But in the late 1930s Japan expanded its Asian influence southward through military force. By 1939, Japanese political leaders were promoting a Greater East Asia Co-prosperity Sphere, which encompassed Southeast Asia and the Indonesian archipelago.

### Social Dynamics

In addition to diplomatic repercussions, economic recovery in the 1930s promoted extensive social and demographic changes. The rapid expansion of zaibatsu, independent firms, and subcontractors was a powerful magnet drawing workers and their families to the nation's cities. The urban populace increased by almost 50 percent in the five years after 1930, and it had almost doubled by 1940. Most of this growth occurred in or near the largest cities, Tokyo, Yokohama, Nagoya, Osaka, and Kobe. Hundreds of thousands of newcomers arrived yearly in these cities after the early 1930s, pressing boundaries farther outward. Older districts filled, and hundreds of new suburbs sprang up.

Under the impact of this rapid growth, Japanese cities assumed some of the features that characterize them today. Most development was unplanned and uncontrolled. In the worst cases, it led to teeming districts near bays and rivers, overbuilt with factories, warehouses, and cheap lodgings. Government reports and newspaper articles convey some sense of what it was like to live in such districts, but one of the most vivid accounts of life among the urban poor appears in Tomioka Taeko's short story "Facing the Hills They Stand." Tomioka herself grew up in a poor urban neighborhood, so she writes with the authority of a witness to the poverty, ill health, alcoholism, gambling, abuse, and child abandonment that afflicted families in such areas. By employing a simple, clipped language, she effectively portrays the baffled, hapless outlook of people who were passive victims of larger forces they barely understood and seldom controlled. Tomioka may exaggerate the misfortunes that befall the family in her story, which trades in hemp bags and iron scrap, but she has created a moving depiction of the struggle for survival in Japan's chaotic cities during the 1930s and 1940s.

There were other urban areas that took on a much different character. Some districts away from ports and rivers developed also with little planning, but were more hospitable to residential settlement. Good quality, single-family housing might mingle with apartment buildings and scattered, small factories. These areas attracted a mix of residents, drawn from the middle and lower ranks of urban society. The best residential areas were often well planned by large-scale developers. These were situated on higher ground, which offered cooling breezes and pleasant views, and attracted new residents from among the managers of banks, insurance companies, department stores, and manufacturing firms. Steady employment and rising incomes enabled these men to relocate their families in the fashionable suburbs emerging on the periphery of the metropolis, especially near Tokyo and Osaka.

The suburb of Ashiya is one such community. Situated between Kobe and Osaka, Ashiya developed as an upper-middle-class settlement in the 1930s. Tanizaki Jun'ichiro has immortalized its social character during that period in one of Japan's most famous novels, *The Makioka Sisters*. Tanizaki was himself an ardent proponent of suburban living, and his novel is written in part to celebrate the virtues of that life. By contrasting the restrained customs of a declining merchant house in Osaka against the bright, languid elegance of Ashiya, he offers an invaluable depiction of suburban culture, family relations, and changing sexual mores just before the onset of war.

While suburbs grew, the old urban neighborhoods being vacated by the new suburbanites, along with the teeming factory and port districts,

**4. Prewar home interior.** *This main room, like one in the house of a modestly well-off urban family in the 1930s, had reed mat* (tatami) *floors, a brazier* (hibachi) *for heating tea water, a kimono chest* (tansu) *against the right rear wall, and a small writing desk against the rear wall with a religious shrine* (kamidana) *above it.* (Courtesy of Patricia S. Allinson.)

attracted legions of lower-status newcomers. Some were families moving into the largest cities after a brief stay in a provincial town. Others were younger sons and daughters moving directly to the city from rural villages. Still others were families leaving farming to try their luck in the big cities. These new urban arrivals found work in domestic service, textile mills, retail shops, small factories, and construction firms.

For about seven years after 1932, many people like these won jobs that provided low but steady income, and they realized a brief increase in their standard of living. This did not prevent some of them from providing the electoral support for the fledgling Socialist Party. Based primarily in the new industrial districts around Tokyo and Osaka, it won 8 percent of the seats in the lower house election of 1937. Modest improvement in their material conditions may, however, have lulled many of these low-status urban newcomers into oblivious acceptance of the government's policies of continental expansion.

Conditions in rural Japan also began to improve in the mid-thirties after a decade or more of agricultural depression. The departure of some tenant families, along with an accelerated outflow of younger sons and daughters, relieved some of the demographic pressure on scarce resources. At the same time, prices for agricultural goods finally began to rise, owing to increased urban demand. Other prices rose, too, but not as fast. Consequently, more farm families were able to pay off some of their debts, restore a measure of economic stability, and even begin to set aside some savings. Not everyone enjoyed such good fortune, however, and poverty, ill health, poor nutrition, and low levels of consumption continued to plague many families. Among those whose fortunes improved, better material conditions may have promoted rural acceptance of imperial expansion, too.

The market was not the only factor assisting farm families in the 1930s and early 1940s. Recognizing the need for secure food supplies under wartime conditions, and worrying about the quality of rural recruits, the government adopted important new agricultural policies. In the 1930s it began allocating more resources to health and social welfare in rural areas and also extended protection to vulnerable farm tenants. In 1941 the government passed legislation to support the price of rice for producers. The effect of these policies was to improve, however slightly, the material conditions of life for disadvantaged groups in rural Japan and to redress, albeit modestly, the balance of power in favor of middling and lower groups. Large landlords, who found their positions jeopardized by these policies, began to downplay their rural holdings and seek returns from industrial and commercial investments in urban areas. All of these changes anticipated postwar reforms that dramatically altered the composition of wealth, power, and status in the countryside.

### Political Forces

The struggle for power in national politics during this period was characterizd by a seething instability. Between 1932 and 1945 eleven different men formed thirteen cabinets. Most governments served for just a matter of months; only one survived for more than two years. Competition for power among elites was fierce. Party politicians fought against bureaucrats, the military, aristocrats, and most especially themselves. Their bickering led to factional infighting, party splits, and new groupings. The influence of the two major parties, which had alternated in forming cabinets during the 1920s, waned, inhibiting their ability to retain popular support and build elite coalitions. Big businessmen, once members and leaders of political parties, drifted toward other allies. Aristocrats maneuvered among everyone, and the military was in competition against all comers.

The military's combative stance resulted from an aggressiveness deeply tinged with racial overtones. Japanese military officers had grown increasingly isolated from society during the early decades of the twentieth century. They entered early into a training program that separated them from the public educational system and placed them in military academies. From their teens onward, they imbibed the authority and discipline of military life. Army officers in particular learned a strategic approach that emphasized the distinctive spiritual strength of the Japanese fighting man, exemplified in massed attacks with bayonets. Men who drank this ideological brew, and who lived out their adult careers amid other true believers, developed unbending personalities that hampered bargaining in national politics. Nonetheless, in the course of the 1930s, military leaders and a faction of high-ranking bureaucrats gradually joined in coalition to achieve a precarious domination over the national government.

To understand the competition among elites, it is necessary to appreciate the broader political and ideological environment in which their contest for power occurred. Looming over the 1930s was a kind of national euphoria nourished by the conquest of Manchuria. Japan had secured a colonial toehold there in 1906, when it assumed control of the South Manchurian Railway and obtained a leasehold over the Liaotung Peninsula after the Russo-Japanese War. For the next quarter century, Japanese military forces in Manchuria, the Kanto (in Chinese, Kwantung) Army, provoked excuses to expand Japanese jurisdiction in the area. In September 1931, they carried out a series of actions that obliged the Japanese government to recognize a military fait accompli: the Kanto Army had seized control of Manchuria. In 1932, the government formalized its authority by creating the puppet state of Manshukoku (Manchukuo, in Chinese). The euphoria of colonial conquest sprang from a variety of emotions, ranging from quiet national pride in being able to play the European game of imperial expansion to a kind of vulgar, chest-beating chauvinism. The latter sentiment prevailed among younger officers in the army and had been the basis for the insubordinate conduct of field-grade officers whose behavior had brought about the conquest of Manchuria in the first place.

Young officers in the army and navy were also responsible for creating a reign of domestic terror during the 1930s. Associating in a series of shifting groups, they conspired to assassinate government officials and business leaders and plotted to seize control of the government. On separate occasions they succeeded in killing cabinet ministers, the head of the Mitsui combine, and perhaps most fatefully, Finance Minister Takahashi Korekiyo on February 26, 1936. Takahashi had begun to recognize how his prescriptions for economic recovery were playing into the hands of firebrands in the military, and he had been trying to alter his policies. Enraged at his threat to military ascendancy, a conspiracy of young officers eliminated a powerful opponent. By this very action, the military positioned itself for increased influence within the government while intimidating civilian opposition.

Amid such domestic turmoil, anxiety over recovery at home and progress in the colonies fostered xenophobia. Leaders began to feel under pressure from what came to be known as the ABCD encirclement. America, Britain, China, and the Dutch gradually became ogres to those Japanese embracing a resurgent nativism. They thought the

United States was trying to keep Japan out of China and other Pacific markets; they feared British intentions in the lucrative Shanghai area; they worried about a surging Chinese nationalism and the civil strife broiling between the Chinese Communist Party and the Kuomintang; and they resented Dutch possession of valuable natural resources in Indonesia. Combined with the domestic terror fomented by chauvinistic and pro-imperial groups, this xenophobia contributed to a bunker mentality among many Japanese leaders.

Some leaders, General Araki Sadao in particular, were in a unique position to deepen these fears among a broader populace. For nearly two years in the late 1930s, Araki served as the minister of education in two governments. Long before this he had been associated with some of the most chauvinistic younger officers, and he had been an exponent of the Imperial Way. This amorphous group within the military had emphasized a reliance on spirit and distinctive Japanese attributes, rather than modern equipment or stategic planning, as the source of military might. Imperial Way adherents had participated in some of the terrorist assaults during the 1930s, and they were firm advocates of Asian expansion. As education minister, Araki exploited his control of the nationwide system of public education to inculcate elementary school children with an intensely patriotic morality. Education to citizenship in the elementary schools had always stressed patriotism, but it now took on a more shrill and intolerant tenor. Grounded on claims about the racial uniqueness of the Japanese people, Araki's brand of patriotism deepened the anxious, defensive mentality of the populace while instilling an irrational false confidence.

A suffocating patriotism silenced the voices of opposition. Special security police hounded the small and diminishing number of opponents of imperial government and foreign expansion. Many members of the Communist and Socialist parties were either jailed or persuaded to recant their views in favor of government policy. Through the 1930s, police and government censorship of writers, producers, journalists, newspapers, and other media grew apace. It was dangerous to give expression to alternate viewpoints, and many distinguished figures retreated in silence rather than risk their lives by protesting against government policies.

Imperial euphoria, domestic terror, xenophobia, nativism, and ardent patriotism created an ideological climate in which the country drifted almost inevitably toward war. Political elites pulled and hauled against one another, with fewer voices advocating moderation and restraint. Terror eliminated some of those voices and silenced others. When plots occurred, conspirators often went lightly punished. The emperor refrained from intervening to regulate the military. Rather than impose stronger controls over dissident officers, the government often relied on the military to restrain itself. This was like putting a fox in a chicken coop. At many steps along the way, therefore, the military—despite often insubordinate and outrageous behavior—found its influence waxing rather than waning. It was able to place more of its officers in cabinet positions and in the prime ministership. It also managed to win the allegiance and support of a group of bright, ambitious, strategically positioned young bureaucrats who provided expertise in the civilian administration of national government. When the army in Manchuria broke out of its northeastern fastness and began an invasion of China in 1937, the nation opted for war essentially without dissent.

## INSECURITY

Japan's military expansion southward into China and Southeast Asia brought insecurity and often wanton death and destruction to millions in nearby Asian nations, while costing the lives of millions of Japanese soldiers, sailors, and civilians. For five years the conduct of war expanded Japanese influence in Asia and the Pacific. By the early 1940s, however, the Allied powers had summoned the men and materiel to begin their own offensive. In 1942 they brought the experience of war to Japanese shores; in 1945 they ended the war under devastating conditions.

### The Conduct of War

For eight long years Japan lived with the insecurities of war. Beginning with the push southward from Manchuria, the conflict quickly spread across most of China. The Japanese offensive focused on major cities on the coast and inland and on strategic communications lines. Confronting strong opposition in some locations, Japan pursued its objectives relentlesssly, especially in a violent attack on Nanking in late 1937. Within two years, Japanese troops had occupied the island of Hainan off the coast of south China.

Drunk with victory, Japanese forces began invading Southeast Asia as well. These actions provoked diplomatic criticism, armed opposition, and economic counterattack. Apparently hoping to enhance its bargaining position, Japan launched a surprise attack against the American fleet at Pearl Harbor on December 7, 1941. This stunning blow brought the United States into the war, but it also encouraged Japan to expand further. At the height of its conquests in 1942, Japan's defensive perimeter stretched from the Indo-Burmese border on the west to the Aleutian, Marshall, and Gilbert islands on the east, and from Manchuria and Sakhalin on the north to Sumatra, Java, and New Guinea in the south.

The reversal of Japan's fortunes began with its defeat in the Battle of Midway in June 1942. Thereafter, Japan fought a losing war as it strove to defend its conquests against a methodical Allied offensive. Gradually but decisively, and at great cost in human life, Allied forces regained ground in Southeast Asia and pushed Japan out of its island bastions. While continuing to fight land and sea battles in the Pacific, the Allies also began to carry the war to the home front with punishing air attacks on major cities.

The first Japanese affected by the insecurities of war were officers, soldiers, and sailors. Although accurate official figures concerning the numbers of military personnel were apparently destroyed in 1945, at least 3 million men, perhaps as many as 6 million, became military conscripts. Official postwar figures reveal that about 1.5 million lost their lives, but that is probably an underestimate. Millions more suffered separation from families, the trauma of battle, disabling injuries, and often permanent inability to readapt to civilian life. Some who survived may have enjoyed the brief thrill of victory, and many wartime combatants still gather to sing and reminisce nostalgically about their experiences. But no one has yet emerged from Japan's Pacific War as a national hero, and few can draw solace from the nation's fate in that conflict.

In an era of total war, noncombatants at home could not escape its effects. For a year or two after the army's invasion of China, military demand drove expansion in heavy industry, jobs grew, and wages rose. It seemed for a moment as if everything would be all right, perhaps even better. But despite early successes, the odds against Japan were too great. Its economy was too weak to support its ambitious designs, and strong opponents were already gathering forces against it.

Some leaders understood the dilemmas that Japan faced. In 1937 they began preparing for a total war by centralizing more authority in key organs of the national government. The first critical institution formed was the Cabinet Planning Board. Established in October 1937, this agency was staffed by savvy, experienced bureaucrats who knew how to organize resources and command cooperation. In the following year, the government won approval for the National Mobilization Act, which gave it special powers to advance the war effort. In the same year the government also nationalized the electric industry to ensure reliable supplies of power during the crisis. Sharp inflation and the appearance of black markets caused the government to pass price control laws in 1939 and to introduce the first efforts at rationing consumer goods.

After its agreement with the Axis powers in 1940, the government began preparations for the New Order, modeled consciously on Nazi organizations. These were formalized in the Imperial Rule Assistance Association, which created an aura of monarchical legitimacy around the nation's bellicose expansionism. In 1941, Japan also began organizing private industry for war by creating self-governing associations (*tosei kai*), which eventually spanned twenty-four sectors, among them steel making, coal mining, and shipbuilding. The tosei kai were meant to advance production and promote the war effort in an economy that remained essentially under private ownership and management. When General Tojo Hideki became prime minister in October 1941, it appeared that Japan was well united to pursue an all-out war effort.

Although this structure of wartime authority looked good on paper, it functioned poorly in practice. The Cabinet Planning Board had smart leaders but limited powers. Price restrictions, rationing, and industrial control were all well intentioned. Implementation proved difficult, however, because local and private groups clung tenaciously to their prerogatives, and the government hesitated to overrule them. The New Order was little more than a shroud covering old habits; it never produced single-party rule or dictatorship. In fact, Japan's wartime governments had difficulty imposing deep, effective control over private industry, civilian administration, and the military services. In any case, the Tojo government faced such severe military and economic challenges that it was doomed to an early demise.

Three circumstances sealed Japan's fate long before surrender in 1945. One was the tiny size of its economy in comparison with its American opponent. Almost half of the nation's labor force was needed to produce food supplies, leaving the remainder to fill the military's ranks and to labor in its factories. The factories themselves were too few and too small to produce the steel, ships, and aircraft necesssary to defeat such a well-supplied opponent. Magnifying this economic weakness was a naval blockade that deprived Japan of the imports and raw materials needed to support its populace, much less to pursue a major war. Beginning as early as 1939, efforts to prevent Japanese access to metals and petroleum hampered its ability to carry out efficient economic expansion. By 1942, the stringent blockades began to force a drop in industrial production and civilian consumption.

Finally, ineffectual manpower programs, in agriculture and industry, contributed to Japan's defeat. Agricultural production declined because military conscription policies depleted the male labor force. During the decade of the 1930s, the number of male workers in agriculture fell by more than 1.2 million. Some 800,000 women tried to take their place, but the net number of farm workers shrank by about 400,000 during that decade alone, with the greatest decline occurring after 1937. Similar trends persisted into 1944. As a consequence, the amount of tilled land fell by about 10 percent. Total farm production fluctuated sharply after 1937, owing to bad weather as well as labor problems. A clear decline had set in by 1942, and 1945 witnessed a precipitous drop in farm output.

Manpower policies for industry were also ill conceived and poorly implemented. The government made little provision for keeping trained managers and skilled workers at their jobs. Instead, the army tended to exercise dominant authority, and it preferred to take all the able-bodied males it could. As a result, factories came to rely on an odd mix of workers. The fastest growing industry in the early 1940s was aircraft manufacturing, and experienced male workers constituted only a small share of its labor force. The majority of its workers were women transferred from the textile industry, boys and girls of school age assigned to factory work, older men and women without industrial

**5. Threshing by hand, 1936.** *Men and women exerted heavy labor to husk grain by repeatedly swinging long bamboo poles with a revolving beater attached to the ends to knock kernels from the mature stalks.*

(Courtesy of Robert J. Smith.)

experience, and Korean labor conscripts formerly employed under atrocious conditions in the coal mining industry. Workers as poorly trained and unmotivated as these undercut efficiency and hampered the wartime production effort in key industries.

In response to such problems, various domestic groups had begun as early as 1938 to establish a patriotic labor front aimed at boosting morale among industrial workers. Government bureaucrats specializing in welfare and labor affairs, business leaders from private firms and trade associations, and even leaders of Japan's nascent union movement all supported this labor front. This patriotic undertaking was not very effective in boosting morale or productivity, but it did produce significant long-term effects. Under the labor front, workers selected their own leaders and were allowed, indeed encouraged, to negotiate with management to improve corporate efficiency under the rubric of the firm as a family. These experiences proved exceptionally useful to labor leaders and union members after the war, when unions were legalized and permitted to strike and to bargain collectively. Unwittingly, businessmen and bureaucrats had provided a wartime training ground for the postwar labor movement.

### The Experience of War

These long-term benefits went unnoticed, of course, by workers preoccupied with the war effort. Material shortages, political wrangling, administrative problems, and food scarcities all combined to reduce the standard of living, especially in urban areas. It was becoming more difficult to obtain necessities as early as 1941. Overall, real consumption may have fallen by 30 percent between 1940 and 1944 alone. Food became especially scarce. By the end of the war, the average Japanese citizen was taking in barely 1,700 calories per day, and rice and other cereal grains accounted for about 80 percent of this intake. The remainder consisted of pickled vegetables, *tofu* (fermented bean cake), *misosbiru* (a bean-paste soup), and the rare piece of fish, under the best of circumstances. Few people were able to obtain fruits, fresh vegetables, meat, eggs, or dairy products. Rationing and prudence dissuaded people from buying clothing, had there been any available. Japan's once proud domestic textile industry was dismantled during the war, its facilities and employees converted to the production of military materiel; so cotton cloth production fell by more than 90 percent from its peak in 1937. Few families sought to build new housing or to repair old, owing to fear, penury, and uncertainty. The growing sense of insecurity was underscored by another pattern of household behavior; many families began saving a far higher portion of their incomes, anticipating even worse to come.

In due course, events bore out their fears. In April 1942, the first of what would later become hundreds of bombing attacks by American aircraft took place. Flying from carriers in the Pacific, B-25s dropped tons of bombs on parts of Tokyo as well as Nagoya, Kobe, and Osaka. These high-level bombing attacks caused limited destruction and loss of life, but they proved to be an experiment from which American forces learned two lessons. First, Japan was poorly equipped to defend against air strikes of any kind. Owing perhaps to overconfidence, or perhaps to scarce resources, the Japanese government and military had few defense plans and limited aircraft, artillery, radar, or other systems to thwart air attacks. Second, given such poor defenses, American flyers realized that they could forego high-level, "surgical" bombing attacks, as they were called in the European theater. Instead they could conduct low-level attacks, flying at a ceiling of about two miles, while raining incendiary bombs on their targets. Japanese cities were densely inhabited areas where most residents lived in small, two-storied wooden structures built very close together. Fire bombs dropped in crowded residential, or mixed residential and industrial, districts caused instant conflagrations that spread quickly and killed indiscriminately.

Even before the earliest bombing raids, some urban residents had begun to drift back to the countryside. Unstable job markets, food shortages, and other problems made rural life seem preferable to the threatening urban atmosphere. First fathers with jobs in the cities sent wives and children to live with families in home villages; then whole families began to leave the cities in larger numbers. Finally, entire schools of elementary children were sent to distant rural areas, where they jammed into dormitories, inns, and stores, away from home and family, the normalcy wrung from their lives. Groups like these formed a mass exodus of some ten million people who reduced the nationwide urban populace by nearly one-third. From the largest cities, the flight was even greater; Tokyo, Osaka, Nagoya, and Kobe saw 55 percent or more of their residents depart in the last years of war.

The 1942 bombings were a warning heeded by some; those who failed to paid sometimes with their lives. Attacks resumed beginning in June 1944. Over the next six months, American bombers flew three dozen sorties targeting most of Japan's largest cities. In 1945 the air attacks were virtually unceasing; over just eight months, American bombers launched almost three hundred raids. Scores of B-29s dropped hundreds of tons of incendiary bombs in withering attacks. Officially, ports, factories, refineries, and transport facilities were the targets, but entire districts of large cities, or in some cases entire cities, were bombed. Vast districts of eastern Tokyo were turned to ash during one raid in March. In subsequent months, attacks against Yokohama pummeled almost two-thirds of the city, driving out hundreds of thousands of residents. A night raid on the remote provincial city of Toyama in early August destroyed 96 percent of its urban area.

The loss of life and property was terrifying. Men, women, and children, some fleeing on their mothers' backs, died by the thousands. The Tokyo raid alone killed more than seventy thousand; other attacks, one hundred thousand or more. Many civilian victims were permanently scarred from burns or maimed by injury. Millions of homes and shops were incinerated.

The United States rationalized the destruction in the name of military necessity. In this case, as in so many others, however, American intelligence was faulty. To the very end, it overestimated Japan's economic capacity for war, and it failed to understand that many sectors of Japan's economy had stalled as early as 1942. In retrospect, the American incendiary campaign, which killed well over one hundred thousand people and drove millions from their homes, seems lacking in military or humane justification.

The same can be said of the horrifying events that ended the war. Given the death of participants, the vagaries of memory, and the ambiguity of the written record, we will never fully understand why the United States employed nuclear weapons against Japan in 1945. We do know that shortly after 8 A.M. on the morning of August 6, the Enola Gay dropped the first atomic bomb used in warfare on the city of Hiroshima. More than one hundred thousand people perished that morning, and tens of thousands of survivors have suffered from the lingering effects of radiation sickness. On August 9, the United States dropped a second bomb on Nagasaki, killing another forty thousand or more. Terrified, exhausted, and uncomprehending, the Japanese people listened six days later to the tremulous voice of Emperor Hirohito announcing Japan's surrender. Eight years after it had begun in earnest, the long nightmare of war finally came to an end.

# CHAPTER TWO

# Revival, 1945–1955

THE EFFECTS OF WAR DID NOT END
with surrender. For years after 1945 the Japanese people suffered
physical and psychological devastation. Cities lay in ruins. Inflation
spiraled. Black markets throve. Families lost fortunes. Jobs disappeared. Incomes plunged. These problems, discouraging in their own
right, were complicated by the presence of foreign occupiers. Led by
American members of the Allied forces, the occupiers set about reforming the Japanese in their own image. The reforms met with widely
differing receptions, depending on their timing, conception, content,
and clients. After a predictably difficult start, the occupiers and the
occupied eventually developed a modus vivendi that produced some
achievements and a measure of satisfaction to both parties. This uneasy
process of cooperation eventually set Japan on the road toward
recovery.

## DEVASTATION

Japanese used the term *yaki-nohara*, or burned plain, to describe their
cities. That is how they looked in August 1945. They were vast ex-
panses of charred ruins. In many areas, as far as the eye could see, what
were once thriving commercial districts, quiet residential neighborhoods, and bustling factory zones were burnt rubble. Almost nothing
was left standing. Sometimes a stone *kura*, or family storehouse, stood
above the ashes, marking the site of an old landlord dwelling or a
wealthy merchant house. Here and there the twisted frame of a bank or

**6. Sendai, 1945.** *A prefectural capital in remote northeastern Japan, Sendai— like many provincial cities—suffered as much from bombing attacks as Tokyo or Osaka. U.S. Army Signal Corps.*     (Courtesy of the MacArthur Memorial.)

office building stretched grotesquely into the air, a startling reminder of previous vigor and habitation.

Japan's largest cities were neither vigorous nor habitable in late 1945. The mass exodus had left many cities mere shadows of themselves, both figuratively and demographically. Tokyo's population dropped from a high of nearly 7 million in 1940 to fewer than 3 million in 1945. Osaka's population fell from more than 3 million to about 1 million. In Nagoya, Yokohama, and Kobe, similar declines occurred. Many of the millions who had fled the cities chose to remain in rural areas for five years or more, and some cities faced such severe problems that authorities banned reentry until 1949. Only in the early 1950s did most metropolitan areas return to 1940 population levels.

The American bombing raids during the fourteen months before August 1945 had destroyed about half of the built-up areas of Japan's largest cities. Some of the worst destruction had occurred in small cities outside major metropolitan areas. The night-long attack on Toyama in August 1945 had killed more than 2,000, injured almost 8,000, and driven nearly everyone out of the city. Only 4 percent of the city was left standing. About two weeks before, more than one hundred bombers had conducted a similar raid on the provincial factory center of Hitachi. In one night they dropped 970 tons of incendiary bombs on the small city. Nearly 1,600 died and another 1,000 were injured. About twenty thousand homes were lost, and 72 percent of the urban area was destroyed.

In the major cities, destruction was somewhat less extensive. Fifty-eight percent of Yokohama was destroyed and 56 percent of Kobe, but in Tokyo the figure was 40 percent and in Osaka, 35. Yokohama and Kobe were the nation's major ports, as well as manufacturing centers, so their harbor facilities and factory zones were heavily targeted. Over six hundred American aircraft dropped more than seven million pounds of incendiary bombs on Yokohama in a morning raid on May 29, 1945. Such overwhelming force immediately destroyed many wharves, factories, offices, and homes; the ensuing fires engulfed other districts. In Tokyo, where the commercial center went surprisingly unharmed, air raids focused on the low-lying residential and factory districts to the east. These were wholly engulfed as bomb-induced fires swept across the flat, densely built areas.

Though less extensive, the destruction in the major cities still had far-reaching consequences. Early postwar estimates placed the number of dwellings lost in 1944 and 1945 at almost 4 million. Some of those homes were destroyed by earthquakes and fires independent of the war, and some were torn down to anticipate or respond to bombing attacks. But 2.5 million dwellings were destroyed by air attacks alone. Most were in the largest cities, and this explains why so many people had to depart the metropolitan areas after 1944. Scarce supplies, falling real incomes, restrictions on reentry, and other priorities all combined to delay reconstruction of these urban dwellings for many years.

Construction delays were also a product of the hidden costs of the war. After 1937, more and more of the nation's resources were directed into the war effort. By the early 1940s an inordinate share of all national expenditures went for military purposes. As a consequence, Japan had to forego the construction of roads, schools, civic halls, and public libraries, as well as private or public housing. These hidden costs, or intangible sacrifices, would have left Japan with a large backlog of construction at the end of the war under any circumstances. Coupled with the extensive destruction of homes and apartments during the war, this backlog postponed the provision of adequate housing until well after 1945.

In the meantime, families remaining in the wartorn cities used every device they could to secure shelter. Some slept in subway tunnels. Others made homes in abandoned trolley cars or bus bodies. Many built ramshackle huts of wooden debris and tar paper. Still others lived in caves, holes dug out of the ground, with a sheet of cloth or a piece of board to close themselves off from the elements. Families of four or five crowded into one-room apartments in some of the old, hastily constructed buildings that did survive the war. The back alleys of Tokyo and Osaka housed thousands of families under these conditions long after 1945.

Securing shelter was a difficult task, but finding food was almost impossible. Harvests were especially poor in 1945, when they fell to barely 60 percent of the prewar peak. Conditions improved slightly in 1946 because rice production and agricultural output both rose. But 1947 was another poor harvest year, and rice supplies fell far short of national needs. Thereafter, agricultural production increased gradually and finally reached prewar highs again in the early 1950s.

Low output was just part of the food supply problem, however. Labor shortages, declining amounts of arable land, and marketing and transport difficulties all made matters worse. Repatriated military conscripts took time to make their way back to family farms. Meanwhile, women, children, the elderly, and urban emigrants were most of the farm workers. Labor shortages caused some land to go uncultivated. Paddy fields devoted to rice production, which had shrunk by almost 10 percent by the end of the war, shrank even more by 1947. Marketing mechanisms broke down because transport systems were destroyed, obsolete, or in disarray. Rural producers consumed much of their own output—by necessity. Urban emigrants, returning soldiers, and civilians repatriated from overseas colonies swelled the rural populace by several million after 1945, imposing immediate, direct demands on an agricultural system already dealing with scarce resources.

The Japanese government did what it could to ensure adequate

7. *Barakku. Cheaply constructed, makeshift dwellings like these in Tokyo were called* barakku, *or* barrack, *in reference to poor military housing; they sprang up to provide shelter in areas devastated by bombing. U.S. Army Signal Corps.*              (Courtesy of the MacArthur Memorial.)

supplies of food, and the United States offered some assistance in kind, although the ground corn it provided was wholly alien to the Japanese diet. Rather than rely on authorities or a reeling commercial market, Japanese producers and consumers reverted to practical solutions. *Katsugiya* were one response. The katsugiya were farm women from agricultural districts near large cities. They won their names because they hoisted large bundles of rice, vegetables, and other farm products onto their backs and carried them directly to consumers. Riding crowded trains or walking long distances, they bartered these precious food supplies for cigarettes, clothing, heirlooms, and money.

Consumers sometimes reversed the process. Carrying cash, shoes, towels, and cigarettes, they boarded the rickety local lines serving rural areas in hopes of finding farmers willing to sell food in exchange. Nagai

Kafu's 1949 short story "The Scavengers" captures with disturbing empathy the plight of such food seekers. A woman of forty and another in her late sixties are the central figures in the story. They find themselves trudging back toward the city laden with farm produce. Chatting along the way, the older woman laments to the younger than she has struggled like this to find food for almost a decade. Tired by their exertions, the two sit down to snack. While they are eating, the older woman appears to have fallen asleep. On closer inspection, the younger woman discovers that she has died. Being sure that no one will notice the body, the younger woman leaves the scene with the older woman's rice bundle. She knows that it will be lighter than the bulky sweet potatoes she is carrying and bring a higher price. On the road she meets a man who buys her rice for cash. Without reflection or remorse, she makes her way home. Kafu's story illustrates how the early postwar struggle for survival forced some to press beyond their physical limits and drove others into ruthless self-preservation.

Kafu's younger woman is a fictional construct, but her plight reflects the realities of the period. Just finding enough food to survive was an overriding task for many urban families, especially during the worst years of 1946 and 1947. Families of middling status were forced to spend 60 to 70 percent of their monthly income on food alone during those years. In contrast, poor urban laborers in 1932 had managed by spending only one-third of their incomes on food. To raise the necessary funds, urban families foreswore all but the most essential outlays. They usually allocated the necessary minimum to educational expenditures, and they did all they could to make sure that working fathers looked respectable. But families otherwise spent almost nothing on clothing and housing. Photographs of city life showing most men in army uniforms and many women in simple cotton garments twice repaired attest to the material deprivation of those years.

The immediate postwar period thus drove many urban families into dire straits. For two, three, and sometimes as many as four years, it took nearly all of a family's combined income just to keep food on the table. This often meant foregoing new shoes or properly repairing the roof. In many cases, families had to spend down savings or sell off valued heirlooms to get by. The early postwar experience thus ensured that when rapid growth occurred in the 1960s many a family would find it a gratifying relief.

To corporate managers and industrial workers, the events of the 1960s would have seemed a complete fantasy from their vantage point in 1945. The number of factories in operation was about 40 percent of the prewar peak. With many factories destroyed and others idle, more than two million industrial laborers were out of work. Even among the employed, minimally paid make-work was common, and the wages that did flow into workers' hands were being constantly devalued by a rapid inflation that set in quickly. All of these problems contributed to the deep economic distress of the early postwar years, especially in urban areas.

A closer look reveals, however, that outright destruction had spotty effects. Japan's aircraft manufacturing capacity was almost nil in 1945. Its textile industry was also producing almost nothing in comparison with the early 1930s, owing more to dismantling than destruction. Iron and steel, chemicals, machine tools, and cement were industries in which production was also very low. In contrast, there were high rates of usable capacity in aluminum refining, shipbuilding, vehicle making, and even in steel making at the site of the original Yahata firm. Often it was not destruction itself but unused facilities that put people out of work and kept industrial output low.

Setting aside for the moment the effects of Allied economic policies toward Japan, there is another crucial explanation for the sluggish pace of economic progress. Isolation from external markets was a fundamental restraint on economic recovery in the first postwar years. With its merchant marine reduced almost to nothing and its currency of essentially no value on international markets, Japan could not easily import raw materials. Without raw materials, it could not produce, sell abroad, earn foreign exchange, or revive the economy. This vicious cycle persisted for several years, while Japan and its foreign occupiers worked through a comprehensive agenda of reforms. In the meantime, the domestic economy stuttered and declined.

Winning a job, finding food, and holding a family together under these circumstances were daunting challenges. A half century removed from these experiences, even those who lived through them had lost the sense of desperation that existed at the time. A vivid depiction of one family's engagement with these challenges remains, however, in Yasuoka Shotaro's novella *A View by the Sea*. The death of the narrator's mother offers the pretext for the tale, but the real story depicts the breakdown of family life during the postwar readjustment. The narrator's father is an army officer who spent most of the war abroad. With the father absent, the son and his mother developed a close relationship while living comfortably on his father's generous military pay. When his father returns after the war, he is a broken man, probably suffering genuine psychological disorders. In addition, he is so ill-suited to civilian habits that he can neither readjust to his family nor undertake compensating work. Forced to change homes frequently, constantly straining to make ends meet, and always on tenterhooks, the family gradually declines into a completely dysfunctional state. The parents quarrel and draw apart, the mother loses touch with reality, and the son leaves home in aimless pursuit of a livelihood. Yasuoka relates his story with frequent use of reminiscing flashbacks in a gentle, elegiac manner. It is a style that artfully veils his jarring portrait of one family's response to the stress and destitution of early postwar life.

## REFORMS

The Allied occupiers who entered Japan in late 1945 seem to have been oblivious to the suffering, poverty, and destruction that surrounded them. It is no exaggeration to say that they behaved with the vision and confidence of world conquerors. For a few brief years they seized the moment and worked vigorously to impose their version of the good society on Japan. The sheer confidence born of victory gave impetus to their efforts. So did the vibrant energies of the New Deal in the United States. Those ideas still influenced American policy at home, and they were carried to Japan by people who themselves had direct experience of American reforms. Additional impetus to reform came from talented Europeans, political refugees from the Hitler regime, who brought valuable skills to bear in such fields as land reform and the law. They sought to institute in Japan an egalitarian order inspired by European political values. These political conditions, personal inclinations, and ideological premises propelled ambitious reform of Japanese society.

### Purges and Preliminaries

The occupation of Japan was officially an Allied undertaking, overseen not only by the United States but also by Great Britain, the Soviet

Union, and eight other Allied powers. In fact and in practice, Americans dominated the collective organs that carried out the Occupation, and American military officers held nearly all the most important positions in the administration. The key organ was the office of the Supreme Commander for the Allied Powers (SCAP), and the key individual was General Douglas MacArthur, who was the supreme commander. Deft at public relations and self-promotion, he became synonomous with SCAP itself. MacArthur relied heavily on a small staff of loyal subordinates, who injected another ideological tendency into the reform efforts: anticommunism. Within two short years, the anticommunist objectives of general headquarters were beginning to thwart reform efforts by the more ardent democrats in the lower ranks of the Occupation staff.

The anticommunist thrust within SCAP was a reflection of a more general American fear of communism. Emerging animosity toward Soviet actions in Europe and growing fear of Communist victory in China were two emotions coursing through the American government by 1947 and forcing officials to rethink policies toward Germany and Japan. Initial policies emphasized a punitive peace and placed severe restraints on economic recovery. Gradually, American policy shifted away from punishment toward reconstruction. Germany would be a democratic bastion against the USSR. Japan would become the workshop of democracy in Asia, to defend against the spread of communism from China and the Soviet Union. This alteration in American strategic objectives fostered a "reverse course" in Occupation policies. Instead of punishing Japan, SCAP turned to embracing Japan as an ally in its war against communism. The reversal of policy, which began as early as 1947, had some effect on many of the major reforms undertaken during the Occupation.

To prevent recurrence of war, expedite reforms, and sweep clean the slate, occupying authorities began immediately to carry out a purge of persons alleged to be supporters of the war effort. Issuing memorandums and relying on intimidation, they forced into retirement men who were members of the thought police, religious officialdom, extremist groups, and the Imperial Rule Assistance Association, a wartime patriotic organization. They did the same to career military officers and former government officials. From the two latter groups, twenty-eight were selected for trial before the International Military Tribunal for the

Far East between May 1946 and November 1948. Seven were sentenced to death by hanging, and eighteen were sentenced to prison terms of seven years or more.

The purge continued under the auspice of an imperial order issued in late February 1946. The targets now expanded to encompass several groups of varying influence. The largest group consisted of former members of the Imperial Reserve Association, a Japanese variant of the American Legion. Many of these men were elderly figures who had done little more than carry out national orders in their roles as heads of local branches. A second group of purgees was made up of about three thousand leaders of private firms in finance, commerce, industry, and the media, including many high-ranking managers in the largest zaibatsu and independent firms. Not all of them had enthusiastically supported the war effort, but they had dutifully worked on behalf of their firms and the nation after 1937. More than three hundred national politicians constituted a third group. Their departure from the political scene, and the removal of the businessmen from the economic scene, guaranteed that a younger cohort of political and business leaders would step to the fore, at least as long as the purge remained in effect.

The fourth and final group targeted by the purge were national civil servants. The Allies had already made the strategic decision to rely on the national bureaucracy to implement their reforms, so they had to deal gently with its personnel. Only a few score bureaucrats were obliged to resign their posts, and the bureaucracy itself was retained with few changes. The Allies did abolish the ministries of the Army and the Navy as well as the previously powerful Ministry of Home Affairs. The latter's functions they reassigned to three new entities: the Ministry of Construction, the National Police Agency, and the Local Autonomy Agency. On the whole, therefore, the bureaucracy escaped significant reform, thus ensuring its centrality in the structure of authority that survived.

There was also a later, second phase of the postwar purge. The first phase, described above, removed from official positions about two hundred thousand alleged contributors to the war efforts. Purge orders remained in effect, however, and in 1950 they were adapted to different purposes. By that time Communist and Socialist parties had made inroads both in elective politics and in the labor movement. Their successes rankled the anticommunist leaders in SCAP. These men, already nervous owing to the Cold War in Europe, Senator Joseph McCarthy's activities in Washington, and the impending victory of the Communist Party in China, once again invoked the purge orders, this time against alleged Communists in journalism and the labor movement. Nearly twenty thousand people were forced from their jobs, and the Japan Communist Party (JCP) and key segments of the public-sector labor movement suffered permanent decline as a result. This marks a clear instance in which the reverse course produced demonstrable changes in the objectives of Allied policies.

### Reforms and Reformers

While removing likely opponents from the political scene, the Allies embarked on a wide-ranging program of specific reforms. Six efforts were of particular importance: the reforms of landholding, labor organization, the zaibatsu, the educational system, the constitution, and local government. Reflecting the bold vision and jaunty confidence of the victors, these reforms touched everyone in Japanese society, whether male or female, young or old, rich or poor, employed or jobless. Their purpose was to rid Japanese society of its prewar evils and to remake it in an American image.

Land reform was an audacious undertaking. A land-rich country like the United States had little experience of small-scale tenantry (outside the South) and essentially no history of land reform efforts. Moreover, the occupying authorities knew woefully little about rural Japan in 1945. There were few language-competent specialists on Japan in universities or government service. Reliable scholarly works on Japanese agriculture or rural life were almost nonexistent. Only one ethnography, based on field studies conducted in the late 1930s, offered a first-hand description of village conditions. Many other books relied heavily on Japanese scholarship on the agrarian problem. Ironically, many of these were written by Marxists whose affection for theory diverted them from the complex realities of the countryside.

The reformers thus operated with an image of rural Japan which placed a small body of landlords atop the shoulders of a large, immiserated tenantry. They overlooked almost entirely the large group of middling farmers whose presence denoted a wider distribution of land than the occupiers at first seemed to realize. Fortunately, the

Japanese farmers and officials who carried out the land reform compensated for these misunderstandings.

Allied officials presented their reform proposals for the Diet's consideration in late 1945. They were eager to create a yeoman farming class that would be the backbone of democracy in rural Japan and efficient producers in a capitalist economy. By early 1946 the first efforts at land reform were underway. The principal objective was to redistribute land so as to reduce, if not eliminate, tenantry in the countryside. Nearly all land owned by absentee landlords was confiscated and redistributed on generous terms to tenants. In addition, resident landlords owning more than 2.5 acres of land (or 10 on the island of Hokkaido) had to relinquish the excess, which was also sold to tenants. Finally, laws were passed that secured the rights of those tenants who did remain, to protect them against the worse abuses of their landlords.

In each village where redistribution occurred, the reformers organized committees of local farmers to reallocate land. These committees usually reflected the proportion of landlords, middle farmers, and tenants in a village. They enhanced the status of middling farmers within their villages, a position that some prewar agrarian reforms had already bolstered, by making them essential political buffers between tenants and landlords. Most committee members were knowledgeable about the value and productivity of area land parcels and assured that, in most cases, redistribution took place in an equitable manner that won the compliance of village residents, especially the tenants, who were the primary beneficiaries. The reformers were less attentive to the rights, and the plight, of those defined as landlords.

If yeoman farmers were to be the backbone of Japan's new democracy in rural areas, their counterparts in the cities were to be union members. At almost the same time that Allied officials drew up their plans for land reform, they were also devising laws to alter the conditions of urban workers. Reformers envisioned these workers as a countervailing power to the interests of large capital. In theory, just as members of pro-Democratic U.S. labor unions in the 1930s had served as a foundation for New Deal social policies, so would organized workers in Japan become advocates for progressive policy making. In addition, Allied reformers hoped that a viable union movement would serve as a schoolroom for democracy. When union members elected their representatives and participated in the governance of their own organizations, they would acquire valuable lessons in democracy.

To achieve these objectives, Allied officials presented draft legislation to the Diet in late 1945. They insisted on sweeping reforms to Japanese labor law, which had prohibited strikes and collective bargaining entirely before 1945. The Allies proposed that all eligible workers be allowed to organize and join labor unions. They also proposed that all workers, whether in the private or the public sector, be allowed to bargain collectively and to strike. The Trade Union Law won quick approval in December 1945 and sparked an enthusiastic response from workers.

Occupying authorities took additional steps to undergird support for labor. They pressed the Japanese government to pass the Labor Standards Law in 1947, providing basic protections for all workers and advanced protections for women and minors. During the prewar era, the national government had monitored labor affairs through a bureau in the Ministry of Welfare, indicating the low status of labor problems. Under the Occupation, this bureau became the core of the new Ministry of Labor established in 1947 to increase the importance of labor issues in national politics.

Labor was to serve as a countervailing power to that of large capital, which in Japan meant the zaibatsu. Allied officials saw zaibatsu influence as intrinsically evil, both in its own right and because the zaibatsu had allegedly collaborated with the military and landlords to promote the war. Some New Deal sentiments lay behind this thinking, because concentrated capital had been an object of criticism in the United States during the 1930s. Partial understanding of the role of big business in prewar Japan also shaped the reformers' views. They were relying again on Japanese scholarship influenced by Marxist analyses. These studies railed against the monopoly capitalism of the zaibatsu and often exaggerated their importance in the prewar Japanese economy. Reformers thus operated with a skewed understanding of these distinctive economic institutions.

Against these sentiments and misunderstandings, however, we must weigh the facts of the late war period. Many of the old zaibatsu profited immensely from military production, especially in the steel, shipbuilding, chemical, and aircraft industries. In addition, wartime centralization of financial organizations also benefited banks and trust companies affiliated with the zaibatsu. As a consequence, the old zaibatsu and some of the new ones, too, truly had concentrated a large share of paid-up corporate capital by war's end. They did exercise a kind of oligopolistic control in trust banking, shipping, international trade, and some spheres of heavy industry, but they did not enjoy an economic monopoly by any means.

Allied plans for reform of the zaibatsu were multifaceted, extensive, and penetrating. To eliminate the concentration of capital, officials confiscated the stock holdings of fifty-six members of fourteen leading zaibatsu families; they also confiscated the stocks and bonds belonging to major zaibatsu holding companies. These shares were then sold on the open market, often to individual buyers. Reformers also eliminated the holding companies themselves, thereby destroying the managerial nerve center of the zaibatsu enterprises. To further reduce the concentration of zaibatsu influence, the reformers ordered large firms, such as the Mitsui Trading Company and Mitsubishi Heavy Industries, to be divided into smaller and less influential parts. Finally, to protect against reconsolidation of power, Allied authorities persuaded the Diet to institute antimonopoly laws and the Fair Trade Commission to oversee them. These laws prohibited interlocking directorships and the kind of internal coordination that had shaped the zaibatsu during the prewar era.

Economic institutions were not the only ones to attract the attention of Allied reformers. They were jangled during the war by the shrill nationalism that gripped the Japanese populace. In their eyes, the military, landlords, and the zaibatsu were all culpable on this count. But perhaps most culpable was the Japanese educational system. Reformers held the schools, especially through their morals (*shushin*) courses, strongly responsible for the irrational ideologies of wartime. Allied authorities directed their changes more at organizational form than curricular content. Where content was concerned, they obliged the school system to cease teaching the morals courses and the patriotic texts developed for the purpose.

When it came to form, Allied officials suffered an almost complete loss of imagination. They simply obliged Japan to reorganize the structure of its educational system according to American norms. The prewar system of education had been thoughtfully calibrated to meet the needs of an agrarian society undergoing a process of rapid industrializa-

**8. Outdoor classroom, 1946.** *Widespread destruction of homes, factories, and schools forced teachers and students to improvise in many ways, for example, by using open-air classrooms like this one in Tokyo. U.S. Army Signal Corps.* (Courtesy of the MacArthur Memorial.)

tion. Although it served in only limited ways as a vehicle of upward social mobility, it did provide the nation with people possessing skills that met job demands—at most times and in most respects. The occupiers imposed a simple 6-3-3-4 system: six years of elementary school, three of middle school, three of high school, and four of college or university. This formalistic change meshed poorly with many aspects of schooling in Japan; it also bred problems that have plagued the educational scene ever since.

The capstone of Allied reforms was a new constitution that went into effect on May 3, 1947. This document was the product of brief, intense efforts by a small group of Americans working under the direction of a young attorney named Charles Kades. The content of the postwar constitution was strongly influenced by a desire to avoid the constitutional dilemmas of the 1930s. Its drafters were especially concerned to eliminate the political autonomy of the military. They wanted to eliminate the prewar aristocracy, the aristocratic upper chamber of the legislature, and the Privy Council, too. And they were determined to trim the political authority of the emperor and to create the foundation for an elective democracy that vested sovereignty in the people, not the imperial institution.

Constantly echoing the language of American political documents, Japan's postwar constitution creates a ministerial form of elective government that preserves the imperial institution as a "symbol of the state." There had been some controversy within American policy circles over the fate of the imperial institution; the constitution retains the office but strips it of all real power. The emperor is granted a number of essentially ritual duties, and he enjoys many perquisites. But the constitution makes clear at the outset that sovereignty rests with the people themselves and that they will elect their legitimate leaders.

A prime minister and cabinet ministers constitute the executive branch of the government, aided by the national civil service in the state bureaucracy. The constitution requires that at least half of all cabinet ministers hold seats in the national legislature. This provision effectively eliminates the need for such informal prewar bodies as the genro and jushin, which had arisen in the first place because the Meiji Constitution did not specify how ministers would be chosen. In practice, nearly all postwar ministers have been drawn from the ranks of elected politicians.

Under the postwar constitution the suffrage is extended to men and women at the age of twenty. They express their political choices by electing representatives to a bicameral legislature, the Diet. It consists of the House of Representatives and the House of Councillors. The two bodies possess almost equal powers, with the representatives enjoying slight precedence on budgetary matters. Unlike the prewar constitution, the postwar constitution makes stronger provision for an autonomous judiciary. It establishes the Supreme Court, which is empowered to supervise the system of lower courts. It also specifies that the Supreme

Court can determine the constitutionality of laws, although it has been reluctant to do so in practice.

The postwar constitution also addresses in unique manner the role of the military. Article 9 states explicitly that "land, sea, and air forces, and other war potential, will never be maintained" and that "the right of belligerency of the state will not be recognized." Nonetheless, the Self-Defense Force (SDF) arose in the early 1950s, euphemistically circumventing the language of the constitution. In tests of the legal standing of the SDF, lower courts have sometimes ruled against it, but the highest courts have consistently upheld its constitutionality. The postwar SDF operates under a cabinet-level agency that functions under the command of a civilian prime minister.

In addition to political rights, the postwar constitution also addresses a wide range of social rights. In particular, it makes a minimal level of social welfare a constitutional guarantee. Women also benefit from a variety of provisions. They are granted explicit equality before the law, a dramatic improvement in their position under the Meiji Constitution. Such equality has had implications for inheritance practices, patriarchy in the home, access to education, and opportunity in the labor market, by strengthening the legal basis for women's rights.

The postwar constitution creates a structure of national authority that differs significantly from the one that obtained under the Meiji Constitution. With sovereignty rooted in the people, elected representatives in the national legislature possess an authority never exercised by their prewar predecessors. They no longer have to compete against a separate military, a privileged aristocracy, or a privy council. Nor do they have to worry about domineering genro. Far more power is now focused in the Diet, thereby granting more prospective influence to political parties and organized interests. Given the circumstances under which the postwar constitution emerged, however, the influence of the bureaucracy already matched, if it did not in fact overshadow, that of the Diet. Consequently, national politics in postwar Japan can be regarded as a continuous contest in power sharing between elected politicians and appointed bureaucrats, provoked and shaped by the constitution itself.

On the day the new constitution went into effect, so did the new

Local Autonomy Law. As a counterpart to the document that structured politics at the national level, this law significantly reshaped the conduct of political affairs at the local level. Allied officials understood that during the prewar era, local government had been essentially an administrative arm of the nation state. Having vested sovereignty in the people, they now wished to create a laboratory for democracy in the communities of the land. Only in this way would the populace develop a direct understanding of how democracy worked at the grass roots level.

The heart of the reform of local government was popular election of executives and representative bodies. At the prefectural level, the voting citizenry was given the right to elect governors and the delegates to prefectural assemblies, in open campaigns and with the assurance of secret ballots. At the city, town, and village level, voters also won the right to elect mayors and the members of local assemblies. To buttress the autonomy of elected local governments, prefectures and localities received more taxing authority than they had previously enjoyed. Initially, they were given more control over local educational matters and over police forces, too. In 1950 the government belatedly passed the Local Civil Service Law to foster a more professional body of local government workers by specifying qualifications for hiring and promotion and by reducing the opportunities for political favoritism.

Many potential changes were embodied in these reforms of local government, but they were often slow to occur. In their early stages, changes in local government paralleled those in national government. Whereas national politics became a contest for power between politicians and bureaucrats, local politics became a contest for power between communities and the state.

It is not surprising that these radical social, economic, and political reforms did not always work out as intended. Allied reformers were often bright, eager, and optimistic, but they also operated with a mistaken, biased, and incomplete knowledge of Japan. Their bold intentions did not always mesh with realities. Moreover, they had to win cooperation from parties that just months before had been fierce enemies. Finally, both the victims and the beneficiaries of reforms held their own views and acted on them as they saw fit. Knowing their time was short, the Allies consciously sought to revise structures, hoping that, over time, these would assure the emergence of new behaviors.

They aimed to create an environment in which democracy would flourish, but they recognized that its maturation would take years to achieve. Sometimes events bore out their hopes, sometimes not. To understand why, we must examine in closer detail how Japanese society responded to Allied reforms.

## RECEPTION

Allied reforms were extraordinary events carried out under unique circumstances. Japan had never been occupied by a foreign power, much less one acting with such authority and conviction. The nation was psychologically depleted by defeat. Large parts of the country lay in ruins, the economy was functioning well below normal levels, and leaders were in disarray. Amid such conditions, the Allies' extensive reforms attacked every vested interest in Japanese society while promising improvements for many disadvantaged groups. It is little wonder that the reforms provoked diverse, fluctuating responses. Two reforms were qualified successes; three were modestly successful while provoking new lines of conflict; and one reform, zaibatsu dissolution, died aborning.

### Political Context

While the Occupation lasted, between August 1945 and April 1952, duly elected governments ruled Japan under the close supervision of SCAP. The leaders of those governments, the stability of their administrations, and the electoral support they received from the populace all served to shape the reception of Occupation reforms. The two men who presided over the first postwar governments were caretakers with limited popular support or legitimacy. One, Prince Higashikuni, was a member of the imperial line, and the other, Shidehara Kijuro, was a distinguished prewar foreign minister. Both were in exceedingly weak positions to challenge the occupying authorities, and Shidehara was probably personally and politically sympathetic to many Allied reforms anyway. The governments they headed posed few obstructions to Allied directives.

The next several governments were also shaky and short lived. Two lower-house elections, in 1946 and 1947, confirmed political disarray in the electorate, too. The first postwar election occurred in April 1946. Five major parties and many smaller ones ran candidates in a contest conducted under unique procedures. No party won even one-quarter of the vote, but a coalition of conservative parties was able to form a government with Yoshida Shigeru as prime minister. This fractious coalition remained in power for just one year, during a period when many major reforms were enacted. Hoping to shore up his support, Yoshida called for another election in April 1947. His hopes were dashed when the Japan Socialist Party (JSP) won a large share of the vote. As a consequence, Yoshida's government gave way to a coalition in which the Socialist Katayama Tetsu served as prime minister. It was his bad luck to govern during one of the most difficult periods of the Occupation. Katayama was unable to deal satisfactorily with the many challenges he faced, and his failures left a black mark on Socialist leadership which it has never overcome. Katayama served for barely nine months before turning leadership over to Ashida Hitoshi. He was in office for only seven months before Yoshida Shigeru pushed him aside.

When Yoshida regained the prime ministership in October 1948, Japan had passed through the more euphoric days of reform. People were growing anxious about economic recovery, and the country was developing a more conservative outlook. Yoshida was able to turn this changing mood to his advantage in lower-house elections in early 1949 and again in late 1952. On both occasions his Liberal Party won less than half of the votes, but it secured a firm majority of seats in the lower house, providing the support he needed to bolster his famous "one-man" rule.

Yoshida Shigeru was already in his late sixties when the war ended. He was a former career official in the foreign ministry, a former ambassador to Great Britain, and the son-in-law of a powerful prewar political figure. Although he was a scion of Japan's conservative establishment, Yoshida was acceptable to the Allies because he had spent much of the war in retirement while out of favor with the military. He was also deft at dealing with American officials. He appeared to give them what they wanted while preserving his own autonomy of action in many areas.

Yoshida did not hesitate to throw his weight around, and he worked diligently to build his power base. One of his most critical and long-lasting accomplishments was his recruitment of former national bureaucrats into his party. This group came to be known as the "Yoshida school." Its members held major cabinet posts while he was in office, and some went on to lead governments themselves after his retirement. During Yoshida's tenure between late 1948 and late 1954, the Japanese government was in a stronger position to negotiate the terms of reform, or, as happened the moment the Occupation ended, to revise reforms.

Yoshida's domineering ways eventually stirred strong opposition. An election in early 1953 cut the strength of his parliamentary majority. Rumblings within his party, and discussions between the Liberal and Democratic parties, were undermining his authority, too. He clung to office until late 1954, when he finally stepped aside at the age of seventy-six in favor of a career politician, Hatoyama Ichiro. Within a year, Hatoyama presided over the merger that would produce, under the Liberal Democratic Party (LDP), a record of conservative longevity that put Yoshida's in the shade.

Japanese governments and domestic politics were two determinants of the outcome of Allied reforms; there were others, too. Timing was a major consideration. Simply put, reforms advanced earliest had the greatest likelihood of easy acceptance. The presence of reform advocates in the Japanese bureaucracy was also critical. Bureaucrats who shared the objectives of Allied reformers could be influential supporters, whereas bureaucrats who opposed reforms made frustrating colleagues. It was even better if bureaucrats had prior experience with the kinds of reforms the Allies were promoting. Two other determinants of reform outcomes were the victims and the beneficiaries of reform. Small, politically weak reform targets could offer little opposition, especially if a reform was going to benefit a larger constituency. But large, influential victims could stall, bargain, and oppose with galling effect, especially when others might suffer from their demise.

These considerations all shaped the reception of reforms from the Japanese side. There were other considerations operating within SCAP, or bearing on it, that shaped reform outcomes, too. The content and conception of reforms were both crucial. Reforms that were clearly conceived to produce a specific outcome often fared well. Those that were ambiguous and overreaching met difficulties. SCAP's own internal politics sometimes affected the way reforms evolved. For example, MacArthur's staff often found itself at odds with lower-level officials advocating more ambitious changes. Finally, international considerations bore strongly on SCAP's activities. Especially after the course reversal, reforms became part of a larger political equation that incorporated far more than just Japanese elements.

### Varied Responses

**Land reform and constitutional revision.** The prize achievement of the Occupation was the land reform. This was a clearly conceived effort aiming at specific outcomes. It began almost as soon as the Allies reached Japan. Its victims were a relatively small group who found themselves in a rather defenseless position politically, because opposing a project that promised to better the conditions of many rural families would have made landlords seem far more greedy than most of them were. The office of the Supreme Commander for the Allied Powers was determined to carry through a land reform, and Washington was strongly behind it. Finally, and crucially, there were experienced, knowledgeable bureaucrats in the Ministry of Agriculture eager to lend assistance.

Despite the scale and complexity of the undertaking, land reform was implemented with relative ease. Bureaucrats, middling farmers, tenants, and even some landlords cooperated enthusiastically to ensure compliance; SCAP lent direction and motivation. And the goals of the reform were achieved in close conformity with their conception.

At the end of 1945, before reforms began, tenants cultivated almost one-half of the farmland in Japan. The reform itself took about five years to carry out. At the end of that period, tenants worked only 10 percent of Japan's farmland. Previously, rural Japan had been a complex of landlords, middling farmers who both owned and rented, and tenants who rented. After the reform, nearly every farm family in Japan owned all or most of the land it tilled. They had become "yeoman farmers," although with a Japanese twist. They worked intensively holdings that were on average only 2 to 3 acres in size; they were more like market gardens than farms. Nonetheless, pride of ownership, combined with government assistance and market stimulants, encouraged farm families to significantly increase their levels of production. Landowning farmers also became the essential electoral supporters of the conservative parties that dominated Japanese politics for the next four decades.

**9. Cultivating prosperity, 1950s.** *Farmers still used animal-driven wooden implements to till fields in this Shikoku village, where farm homes were assuming a more prosperous look than in the 1930s.*

(Courtesy of Robert J. Smith.)

New farm owners fared well in part owing to the rapid inflation of the late 1940s. They bought their land at early postwar prices but paid for it with the inflated currency of later years. In contrast, the landlords, who lost their property through confiscation, suffered twice over. They lost the land itself; they also saw the value of their compensation reduced to little or nothing by the same inflation that so advantaged the buyers. After the Occupation, landlords pressed for redress through the legislature and won modest concessions.

From the perspective of Allied reformers, the postwar constitution has been another major achievement of the Occupation. Like the land reform, the constitution enjoyed strong backing from SCAP and Washington, and it was clear in its contents and objectives. An attempt by a Japanese committee including former prime minister Prince Konoe Fumimaro to forestall constitutional reform in 1945 with a slightly revised version of the Meiji Constitution helped SCAP to discredit conservation forces in Japan and muster some popular support for its own document. Promulgated early, when governments were disorganized and opposition to reform was difficult, the constitution passed through Diet deliberations with minimal obstruction and became law quickly. Since 1947 it has defined most of the rules of the game in Japanese politics, and it has won many adherents and defenders among the Japanese people.

Some groups in Japan have perennially criticized the new constitution, however, and sought its revision. They decry the secrecy under which the draft was written. They deplore the formalistic debates surrounding its passage in the Diet. They resent the imposition of a document so Anglo-American in its rhetoric, theory, and content. Conservative politicians, former bureaucrats, and a motley collection of right-wingers made up the groups that spoke out most vehemently against the constitution in the late 1940s and 1950s. They were never able to marshal the support necessary to revise the constitution, however, and it has persisted unchanged since 1947. But voices calling for constitutional revision can still be heard.

A salutary conjunction of events made it possible for the Allies to carry out land reform and to produce a new constitution. In both cases, a large group of beneficiaries ensured both acceptance and protection of the reform efforts. Both reforms provoked opposition, but opponents were never able to alter the outcome.

**Labor, local government, and education.** Three other reforms produced mixed and ambiguous results. Initial changes in labor, local government, and education went smoothly enough. New laws were passed and new structures established. In every instance, however, these changes provoked forms of behavior among Japanese beneficiaries which Allied authorities had not fully anticipated. Moreover, SCAP itself antagonized many beneficiaries of these reforms when it pressed the Japanese government in 1948 to cut back on rights granted earlier, especially the right of public employees to strike. Organized workers responded to these cutbacks with vigor, and they set in motion new modes of political conflict which persisted for nearly four decades. To put these general observations in context, and to appreciate the results of these three reforms, it is first necessary to examine the labor movement that arose after late 1945.

Legalization of labor unions met with an enthusiastic response. Workers who had belonged to the wartime labor front took advantage of their experience to organize enterprise unions, that is, unions whose members all came from the company where they worked. This practice was in keeping with the wartime, and even prewar, emphasis on the firm as a family. The strong preference for enterprise unions has lent a distinctive pattern to the postwar labor movement in the private sector. Unions have been strongest at the level of the individual firm, and industrial federations and national centers have been commensurately weaker. Amid the early postwar enthusiasm, members of one small firm were so supportive that everyone joined and the company president became the union head! This kind of naïveté soon disappeared, however, while organization rates continued to climb, peaking in 1949, when 56 percent of all eligible workers had joined a union.

Blue-collar industrial workers in private-sector firms were not the only ones to organize. Some of the largest and most politically oriented labor unions emerged in the public sector, at government enterprises such as the national railways, the postal service, and the telephone monopoly. These unions organized quasi–blue-collar workers who served as station attendants, postmen, and telephone operators. Many white-collar workers in government service also joined unions. They included low-ranking bureaucrats in national ministries, civil servants in prefectural and local governments, and teachers in elementary and secondary schools. Many of these people were college-educated and developed a strong ideological attachment to the union movement. They also recognized full well that their terms and conditions of employment were largely determined by public entities: the national government, prefectural governments, or local governments.

In the immediate postwar period, many public-sector labor unions came under the leadership of members of the Communist and Socialist parties and as a consequence allied themselves politically with those parties. Union members provided the candidates, money, organization, and votes that put Socialists and Communists in the Diet beginning in 1946. These relationships further strengthened the adversarial tendency of the union movement.

As financial conditions worsened during the early Occupation period, public-sector workers saw their real incomes decline drastically. Wage increases did not keep pace with inflation, and inflation ate up the low wages they did receive. Union members in general, and public-sector unionists in particular, became more militant. To draw attention to their plight, union leaders announced a general strike for late January 1947.

This aborted event proved to be a major turning point in Japanese labor history. The general strike was abortive because General Mac-Arthur prohibited it. Workers rather meekly accepted his order on that occasion, but they continued to press for wage increases and improved working conditions. By mid-1948, conditions had so deteriorated that two groups of government workers threatened to go out on strike. MacArthur again prohibited their actions, but this time he followed up with a letter to the new Ashida government urging it to withdraw the right to strike from government workers. Weak and short-lived, the Ashida cabinet complied. In succeeding months, labor laws were rewritten to deny all government workers the right to strike. In addition, new laws came into effect that denied white-collar workers in the national government and in prefectural and local governments the rights to organize unions and to bargain collectively. Instead, they would be allowed to join professional organizations, but those organizations would not be able to bargain over the terms and conditions of their employment.

These actions, carried out at the behest of SCAP, were a clear retraction of rights once legally granted to workers and unions. The response was wholly predictable. Public-sector workers in national and local governments, the JSP, and the JCP were outraged. They felt betrayed by Americans whom they had once seen as allies and benefactors. Their betrayal provoked a new level of opposition to U.S. policy, and it drove a deep wedge between the United States and progressive forces in Japan, a wedge that has never been removed.

MacArthur had taken his actions for two principal reasons. He felt personally that to strike against one's government was treasonous. His views were no doubt shaped by his life as a military officer from a family of military officers, but they were no less genuine as a result. He was also growing distressed by the influence of Communists in Japan at a time when the Cold War was intensifying and Communists in China were nearing a takeover of the mainland. In his mind these conditions called for order and stability, rights be damned.

This contentious political environment surrounding the labor movement after early 1947 provides the context in which to examine the consequences of labor, local government, and education reforms. Where labor was concerned, SCAP's pertinent actions after 1948 produced two significant long-term effects. One was a form of policy paralysis; the other, a gradual weakening of the labor movement.

Policy paralysis isolated labor and the progressive parties politically. Public-sector workers grew preoccupied with restoring the right to strike. After a new national union center called Sohyo was formed in 1950, most public-sector unions affiliated with it. For decades Sohyo placed the restoration of the right to strike at or near the top of its political agenda. It also adopted a set of policies and a pattern of participation that led to strident, adversarial posturing against conservative elements in the Japanese polity. Captured by a constituency of public-sector workers, Sohyo and the JSP failed to develop programs that would address a broader spectrum of society; instead, they were paralyzed by the policies that public-sector unions favored. In all of these ways, the largest union center and the JSP found themselves frozen on the left, appealing to a finite body of supporters. The JSP, along with the JCP, managed to win about one-third of the seats in the lower house during the 1950s, even under such circumstances; but they were never able to break out of their partisan redoubt to form a majority in the Diet.

The labor movement was also weakened in many ways by SCAP's actions. The new and revised laws drastically constrained the ability of many workers to use the economic and political weapons once available to them. In addition, SCAP's changing view of organized labor was a signal to Japanese employers that they could take a tougher stance against unions, and managers began doing so immediately. At major firms, such as Toshiba and Nissan, company officials collaborated with more docile second unions to replace the original unions, whose mem-

bers were more adversarial. Under the conservative Yoshida government, managers took advantage of the second phase of the purge to
root out alleged Communists, and they exploited difficult economic
conditions in 1949 and 1950 to simply fire troublesome union leaders.
As a result of this managerial counterattack, the union movement went
into decline. Membership began to fall in 1949, and organization rates
dropped to 33 percent in the late 1950s. In the early postwar period,
unions had been among the most vibrant and potentially powerful
political forces in Japan. Within a decade, they were a fractious, casti-
gated minority isolated on the political left.

In local government reform, the intent was to assure greater autonomy for prefectures, cities, towns, and villages, and the Local Autonomy Law of 1947 explicitly granted many of those assurances.
Beyond the law, the Allies also diminished the powers of central officials who might want to thwart reforms. After abolishing the old
Ministry of Home Affairs, they assigned officials responsible for overseeing local government to the Local Autonomy Agency under the
Office of the Prime Minister, hoping thus to enable local governments
to develop without intrusive supervision from above. But Allied reformers underestimated the determination of former officials from the old
Home Ministry who staffed the new agency—men who never abandoned their desire to preserve every ounce of control over local affairs.
Central officials sought control through three avenues: finance, duties,
and personnel. They tried to keep local governments dependent by
forcing them to rely on central government grants, rather than
local resources, for their operating revenues. They subordinated local
governments by requiring them to carry out a wide range of duties
mandated by the national government, and they tried to subvert
local autonomy by appointing incumbent and retired central government officials to the best administrative positions in cities and
prefectures.

Local officials resisted such personnel appointments strongly. Al-
lowing central bureaucrats to fill the best positions in local government
put a ceiling on salaries and promotions for those who had come up
through the ranks, and it was a transparent intrusion on local autonomy. Although the law prevented local officials from joining a
"labor union," they nonetheless formed an organization that looked,

thought, and acted like a union rather than a professional organization. Called *Jichiro* in Japanese, it is a direct counterpart to the American Federation of State, County, and Municipal Employees. By treading a fine line between blatant self-serving and public altruism, local officials used Jichiro to defend the interests of its members against state interference in community affairs.

The schools also became a site of conflict between organized workers in communities and educational authorities in the central government. School teachers were strongly politicized in the early postwar years by poor conditions and low pay. Many urban schools had been destroyed, and students learned in any environment available: hallways, playgrounds, parks, and abandoned buildings. Pay did not keep pace with inflation, and teachers—like so many others—struggled just to find food. Many joined a national teachers union called Nikkyoso to give collective expression to their demands. Many Nikkyoso branches affiliated with the Communist and Socialist parties, a move that further radicalized the teaching profession.

A central ministry of education had exercised control over Japan's public schools since the late nineteenth century. Staffed by conservative men, it opposed the progressive parties and their policies. As more teachers joined unions affiliated with the political left, tensions grew between the ministry and Nikkyoso. Cool to Allied reform efforts from the outset, bureaucrats in the central ministry strove to restore the educational system to norms more in keeping with the prewar era. Determined to make the schools a bastion of democracy, the teachers in Nikkyoso defended the schools against the intrusive conservatism of the center. Although these tensions between central bureaucrats and local teachers have waxed and waned, they have persisted throughout the postwar era.

In labor, local government, and education, therefore, the consequences of reform were ambiguous and contested. The reformers achieved some of their objectives at the outset with the passage of laws that key constituencies eagerly exploited. But in every case, unanticipated developments created new lines of conflict. Public-sector workers, especially in the national railways and the telephone monopoly, entered a long-standing competition with their public employers with a significant effect on partisan politics. Organized workers in local government became opponents of a central government eager to chip away at local autonomy. Teachers joined in defense of the schools against conservative bureaucrats in the Ministry of Education. Paradoxically, therefore, progressive interests—abandoned by SCAP during the reverse course—were among the strongest defenders of Occupation reforms.

The patterns of conflict and cooperation that evolved out of these reforms significantly reshaped political divisions in Japanese society. During the prewar era, higher-ranking groups at the center held a preponderance of power, whose exercise was seldom questioned. Thus central ministries issued orders to school teachers and officials in local governments and fully expected them to be obeyed. There was little conflict from the bottom up. This pattern of power has changed during the postwar era, owing to the circumstances under which Occupation reforms were implemented and received. For the most part, local officials, educators, and communities comply with central government orders, and this ensures a continuation of some degree of cooperation between the center and the locales. But ever since the early postwar period, there has been a threat of conflict, too. Local officials contest central government policies, teachers subvert ministry directives, and communities strive for independence from the center. Their behavior actually gives life to political expectations inherent in Allied reforms. Contesting the center also ensures constant bargaining between a national government eager to direct social change from above and local groups striving to expand their autonomy from below.

**Zaibatsu dissolution.** The final category of reform is one that, to a large extent, died on the vine. From the outset, the Allies worked on breaking up zaibatsu with a crude blueprint in mind. Approaching reform heavy-handedly, unmindful of the full implications of their efforts, they encountered difficulties along the way. When the reverse course picked up momentum, Washington's views began to differ from SCAP's, and branches within SCAP began to differ among themselves. Beyond these problems, there were no clear beneficiaries of zaibatsu dissolution. On the contrary, Japanese in many walks of life thought that it produced only victims. Many believed that breaking up such large firms would weaken the economy as a whole, reduce jobs, and undermine living standards. Even workers and consumers had reservations, and of course zaibatsu managers were resistant. Finally, the bureaucrats concerned showed little enthusiasm, either; for they were schooled in German economic theories that praised the virtues of cartels and economic concentration.

Zaibatsu reform did achieve some of its objectives, but it fell short of its most ambitious aims. Zaibatsu families were nearly impoverished when their assets were confiscated. The holding companies were effectively eliminated. The previous mechanisms of financial and administrative control were destroyed. Some individual firms were temporarily broken up; but before this latter task could be fully implemented, the reverse course dissuaded SCAP from following through on all its plans. Moreover, it never did reform the zaibatsu banks, so they endured largely unchanged. Well before the Occupation ended in 1952, SCAP had essentially abandoned interest in reforming the zaibatsu. If anything, it began to wink at efforts to restore them. This enabled former zaibatsu groups to persist in a new guise and to play a central role in promoting Japan's recovery.

## RECOVERY

Economic recovery from the devastation of war was a slow, lurching process. For more than three years after surrender, Japan floundered economically. Allied policies played a major role in postponing recovery, but there were other complications as well, isolation from international markets, scarce resources, and low demand being three of the most important. After 1948, the reverse course, the Korean War, and the peace treaty all helped remove obstructions to growth. By the early 1950s, Japan had made considerable progress toward restoring the economy to its former standing.

American bombing at the end of the war had returned the Japanese economy to a sort of dark age. Vast stretches of urban areas were flattened, and a significant share of the nation's ports and factories were inoperative. Millions of people had been forced back to the countryside, so rural villages were crowded and underproductive. Transportation systems were ruined, decrepit, or outmoded, and investment capital was scarce. The lack of a merchant marine closed Japan off from export markets and complicated imports of needed materials. Consequently, inflation raged unchecked for more than two years, and black markets flourished.

Allied policies prevented Japan from addressing many of these problems during the several years that Washington was determined to

**10. Industrial district.** *This area near downtown Tokyo was leveled in places by fire and pockmarked by bomb craters, but some power plants, factory sites, workers' dormitories, and storage tanks escaped destruction, facilitating economic recovery. U.S. Army Signal Corps.*

(Courtesy of the MacArthur Memorial.)

impose the punitive peace, demilitarize, and ensure that Japan not wage war again. This meant prohibitions on rebuilding heavy industry and continued isolation from international markets. Moreover, such reform policies as zaibatsu dissolution actually complicated recovery. They dispersed capital, diminished economies of scale, and undercut managerial control. The purge also removed influential business figures, whose departures harmed individual firms and the economy as a whole. In addition, prospective reparations payments posed widespread uncertainty for businessmen and government officials alike. As long as reform, revenge, and reparations were the keynotes of Allied economic policy, Japanese officials, managers, workers, and consumers all found recovery difficult.

The punitive, reformist nature of Allied policy changed as the reverse course advanced. The Allies began to downplay zaibatsu dissolution, and they lifted many of their restrictions on the economy. They also began to ponder how different policies might promote Japan's role as the workshop of democracy in Asia. In 1948, Occupation authorities invited a Detroit banker named Joseph Dodge to examine financial conditions in Japan and recommend changes. The nine principles of economic stability enacted in early 1949 became known as the Dodge Line. It was a program of monetary stabilization intended to slow inflation, regulate credit, and put the Japanese currency on a sound footing. The Dodge Line resulted in deflation, job layoffs, and painful cutbacks in many sectors, but it also checked inflation and set many companies on firmer ground.

Dodge's recommendations were harsh but effective, and they might have put the economy on the road to recovery on their own. But they received a wholly unanticipated boost when the Korean War began in mid-1950. Partly out of necessity and partly out of design, the United States opted to rely on Japanese suppliers for many wartime needs. These purchases stimulated demand in such key industries as textiles, chemicals, vehicles, steel, and coal mining. Firms that geared up to meet war orders made quick profits, which they reinvested in new factories. Under this stimulus, the industrial sector finally enjoyed a resurgence.

In addition to the reverse course, the Dodge Line, and the Korean War, a new security arrangement played a role in promoting Japan's economic recovery. Most of the Allied nations signed a treaty of peace in September 1951, which restored Japan's autonomy in the following year. At the time of the peace treaty, the United States concluded a joint security pact with Japan. It permitted the United States to station troops in Japan in order to preserve peace and security in Asia, and it obliged Japan to defray some of the expenses for those troops. The United States was also permitted to defend Japan against external attack and could be called on to suppress internal troubles at the behest of the Japanese government. Under the terms of this pact, the United States became the mainstay of Japan's defense.

Japan had been allowed to remilitarize beginning in 1950. In 1954, the Self-Defense Law established a 150,000-man Self-Defense Force with ground, air, and sea contingents. This small military force operating under the American nuclear umbrella required that Japan spend just a small portion of its GNP for military purposes. Whereas Japan had once created tragic distortions in its economy by spending as much as 60 percent of the nation's output to underwrite military adventurism, the new security pact eventually made it possible to spend less than 1 percent of GNP for defense, leaving far more of the nation's resources available to private enterprises, as profits and investment capital, and to families, for consumption and savings.

The benefits from Korean War demands, defense economies, and Allied policies were valuable stimulants to the still-small economy of the early 1950s. Military demand increased profits. Profits spurred investment in new factories. New factories created more jobs. Jobs meant steadier incomes, rising levels of consumption, and growing family savings, which were quickly channeled into more, and more productive, investment. This new virtuous cycle was the final ingredient needed for recovery.

The modern industrial sector was the prime beneficiary of this virtuous cycle. Even before the Allies changed their policies, the Japanese government had laid plans for a recovery by focusing on four strategic industries: coal mining, steel making, shipbuilding, and chemical production. In the early postwar era, coal was the principal source of energy in Japan; it would be needed to fuel industry once recovery began. Government officials, economists, and businessmen viewed steel as the core of Japan's reconstructed industrial economy. It would provide the material for ships, vehicles, construction needs, and exports. Reconstruction of the shipbuilding industry would generate demand for steel, create jobs, earn foreign exchange, and restore the nation's commercial shipping fleet. Chemicals received priority because synthetic fertilizers could be used to increase productivity on the farm. Agricultural self-sufficiency was imperative under the conditions of the late 1940s, and increasing food output was essential. As a consequence of efforts made between 1946 and 1950, these industries were well prepared to meet some of the demands the Korean War made.

Other industries in a more precarious state also received a much-needed boost from war orders. Toyota and Nissan won orders for trucks which returned these firms to financial solvency and set them on the path to future expansion. The Kubota Works used its profits from military requisitions to increase production of construction and farm equipment. Toshiba and Hitachi both benefited from Korean War demands. So did the textile industry. For a brief moment during the 1950s, it almost regained its prewar eminence. Exports and imports remained below their prewar highs for several more years. But thanks to the stimulus provided by special procurements for the Korean War, Japan's industrial output had reached the point of full recovery around 1955.

Farm output, too, reached prewar highs in the mid-1950s. Heavier use of synthetic fertilizers and insecticides enhanced productivity. But most gains were achieved as they always had been in rural Japan: large numbers of workers used manual techniques to farm small plots intensively. Few gains occurred through mechanization, because trucks, tractors, and other mechanical devices were still rare on most farms. In contrast, farm labor was plentiful, because most city emigrants and returnees still remained in the villages through 1955.

Many farm families were demonstrably better off. They were benefiting from the increased output of rice and a government program that supported the prices paid to producers. In addition, they had increased their incomes through diversification into other agricultural products, such as fruits, vegetables, and poultry, and by taking nonfarm jobs. Higher income from farm products and supplementary income from a job in town had brought many farm families to a standard of living that compared favorably with urban levels.

City residents, too, had seen dramatic improvement in living standards. A year after the war ended, urban consumption levels fell to less than half of what they had been in 1935. These sorry conditions actually worsened in 1947. Finally, in the late forties, a slow turn-around began, and during the early 1950s, living standards gradually improved. For most families, the mid-fifties marked the return to a level of consumption many had not enjoyed since 1935. It was now possible to buy new shoes and new school uniforms for the children. Families could finally patch the roof and replace the moldy *tatami* (floor mats) as well. Major appliances were still out of reach for many. One struggling middle-class family bought its first radio in 1956, and the purchase reduced the father's retirement savings by 10 percent! It would be years before most city dwellers could contemplate buying a family car or

**11. Transplanting rice by hand, 1952.** *Using the labor-intensive methods of agricultural technology that prevailed before the 1960s, four farm women and a small assistant gather seedlings from a rice bed for transplanting, in the same backbreaking fashion, in the flooded paddy fields nearby.*

(Courtesy of Robert J. Smith.)

moving to a new home. But, in the wake of a decade or more of material deprivation, even such modest gains as new clothes and dry ceilings were a source of contentment and satisfaction.

Shono Junzo captures these sentiments in a prize-winning story titled "Still Life," which depicts an urban family in the 1950s. Shono portrays a mother and father and their three children engaged in mundane activities: reading papers, going fishing, telling stories, keeping pets, making doughnuts, drawing pictures, sharing toys, losing things, taking baths, and visiting friends. There are hints of difficult times now passed, when the father reflects on his wife's extravagance in buying a stuffed animal for the children or a fedora for him. But there is none of the despair and dysfunction that permeates Yasuoka's image of an earlier period. Rather, Shono's sketches of minor incidents from daily life celebrate a return to normalcy that finally took place in the late 1950s.

The society that emerged out of war and reconstruction was markedly different from that of 1932. Wealth, status, and power had been thoroughly reconfigured. The war had destroyed many sources of wealth, and the postwar reforms had altered others. Most members of the aristocracy lost nearly everything, whether savings, stock shares, rural land, or urban property. The once fabulously rich zaibatsu families were stripped of their assets. Most large landowners lost their holdings, and many small landowners were nearly impoverished. With the elimination of the prewar military, another group of high-income earners left the stage. Even urban families of only middling status saw their homes destroyed by bombing and spent their assets to survive. Wartime experiences and Allied reforms drastically narrowed the vast disparities in wealth characteristic of Japanese society in the early 1930s.

The loss of wealth also reduced the status claims of many groups. The aristocracy was partly discredited by its complicity in the war effort and fully abolished by Allied reformers. Prewar aristocrats and their descendants never lost the personal and familial ties that would always assure them a place in society, but they did suffer a severe loss of privilege. So did military figures, who had long been among the elite in Japanese society. In rural Japan a new body of owner-farmers rose to share the status that landlords had once monopolized. And the stature of old-line urban families diminished, too, especially in those cities where bombing destroyed the physical and social underpinnings of neighborhood life.

Under these circumstances, power became far more widely dispersed than before. Aristocrats and military figures lost all their formal power. Land reform undercut the power of landowners in village politics, and physical destruction and resettlement did the same to many old-line power brokers in urban areas. In place of these dispossessed groups, a broader and more egalitarian electorate assumed greater influence in both local and national politics. The elected officials they returned to the House of Representatives became leading figures in national affairs. Bureaucrats and businessmen joined these politicians to form a power elite that would preside for the next two decades over a period of exceptional economic growth.

# CHAPTER THREE

# Growth, 1955–1974

"THE ERA OF HIGH-SPEED GROWTH"
is the mantra used to characterize the two decades after 1955. It has
been repeated so often that it may seem trite, but there is no other way
to understand this period. Growth overshadowed everything. It also
consumed everyone's energies and attention. And its consequences
reached into every nook and cranny of Japanese society.

Many preconditions for growth were already evident in 1955, although few observers fully appreciated them at the time. Growth was
more than a process of economic change. Political and social forces also
contributed to rapid economic development. Development, in turn,
reshaped political, economic, and social relations within Japan. As a
result of these changes and the exceptional performance of the Japanese
economy, Japan found itself ranked in company with the advanced
industrial nations of Europe and North America by the end of this
period.

## PRECONDITIONS

Japan was well positioned by 1955 for an ambitious effort at economic
growth. Its occupational and demographic structures embodied features useful to the purpose. The nation's workers—farmers, laborers,
and managers alike—possessed skills and motivations that would expedite growth. The experiences of war and reconstruction had created a
psychological environment conducive to expansion, and the nation had
corporate organizations primed for economic advance. From a com-

parative international perspective, it may have seemed that Japan was destined for a modest future, but that was not the case.

The most striking feature of Japan's occupational structure in 1955 was the predominance of the agricultural sector. Nearly 16 million workers still toiled on Japanese farms; they constituted 41 percent of the nation's labor force. In the same year, West Germany's farm sector employed 18 percent of the labor force; the United States', 9 percent; and England's, 4 percent. The larger size of Japan's agricultural sector was a result of recent historical experiences: partial industrialization brought to a halt by war and defeat, an influx of urban returnees after the early 1940s, and a second influx of overseas returnees after 1945. These two groups of returnees had swollen the rural labor force to more than half of the national total at one point, and many of them still lived in rural villages in 1955.

As long as these groups resided in rural areas, they were an underemployed source of labor. There was simply not enough work to keep them fully occupied, and some of the work they did had doubtful value. Many returnees were men in their twenties and thirties with limited educations and spotty job records. But they were able bodied, energetic, and in most cases eager for steady work. They did not have the skills to win jobs in prestigious commercial or manufacturing concerns, but they were ideal candidates for jobs in the small and medium-sized enterprise sector, the construction trades, and the service industry. As more such jobs became available, men like these rushed to take them. They quickly left the villages and joined other rural emigrants flowing into Japan's booming cities after the mid-fifties. Highly mobile, surplus, adult labor from rural districts was thus one precondition for high-speed growth.

Another was an abundant supply of young workers. The nine largest yearly cohorts in Japan's history were born between 1940 and 1950. The years 1944 and 1945 witnessed low birth levels, owing to the chaos and destruction of the last years of war. But in the preceding four years and in the following five, 2.2 million children or more were born each year. In the 1950s most workers entered the labor force at about fifteen years of age, after completing nine years of formal schooling. When high growth rates began, therefore, fifteen-year-olds from these large birth cohorts were just beginning to take jobs. For the next decade, they provided a steady stream of new entrants into the rapidly expanding manufacturing concerns and service enterprises of the country. They formed a large, educable, flexible, and cheap source of labor.

Japan benefited not only from the sheer numbers of workers available. It also benefited from the attributes of those workers, whether they were farmers in villages or laborers in cities. In rural areas, farm families looked with some optimism on their economic prospects in 1955. Rural living standards were improving, and new, labor-saving devices both for the field and the home were beginning to appear. Under these conditions, an experienced generation of older farmers was willing to invest its energies in farm improvement. Many of them were also able to persuade a son to stay home as a successor with good prospects of his own. For these reasons, older farmers and their younger heirs were available both to preside over a revolution in farm production and to provide the basic food requirements for an increasingly more urban populace.

In urban areas, there was also a supply of workers with attributes needed for economic expansion. Wartime destruction and reconstruction delays had put millions of industrial laborers out of work, but many of them stood ready to assume jobs that became available. Some of them had acquired industrial work experience during the war, and others had been lucky enough to maintain their skills by hanging on to some kind of job after the war. These experienced, adult workers became the core of the industrial labor force after 1955, and they provided the shop-floor supervisors who integrated the young school leavers into the labor force.

Japan also possessed a body of experienced, white-collar managers with indispensable skills. The origins of professional management in Japan can be traced to the late nineteenth century. Government enterprises, the embryonic zaibatsu, and the new textile industry were the organizational nurseries in which a significant number of white-collar managers first grew. Seldom trained in professional schools of business, they usually learned management on the job. Skilled managers were still a small group in the 1920s, but their numbers grew in pace with the economic expansion after 1933. During the late thirties and the early forties, this growing body of white-collar professionals developed essential skills in administering private firms. Many of them were only in their forties when rapid growth began in the 1950s. From this cohort of managers Japan drew the leadership for individual firms, restored zaibatsu groups, trade associations, and peak business organizations over the next two decades.

Farmers, workers, and managers were all highly motivated to invest their energies in a program of economic growth. Nearly everyone in these groups had suffered from material deprivation. Some farmers had struggled to stay afloat and to get ahead in a shaky agrarian economy since the 1920s. In 1955 they were finally enjoying the benefits of an improved standard of living. Yet it was a standard still only slightly above that which many had achieved momentarily almost two decades earlier. Workers, too, were finally attaining a living standard that some had fleetingly enjoyed in the mid-1930s, but they now had higher aspirations.

Managers were driven by more complex motivations. Some observers have asserted that Japan's managers were determined to win the war by economic conquest after 1945, when they pursued high-speed growth with such fervor. There is a hint of truth to this otherwise uncharitable claim. Many Japanese managers in the 1950s and 1960s were competitive, patriotic men; this only stands to reason. They were products of a school system that cultivated patriotism early on. They were impressed at an early age when Japan flexed its muscles in a victory over Russia. They were young adults in the 1920s, when the United States forced the Japanese to swallow a raw insult by barring them from entry through migration. And they spent a long stretch of their lives in midcareer participating in a war against the Allied powers. They were also by nature competitive people who had achieved their positions by dint of hard, personal effort.

These men were animated by far more, however, than a warlike compulsion to achieve victory over the United States. They cherished a passion to improve Japan's stature, economically and diplomatically, and a need to efface the humiliation of defeat. They were seeking status and acceptance among the major powers. Moreover, like farmers and laborers, they had ample incentive to better their own material conditions and those of their children and grandchildren.

Among laborers, pent-up material demands eventually fostered moderation in union behavior. Even before the era of rapid growth, a kind of cooperative unionism had begun to appear in the private sector. By 1955 the activism of the early postwar years had faded significantly. At many large firms, docile second unions had replaced more aggressive predecessors. Many adversaries of management had been fired or purged, and most remaining workers were eager to stay on the job in order to increase their incomes. They accepted the managerial notion that they were all members of a common family, striving to achieve what was best for the company as a whole. Union members with such attitudes opposed work stoppages, and they came to balance their wage demands against the financial status of the firm. This labor moderation nurtured an already strong commitment to economic goals and smoothed the political process of growth.

Japanese business experiences offered other preconditions to growth. There were many individual firms and enterprise groups with long histories of successful achievement. Moreover, many firms had acquired valuable experience in the years after 1932. They had learned how to raise capital, build factories, hire labor, marshal resources, oversee production, and market output in a rapidly changing economic environment.

Two other business developments served the Japanese economy well after 1955. One was the patterning of financial practices. For two decades, a few major commercial banks had been developing expertise in providing loans to private firms as their main source of capital. Some of these commercial banks were affiliated with the former zaibatsu; others were large regional institutions. After 1955 the relations among these banks and their customers became stronger and even better articulated.

In addition to banking relationships, Japan had unique institutions that fostered strong commercial relationships: large international trading organizations known as *sogo shosha*. The sogo shosha had originated in the 1870s to import raw materials and other products from abroad, to sell Japanese exports overseas, and to serve as commercial intermediaries within Japan. The two largest and oldest sogo shosha were associated with the Mitsui and Mitsubishi groups. By 1955 they had almost a century of experience in dealing with international markets—experience they put to good use during the next two decades.

Despite these obvious advantages, few anticipated how successful Japan would become—understandably given Japan's minor role in the international economy in 1955. The one nation that had escaped destruction during World War II while developing a much larger eco-

nomic base was the United States. Ten years after the war it stood head
and shoulders above the other industrial democracies. If we index the
GNP of the United States in 1955 at 100 (with comparisons based on
the U.S. dollar), we find that the next largest GNP was England's at l4.
France followed at 12 and West Germany at 11. Japan came in at a
mere 6, making the American GNP more than sixteeen times larger.
Similar disparities existed in most key industries across these economies. To cite just one example, the United States led the world in raw
steel production in 1955. If its output is indexed at 100, the other
countries ranked as follows: West Germany, 20; England, 19; France,
12; and Japan, 9. In other words, the wide economic gap that had
existed between Japan and the United States in the early 1930s still
persisted in 1955. That gap would soon narrow rapidly, however,
under the impact of Japan's high-speed growth.

## PROCESSES

The processes underlying rapid growth had political, economic, and
social elements. In the political arena, the leadership and the citizenry
entered into a compact that provided a high degree of stability. This
compact endorsed economic growth as the nation's highest priority,
and it supported political integration in pursuit of that goal. Political
stability also provided an environment attentive to the needs of business
enterprises, both large and small. Enterprises joined together to marshal
domestic resources in pursuit of economic growth. Businesses were also
able to exploit a unique conjunction of international factors that served
their objectives. The rapidity of growth created widespread social
change, especially a high level of occupational and geographic mobility.
Although social changes were disruptive and widespread, they never
reached destructive proportions. Consequently, the populace adapted
to economic imperatives that ultimately improved the material lives of
millions.

### Political Processes

Political stability during this era rested on a compact between voters
and the Liberal Democratic Party (LDP). Throughout these decades the
electorate returned a majority of LDP members to the Diet. The LDP
majority, in turn, endorsed growth as the nation's highest priority and
pursued policies conducive to its realization. In this effort, the LDP had

the support and cooperation of the national bureaucracy and numerous interest groups. The LDP also enjoyed a domination in local politics that helped to integrate national policies and local efforts. Some groups were damaged by the LDP's policies and others contested them openly. Their actions guaranteed tensions in the polity and ensured that the LDP could not act entirely unchecked. But opposition groups never became so strong that they deterred power holders from pursuing their objectives, and they were never able to win power themselves.

**The governing coalition.** The LDP was formed in November 1955, as a merger of the two parties that had led most postwar governments, the Liberals and the Democrats. Those parties traced their origins to the beginnings of parliamentary politics at the turn of the twentieth century. Owing to this history, the newly united LDP could count many groups among its prospective supporters: big business, the small and medium-sized enterprise sector, the retail trades, most farmers, some industrial workers (including some union members), and some white-collar city dwellers.

The LDP was a parliamentary party whose character was determined by the backgrounds of its national legislators, especially members of the House of Representatives (HOR). LDP legislators fell into four categories. About one-fourth of them began their careers as bureaucrats in national ministries. They usually stayed until they reached one of the highest posts available to a career civil servant and then entered elective politics in their late forties or early fifties. A second group of almost equal size began their careers as elected politicians in local government, often as city mayors or prefectural assemblymen. They, too, usually entered the Diet in their forties or fifties. A third group were businessmen. They usually continued to operate their small local or regional enterprises while serving concurrently in the Diet. A fourth group was more disparate: journalists, lawyers, doctors, academics, and self-employed professionals.

Former bureaucrats provided most of the party's leaders in the two decades after 1955. Indeed this was an era of leadership by bureaucratic elites, because former bureaucrats were prominent among the nation's business leaders during this period, too. The three men who held the post of party president, and thus prime minister, between 1957 and 1972 were all former high-ranking bureaucrats. Kishi Nobusuke (prime minister between 1957 and 1960) had been a key official in the Ministry of Commerce and Industry before the war and a minister of munitions in the wartime cabinet of General Tojo Hideki. After his release as a Class A war criminal after the war, he reentered elective politics and played a major role in guiding the merger of the Liberal and Democratic Parties. Ikeda Hayato (1960–1964) had been a high-ranking official in the Ministry of Finance before and during the war. He was one of the first bureaucrats whom Yoshida Shigeru recruited into his Yoshida school (described in Chapter 2) and the first member of the school to become prime minister. Another early member was Sato Eisaku (1964–1972). He had been an official in the Ministry of Transportation before entering elective politics. Many of the men who served as cabinet ministers under Kishi, Ikeda, and Sato were also former bureaucrats who had become elected politicians.

The former bureaucrats were politically adroit and well connected. They made some of their contacts as students in higher schools and universities before the war, others while working with businessmen and politicians during the war, and they acquired valuable knowledge and experience during their bureaucratic careers. Such knowledge and contacts made it possible for LDP leaders to develop easy relations with incumbent bureaucrats and major business figures during the years of rapid growth. Personal relationships, and the common outlook on national needs that these men shared, fostered consensual support of economic growth at the highest political, bureaucratic, and economic levels.

In addition to powerful elites, many interest groups also lent their support to the LDP. One supportive interest group was an agricultural association called *Nokyo*. It incorporated almost all farmers in the country under its umbrella; they used Nokyo to articulate their political demands in the capital. Another was a peak business association known as Keidanren. It represented the interests of the largest industrial, financial, and trading firms in Japan. Keidanren worked closely with the government to promote public policies that brought private benefits to large corporations. Other interest groups that backed the LDP included trade associations that articulated the political demands of individual sectors, such as steel making, shipbuilding, electronics, and banking. Still other pro-LDP groups were drawn from the ranks of small and medium-sized enterprises and the small-scale retail sector.

These various groups sustained the LDP with financial contributions and the votes of their members. They made their interests known by lobbying LDP legislators, by approaching bureaucrats, and by conducting publicity campaigns on the streets and in the media. They did not always get everything they wanted from the LDP, of course. But as long as the economy grew at rapid rates, the ruling party was able to satisfy a surprisingly large share of their demands.

Interest groups came together in support of national policies in one distinctive venue, the *shingikai*, consultative committees established by law. Shingikai were usually attached to an individual ministry or to the prime minister's office. Their purpose was to advise a minister or the prime minister on policies in a specific area, such as industrial structure, tax changes, or agricultural programs. Shingikai members were drawn from representatives of interest groups immediately concerned with the issues at hand. Thus bankers and economic specialists dominated shingikai on tax policy. Business leaders, union members, consumer representatives, journalists, and others sat on the large industrial structure committee. In this way, shingikai served as a preliminary forum in which contending views about policy changes could be discussed and a kind of consensus ironed out. Shingikai reports often became the foundation for future legislation. Participants in shingikai discussions, along with the groups they represented, were then obliged to support the legislation that subsequently emerged. These mechanisms functioned both to build consensus and to ensure compliance with national goals.

**Policymaking.** One of the most emblematic policies of this era was the Income-Doubling Plan of 1960. Promoted through the personal and political efforts of Ikeda Hayato, this plan aimed to double both the national GNP and personal incomes. It also prescribed rapid growth under conditions of full employment by setting ambitious goals for investment, production, and exports. Much to the surprise of its critics, the Income-Doubling Plan achieved most of its goals well before their target dates. Many factors were responsible for this achievement, as later sections of this chapter explain. The early success of the plan gave a sharp boost both to Ikeda's personal stature and to the political fortunes of the LDP itself. Thereafter, most of the credit for economic growth redounded to the benefit of the ruling party.

The Income-Doubling Plan was essentially a political document that set broad targets for economic growth. In carrying out the plan, the government employed tax breaks, some direct assistance, a great deal of indirect assistance, and administrative guidance, or *gyosei shido* (directives from a government ministry). Gyosei shido were based as much on the political status and prestige of the directing ministries as on written laws. Guidance occurred when an official from the Ministry of International Trade and Industry (MITI) made suggestions to a steel firm, or when a bureaucrat in the Ministry of Finance (MOF) offered direction to a bank. In these circumstances, the private enterprise usually heeded their words, both out of respect for the ministry and out of concern for self-interest. Bureaucrats could make life difficult, and compliance was usually a wiser response than defiance. Gyosei shido was thus a vehicle the bureaucracy used to assist the LDP in carrying out parliamentary policies; it could also be used to pursue the goals of the ministries themselves, regardless of LDP actions.

In addition to the informal authority that inhered in administrative guidance, the bureaucracy also had formal responsibility for implementing laws passed in the Diet. Japanese laws were often very brief, consisting of just six to eight pages of concise, general guidelines. The bureaucracy therefore enjoyed considerable discretion when implementing and interpreting them. In most cases, however, the bureaucracy and the LDP were in agreement on the broad outlines of economic policy, and they usually—although not always—worked in tandem to achieve common objectives. Laws and regulations of special importance during this period shaped policies in two major areas: finance and agriculture.

Financial policy functioned to benefit large-scale industrial enterprises. Implemented primarily through the Bank of Japan and the MOF, financial policies were intended to keep the costs of capital low so that the largest and most productive firms could expand rapidly. Smaller firms that were less efficient producers were obliged to pay higher costs for their capital. The MOF established controls over corporate financing that restricted the growth of a corporate bond market, and it discouraged reliance on the stock market for corporate funds. Stock speculation had created a volatile economy during the prewar era, and postwar officials did not want to repeat that experience. Postwar financial practices fostered close ties between banks and their major creditors and also created efficient mechanisms for financing rapid growth of leading industries. They also enabled

Japanese corporations to pursue long-term, strategic development rather than short-term, tactical moves aimed at paying dividends and satisfying shareholders.

With control over the allocation of foreign exchange and imported technology, MITI augmented these policies. Between 1949 and 1979, MITI enjoyed the legal authority to channel often-scarce foreign currency toward large firms that would use it most effectively in pursuit of national economic goals. The ministry also had the right to approve the importation of technology from abroad and used this right to direct such resources toward large firms as well. Thus MITI could employ its administrative authority, for example, to allocate dollars to an expanding firm in a growing industry that wanted to buy the latest machine tools from the United States.

By controlling both foreign currency and technology approvals, MITI promoted national goals at the same time it advanced the private interests of the corporations and the industries that benefited. These practices created a complex web of cooperation, primarily between the late 1940s and the late 1960s, that has become famous in the United States as Japan's "industrial policy." Industrial policy was one, short-lived ingredient among many that contributed to Japan's rapid growth between the fifties and the seventies.

Agricultural policy was characterized in one sense by a bald exchange relationship between the LDP and farmers. The LDP appeared to offer assistance to rural areas in return for the farm vote. One important form of government assistance was a price support program for rice, to assure farmers of a high and rising return on their rice output. The government also restricted the import of rice into Japan. Other forms of assistance included extension services, financial grants for rationalizing land use or diversifying production, and investments in better roads and sewer systems to improve the quality of life in rural areas. The government also encouraged private construction of new factories in agricultural regions, to increase job opportunities off the farm and thus enhance the incomes of farm families.

LDP politicians and their rural clients were certainly scratching each other's backs, but there was more to this exchange than is immediately obvious. Many LDP politicians had grown up in rural areas and experienced the poverty of the prewar agrarian economy, and they above all wanted to prevent a repetition. By developing policies that stabilized rice prices and offered extra income to farm families, they were consciously easing the transition from an agrarian to an industrial society. Their policies enabled many farm families to remain in their home villages, to continue to work on their farms, and to realize the benefits of a growing economy, too. This arrangement preserved a large body of increasingly well-off consumers whose demands continued to feed economic growth. It also enabled Japan to avoid the kind of poverty, unemployment, and social distress that have appeared in many societies during periods of rapid industrialization.

The Japanese government pursued many policies in support of economic development; it also refrained from adopting others, and these omissions are equally important. One thing the Japanese government foreswore was a large defense establishment. Defeat in war, the atomic bomb, a more peaceful world, and the American nuclear umbrella all deterred Japan from spending lavishly on defense. By the 1960s, defense outlays equaled a bare 1 percent of the GNP. This left almost all of the nation's resources to be used for peaceful purposes of investment, consumption, and savings.

Japan did not develop a very generous system of public welfare during this period, either. By avoiding the taxes and expenditures such a system would have required, it left a larger share of the GNP in private hands. This choice probably enabled Japan to invest in new factories at a more rapid rate than other countries, such as Sweden and Great Britain, whose economic choices favored welfare and income redistribution over private capital formation. Also in contrast with some European countries, Japan did not nationalize any industries after the war. It left nearly all the manufacturing sector in private hands. It is difficult to measure the economic benefits of this choice. If the experience of Great Britain is any guide, however, leaving the private sector to pursue its own interests avoided a rash of nagging political and economic problems. Finally, again in contrast with European as well as North American countries, the Japanese government never became a large consumer of goods and services. This policy, too, left more resources in private hands, and it certainly contributed to the growth in disposable family incomes. In fact the government was often able to cut income taxes during this period, aided by rapidly rising revenues in the face of limited outlays.

The national government was not the only public entity to promote economic growth. Local governments did too. In most locales, political candidates ran without party affiliation, for two reasons. Partisan politics had not fully penetrated to the municipal level, and candidates and voters both tried to maintain the fiction that their communities were united around common goals. Nonetheless, local residents understood full well which politicians were affiliated with the LDP and which with the opposition. Most local politicians, in some communities as many as 80 percent, were LDP supporters. They shared the party's goals, and they achieved them by supporting LDP Diet members.

In return for their support, local conservatives relied on what came to be known as the "pipeline to the center" to get what they wanted for their communities. The pipeline brought government assistance in many forms. Most of it was in fact distributed according to complex formulas designed to minimize political favoritism. But this did not prevent the LDP and its politicians from taking credit for most local improvements—such as a surfaced road, a new bridge, or a railway station—subsidized with national funds.

In addition to collaborating with the central government to carry out national policies, many localities during this era undertook their own initiatives as well. Inviting into the community large firms needing factory sites became a widespread practice among local governments in the 1960s. Cities and towns would often pay the costs of developing land parcels for industrial use. They would also offer companies real estate tax holidays for several years, in the hope of luring a new auto plant or electronics factory. Through this process, local communities reaped both immediate returns, in the form of more jobs and better incomes for local residents, and later returns, in the form of a larger tax base. Unfortunately, some communities suffered heavy costs, too, when the firms they attracted caused severe environmental pollution.

These local undertakings illustrate the postwar pattern of cooperation and conflict between communities and the state first noted in Chapter 2. Support for the LDP and its politicians, and reliance on the pipeline to the center, were forms of cooperation. By adopting them, communities pursued their own interests as they subordinated themselves to the center. In contrast, local initiatives to bring in companies were an assertion of autonomy. Such initiatives promised to increase the local tax base and to decrease reliance on the center for financial assistance.

**The opposition.** Many Japanese citizens lent their political support to the complex, integrated structure of consensus that promoted economic growth. Some, however, did not. Opponents at the national level were drawn from the ranks of the progressive parties, in particular the Japan Socialist Party (JSP) and the Japan Communist Party (JCP). Union members in the public and the private sectors, farmers with lingering ties to the prewar tenant movement, and discontented, young, low-status, white-collar workers in the cities provided these parties with their electoral support. Both the JSP and the JCP maintained a shrill, rhetorical, public opposition to the LDP throughout these two decades, although the JSP did cooperate with the LDP on some issues behind the scenes.

Two other political parties appeared for the first time during this era. One was the Democratic Socialist Party (DSP), which originated in 1959 when a group of moderates split from the JSP to form their own party. They aligned themselves with a national union center called Domei, which originated in 1954 and represented the interests of workers in private industry. The moderate character of both party leaders and union supporters cast the DSP in a centrist mode and led to alliances with the LDP on a range of issues. Another centrist party appeared on the national scene in 1967 when the Clean Government Party (CGP) returned its first members to the Diet. Drawing its support from an evangelical Buddhist sect called the Soka Gakkai, the CGP advocated moderate policies, too, by stressing better provision of social welfare in particular.

The partisan segmentation that grew after the 1960s reflected the increasing diversity of Japanese society itself. It did not, however, pose a threat to the stability of LDP rule. In the six HOR elections held between 1955 and 1972, the LDP secured a comfortable majority of seats in every one. Its share of the popular vote drifted steadily downward, however, from 58 percent in 1958 to 47 percent in 1972. This was an ominous trend for the LDP, but its full impact was not felt for another two decades.

Political parties were not the only ones to contest LDP policies in these years. Two other groups provided some especially visible opposition: coal miners and students. During the 1950s, Japanese political, bureaucratic, and business leaders gradually decided to adopt petroleum as the nation's primary energy source. This choice required a de-emphasis of the domestic coal industry, and in the 1950s, private firms adopted rationalization programs that required massive layoffs. The symbol of opposition to the layoffs was a strike at the Miike Mines of the Mitsui company in 1959 and 1960. Despite a prolonged, united effort, the strikers failed to achieve their objectives. Thereafter, cutbacks in the coal industry continued apace. When the Miike strike ended, nearly three hundred thousand miners still toiled at working mines across Japan; by 1972 the remaining mines employed about forty thousand workers. These changes not only reduced the absolute strength of the union movement but sent a chill through the hearts of many union members in other industries, especially steel. Their increasingly more moderate, cooperative behavior was reinforced by these events.

Students expressed their opposition to the LDP and its policies most vociferously in 1960, when the security treaty signed in 1951 came up for renewal. In alliance with progressive intellectuals and labor unions, students opposed the treaty because they believed that it aligned Japan with the United States in an anticommunist crusade. They preferred neutrality or alignment with nations in the Third World. Students also opposed Kishi himself, in his role as an elderly, conservative politician tainted by his wartime record. Students and their allies organized mass demonstrations in the streets of Tokyo and around the Diet to promote their goals. They failed to prevent passage of the treaty, but their efforts probably did cut short Kishi's tenure as prime minister.

Kishi's successor, Ikeda Hayato, responded to the students by taking a more low-key approach that emphasized economic issues on which people agreed, rather than diplomatic issues on which they differed. Frustrated by their failures, many students joined cells of factionalized, leftist student groups. Operating mainly underground, these groups burst onto the scene again in the late 1960s, when student opposition to the Vietnam War cropped up in national capitals around the globe. Once again, however, students saw their demands ignored and their efforts thwarted. Their opposition did little to change the entrenched powers of the LDP.

### Economic Processes

The impregnable political position of the LDP and its economic policies were necessary, but not sufficient, conditions for high-speed growth.

Growth was not just the outcome of a political program conceived by a ruling triad of politicians, bureaucrats, and businessmen and implemented by a nation working as one. Politicians, bureaucrats, and businessmen did play their roles in promoting rapid growth, and many groups within Japan did their part, too, even when they worked at cross purposes. But to fully appreciate why such rapid growth occurred between 1955 and 1974, we must adopt a broader, indeed global, perspective. Growth was the product of a temporary conjunction of factors, both domestic and international, which many groups in Japan exploited to their material advantage. Understanding the economic features of this process thus requires an analysis of international forces as well as domestic.

**The international environment.** Four aspects of the international economy contributed to Japan's economic success: secure access to relatively low-cost raw materials; currency exchange-rate stability; open world markets in which to sell exports and buy imports; and booming international demand for manufactured products. Japan had to purchase raw materials abroad if it was going to become a manufacturing giant; for its own resources were inadequate to the task. It had limited supplies of coal and a few metals, but it could not satisfy domestically its demands for petroleum, iron, bauxite, and numerous other commodities. Winning secure access to raw materials and energy sources that were low in price was a real boon to the Japanese economy. It was an even greater boon to obtain steady supplies of major imports, such as petroleum, at costs that actually fell between the late 1950s and the early 1970s. Japan's reputation as a low-cost producer of high-quality manufactured goods arose from temporary opportunities like these.

A stable regime for international currency flows was one major achievement of the post–World War II settlement among the Allied powers. Allied leaders laid the essential foundations for this system at Bretton Woods in 1944. The system was implemented through the International Monetary Fund (IMF), which was established in 1945 to operate under the auspices of the United Nations. Stable currency exchange policies created a predictable monetary environment and smoothed the pursuit of international commerce. The former Allies, and in due course Japan and West Germany, constructed on this foundation a liberal system of international trade that functioned well until the early 1970s.

A policy of open markets further encouraged cooperative behavior in international trade. Agreement on this issue had to await the revision in economic policies toward Germany and Japan, so open trade regimes did not emerge until the creation of the General Agreement on Tariffs and Trade (GATT) in 1948, which established a mechanism for encouraging open markets, reciprocity in trade, and cooperative efforts to improve international commerce. Japan won GATT membership in 1955 and went on to enjoy the benefits it conferred on a nation so dependent on imports and so advantaged by exports.

The IMF and GATT created a markedly improved environment for international commerce. The result was a two-decade period of booming growth in global trade. In the twenty years after 1953, the total volume of manufactured goods exported around the globe increased by six times, and the dollar value of world exports by more than seven. Old markets in Europe and North America expanded rapidly, and new markets arose in Asia, Africa, and Latin America. Everyone seemed eager to trade.

Japan rode this wave of trade expansion as agilely as any other nation. Between 1955 and 1974, the dollar value of Japanese exports increased twenty-five times over. So did the value of its imports. Japan found itself poised to supply exactly what the world was demanding in greatest quantity: steel, fabricated metal products, ships, and precision equipment. Near the end of the era it added automobiles, business equipment, and audio and video appliances to this list. The sale of these exports earned the currency Japan needed to pay for its imports: petroleum and other energy sources, industrial raw materials, and food products. Despite having been almost shut off from the outside world in the early postwar years, Japan accounted for more than 6 percent of the world's exports and an equal share of its imports by 1974.

It is important to add another perspective to these figures. Although Japan had become one of the world's largest exporters and importers, foreign trade still accounted for a relatively small share of its overall economic activities. Exports were equal to about 11 percent of the GDP in 1974, and imports were just slightly higher. In this sense, Japan was far less reliant on foreign trade than many other countries. A small country such as Belgium, which traded extensively with its nearby neighbors, was four times more reliant than Japan on foreign trade. Even the much larger economy of West Germany was twice as reliant. Exports and imports were a necessary component of the Japanese economy in this era, but it is essential to bear in mind that Japan's domestic market absorbed about 90 percent of what it produced each year between 1955 and 1974.

The sogo shosha were ideal institutions to mediate Japan's role in this expansive international economy. They had decades of experience in finding raw materials, in transporting bulk commodities to and from Japan, in financing trade activities, and in educating Japanese producers about markets abroad. During this era six giant sogo shosha assumed preeminence in offering these services. Three were descendants of the old zaibatsu and maintained their names: Mitsui, Mitsubishi, and Sumitomo. They dealt primarily with firms bearing the same old zaibatsu name, but they also worked on behalf of other firms, especially in the steel industry. Three other sogo shosha—Ito Chu, Marubeni, and Nissho-Iwai—served the needs of firms in the three different groups to which they belonged, while working with other, nonrelated firms, too. These unique organizations linked Japan to international markets by handling as much as half its imports and exports in some years. They also functioned as catalysts in the development of the domestic economy by helping to shape the internal response to external demands.

**The domestic context.** To satisfy export demands and meet domestic needs, Japan had to integrate rapidly expanding production at home. Mobilizing capital, making investments, and exploiting technology were three essential tasks, which Japan carried out by directing the lion's share of resources to large firms, some old and some new. At the same time, it was necessary to foster the parallel expansion of small and medium-sized enterprises. The country met all of these challenges, and output and productivity grew at extraordinary rates. Manufacturing benefited most from these changes and agriculture the least.

Capital for investment purposes was still scarce in Japan in 1955, posing difficulties for firms that wanted to invest in new factories. During the next decade, however, an effective system of industrial finance evolved. Internal financing provided about 40 percent of the capital needs of firms in the manufacturing sector. These funds were generated by the firms themselves, in the form of depreciation allow-ances or reinvested profits. The remaining 60 percent of industrial investment came from a variety of external sources. Some came from corporate bonds, despite MOF restrictions on their issuance. A very small share came from the sale of equity on the stock market, and another small amount came from foreign sources. But the largest share of external financing came from bank loans, which were dependent, in turn, on the accumulated wealth of small savers. It was they who financed much of Japan's investment, both public and private, during this period.

Families, individuals, and small proprietors made up Japan's small savers. They were not, for the most part, very wealthy, and they did not have very large incomes in 1955. They had, however, a strong propen-sity to save. Depression, war, and reconstruction had all persuaded older people to set money aside, because they never knew what might happen next. They maintained the habit of saving long after the war. Younger people saved during this period for other reasons: to pay for future consumption, such as the educations and weddings of their children, and the new homes that many wanted to buy. In the absence of a generous system of social welfare, people also realized that they needed to save for their own retirements. Given these considerations, Japanese families saved at unusually high rates. At the beginning of this period, families put aside, on average, about 13 percent of their dispos-able incomes. As the economy grew and wages rose, they saved a little more each year. By 1974 the average family was saving 25 percent of its disposable income, a rate four to five times higher than the American savings rate.

Small savers placed their money in two types of financial institu-tions: the postal savings system and banks. Millions of families found it convenient to stop off at the corner postal branch and deposit small sums as they became available. These accounts paid interest at competi-tive market rates; they also offered an opportunity to evade taxes on interest, something the government winked at for many years. The central government mobilized postal savings for public investments through an off-budget account known as the Fiscal Investment and Loan Program. This program loaned funds to government entities that invested in public housing, small and medium-sized enterprises, trans-portation and communications networks, improvements in the living environment, and export promotion activities. In all of these ways the central government exploited funds gathered from small savers to underwrite public investments that facilitated economic growth. These procedures had the additional benefit of keeping taxes low.

Funds accumulating in accounts that small savers held at banks, especially the largest commercial banks, underwrote private investment. The commercial banks converted their deposits into short- and long-term loans to private businesses. They strongly favored the largest firms for this purpose and consistently loaned more than half their funds to giant entities that constituted less than 1 percent of all firms. During this period, the sectors of the economy that absorbed the most private investment capital were the electric power, engineering, steel, and chemical industries. The textile industry also borrowed large sums as it shifted production from the natural fibers to synthetic. Between 1955 and 1974, private investment varied between 10 and 21 percent of GNP per annum, but it averaged about 18 percent each year. This rate, too, like the savings rate of Japanese families, was exceptionally high by international standards. It guaranteed the rapid expansion of factories and an attendant increase in jobs and incomes.

There were six commercial banks that played a special role during this era. Four of them were direct descendants of the old zaibatsu banks: Mitsui, Mitsubishi, Sumitomo, and Fuji (the postwar successor to the Yasuda Bank). The other two were the Daiichi Bank (which later became the Daiichi-Kangyo Bank) and the Sanwa Bank. As the fifties progressed, these banks began to assume the financial role that former zaibatsu holding companies had once played. They became the principal source of investment capital for the firms associated with them; they purchased more and more of the shares of those firms; and they came to play a guiding role in shaping the development of those groups.

The groups (sometimes actually called *guruupu*, in Japanese) became known as *keiretsu*, or affiliated firms. In the Mitsui, Mitsubishi, and Sumitomo groups, most of the major firms linked to the bank bore the name of the zaibatsu itself. In the Fuji group, firms once underwritten by the Yasuda financial interests predominated. They were often firms located in eastern Japan, such as Hitachi, Nissan, and Japan Steel Tube. The Daiichi group brought together two former, small zaibatsu groupings, the Furukawa and the Kawasaki. The Sanwa Bank created a network of firms located primarily in the Kansai Region around Osaka.

The postwar keiretsu were even more diverse than their prewar predecessors. In addition to the commercial bank situated at the hub, each keiretsu usually had two other financial institutions, an insurance company and a trust bank, that could provide loans or investment capital. Each also included one of the six large sogo shosha, which served the marketing needs of group members. Most keiretsu had some exposure to the retail sector through a major department store, sometimes owned by a private railway, such as Tokyu in the Tokyo area or Hankyu in the Osaka region. And each group had a variety of manufacturing concerns that offered it a presence in nearly every major industry: steel making, chemical production, electrical machinery, synthetic fibers, construction, shipbuilding, and food processing, to name the most important.

Postwar keiretsu differed from the prewar zaibatsu in several ways. They did not have holding companies to provide direct, formal authority over firms. The family members who controlled the zaibatsu were removed from power after the war and did not play a managerial role in the keiretsu. Interlocking directorships were prohibited by law after the war, so formal control through managerial assignments was not possible in the keiretsu.

The keiretsu did bear some resemblances to the zaibatsu in other ways. In place of the holding companies, banks shaped keiretsu development by providing funds and advice. Banks shared their influence with conferences of company leaders; they met on regular occasions to provide informal coordination among keiretsu firms. More than formal authority, therefore, informal ties that keiretsu firms found mutually beneficial drew them together in cooperative alliance. These ties included shared identity with a lead bank, common brand names, crossholding of shares, marketing coordination, intergroup sales and purchases, and informal personnel relationships.

The keiretsu were a direct product of the prewar history of Japanese business development and a shrewd response to the exigencies of a booming, postwar international economy. They played a major role in promoting Japan's rapid growth, and they controlled a large share of capital and markets in the industries where they were represented. But they were by no means alone in fostering the gains of this period. As descendants of the zaibatsu, they were well positioned in manufacturing sectors that had been important through the early 1940s, including mining, chemical production, shipbuilding, and some parts of the steel and engineering industries, but they had been slow to enter some of the newest industries, such as auto making. In the postwar era, they were even slower to develop a presence in some of the fastest-growing industries, such as consumer electronics.

Therefore, alongside the surviving zaibatsu enterprises, a contingent of newer, independent firms emerged that in time won high standing in the industrial economy. These firms included Toyota and Honda in the auto industry; Matsushita, Sony, Sharp, and Sanyo in consumer electronics; Fujitsu in computers; Komatsu in construction and farming equipment; and Maruzen and Idemitsu in the petroleum industry. Rapid growth depended on the continued presence of the old zaibatsu in their new guise as keiretsu, but it also depended on the entrepreneurial drive of new men bucking the odds to form new industrial giants.

One thing the new men did especially well was to exploit the latest technology. They utilized new technology from abroad, through direct purchase, royalty arrangements, or joint ventures. Steel making, electrical machinery, and chemical production all became far more productive as a result. They also built their own laboratories and institutes in which they pursued research and development under private sponsorship. Japanese firms also achieved many technological gains by adapting and improving processes introduced from abroad; in fact improvements in production processes made a major contribution to higher productivity levels, especially in the auto industry. Finally, Japanese firms found practical applications for inventions that sometimes went unused elsewhere. A small communications company discovered in the late 1950s how the transistor could be exploited to make portable radios. Its application revolutionized consumer electronics and eventually made Sony a household word.

Favored by history, access to capital, and their own resources, the largest firms made the fastest gains and accumulated the largest profits during this era. Although they represented less than 1 percent of all manufacturing firms, they employed about 17 percent of the industrial labor force and accounted for about 26 percent of the value added in the production process. The balance of the industrial labor force toiled in the small and medium-sized enterprise sector.

This sector also experienced sweeping changes after 1955. It added more than 260,000 new factories and nearly five million workers. The value of its output increased almost five times over. Its political influence rose perceptibly as it organized to articulate its demands to politicians and bureaucrats. The Basic Law for Small and Medium Enterprises, passed in 1963, laid the foundation for a more rational and attentive treatment of these firms by the government. In addition, many large final producers in such industries as auto making and electrical equipment devoted increased attention to their smaller parts suppliers. Owing to these changes, many small and medium-sized enterprises improved their managerial practices, their efficiency, their working conditions, and not least, their profitability. Some small firms, such as Nippon Denso, were so successful that they became giant enterprises themselves. In the best years, small firms often made higher profits on their capital than large firms. These achievements created a body of small entrepreneurs who became a major influence in the communities and regions where they operated and in the inner circles of the local LDP.

Integrating capital, investment, and technology in this diverse industrial context produced extraordinary returns for Japan. Between 1955 and 1974 the average *real* rate of growth was 10 percent per annum. It is difficult to appreciate what this figure means. An investment earning interest at 10 percent doubles in value at seven-year intervals. The Japanese economy, too, was doubling in size every seven years. Under those circumstances, people often joked that Japan was always "under construction," and so it seemed. Overnight a quiet, grassy field would hum with activity as bulldozers arrived to build a factory site. Or a pleasant residential street might suddenly become a subway route attracting trucks and cranes all hours of night and day.

We can measure such changes in more concrete ways. The production of commercial shipping tonnage increased 5 times over in the two decades after 1955. Steel production increased by about 13 times. Machine production rose 39 times, and auto output climbed 197 times. Obviously, some of these increases are a function of small initial bases, but that does not gainsay the record of the Japanese manufacturing

**12. Medium-sized factory.** *Many factories like this one, which manufactured auto parts under contract to Toyota Motors, sprang up amid centuries-old paddy fields during the rapid growth of the 1960s and 1970s.*

(Gary D. Allinson.)

sector in this era. Starting from a modest position in 1955, Japan became one of the world's most important manufacturing nations in the course of two short decades.

There is another segment of the domestic economy whose conditions require discussion in a more sober tone. The agricultural sector underwent some wrenching adjustments during this era. In less than twenty years, the total farm populace dropped from 36 million to 23 million. About 1 million families left farming entirely. New jobs in the cities may have brought steadier incomes and a gradual improvement in their standard of living, but the loss of so many children, relatives, and entire families was a heavy social blow to many small communities. Some of them never recovered.

Those who remained on the farm experienced a quiet revolution in their own lives. A principal cause of change was mechanization. Beginning in the late 1950s, labor-saving devices were introduced into farm areas with increasing rapidity. Mechanical threshers were among the first new devices; they saved hours of time once spent husking rice. Mechanical plows were next; they eliminated days of backbreaking labor preparing fields for transplanting. By the late 1960s, sprayers, grain dryers, mechanical planters and harvesters, and small trucks were becoming more widespread. All of these devices enabled farm families to maintain their plots with a much reduced investment of labor.

Freed from time-consuming chores, fathers, wives, and children who remained on the farm could seek extra income off the farm. The luckiest were able to secure full-time, well-paid work as school teachers or local officials. Others had to make do with seasonal jobs in a local factory or daily labor on a construction project in a nearby town. The least lucky were forced into *dekasegi*, or short-term itinerant labor. Dekasegi workers usually left home after the fall harvest to travel to the Tokyo and Osaka regions, where they stayed in cheap lodgings for five or six months while they worked long, grueling hours on construction gangs. With the arrival of spring, they returned home for the rice-planting season. In the 1960s, hundreds of thousands of farm families suffered annually from the social stress imposed by this labor system.

Farm households were forced to invest energy and ingenuity and to make sacrifices in their struggle for survival. Farmers in remote areas with poor soils and short growing seasons had difficulty making ends meet, whereas farmers in temperate regions producing fruits and vegetables for urban markets did quite well. By combining income from outside work with earnings from agriculture, the average farm family was able to maintain a standard of living that approximated the urban level in most years during this period. Even with the much smaller labor force, Japan's farmers were able to satisfy almost all domestic demand for rice, fruits, and vegetables. The total value of farm production thus increased five times over during this period. By the end of the period, however, changing dietary habits were attracting imports of other food

**13. Threshing rice mechanically, 1974.** *By husking and bagging rice simultaneously, machines like this made it possible for one person to do the work of four.* (Courtesy of Gail Lee Bernstein.)

**14. Transplanting mechanically, 1974.** *The introduction of mechanized rice transplanters made it possible for one man to relieve many farm women from long hours of arduous labor and free them to earn cash incomes from jobs outside agriculture.* (Courtesy of Gail Lee Bernstein.)

products, such as wheat, soybeans, and meat, that Japanese farms were ill suited to produce. The arrival of these imports made future prospects in farming much dimmer for a son in 1974 than in 1955.

The era of high-speed growth was a distinctive episode in Japan's economic history. Rapid growth occurred because many domestic and international factors came together at the same time. A long period of material deprivation caused by depression, war, and reconstruction made people hungry for a better standard of living. These consumer demands coincided with the need to rebuild wartorn economies in Japan and Europe. Demand created a domestic and international market for goods that Japan was well-equipped to produce. The nation took advantage of its managerial experience, its labor skills, and its institutional resources to channel capital, investment, and technology into an efficient system of high-quality production. Secure supplies of low-cost raw materials, easy access to world markets, and a stable currency regime facilitated Japan's ability to pursue its economic goals. Steady jobs at higher wages for increasing numbers of workers encouraged high levels of consumption and savings. Consumption sustained demand, savings generated investment capital, and the economy continued to grow at rapid rates—as long as the right conditions obtained.

### Social Processes

High rates of economic growth stimulated extensive social changes. Occupational and geographic mobility were especially pronounced, as millions of workers took new jobs in different parts of the country. Faced with severe challenges in providing housing and public services to fast-growing populations, cities expanded and new suburbs arose. New modes of social interaction promoted a new style of family life in urban areas, leading to some new roles and attitudes—though the position of women did not radically change. The educational system expanded to serve the needs of public and private employers. Wealth came to be distributed more equally and more extensively, and social status underwent subtle change. New status markers, higher levels of education, and more widespread wealth gradually nourished a more politically self-conscious citizenry. Near the end of this period, grass roots dissent over environmental problems provided an early sign that rapid growth could not continue indefinitely.

**Mobility.** Occupational mobility completely realigned the allocation of jobs in Japanese society. In 1955, Japan's occupational distribution looked like that of many countries in the early stages of industrialization. Farm workers and others in the primary sector (fishermen and foresters) formed 41 percent of the labor force. The secondary sector, which included mining and construction workers as well as industrial laborers, occupied only 23 percent of the work force. The tertiary sector, which included workers in commerce, various service trades, the professions, and government, accounted for the remaining 36 percent.

During the next twenty years, this picture changed dramatically. Farming and mining experienced drastic reductions in their labor forces. Mining jobs declined by more than 75 percent, reducing that industry to a tiny remnant of its past. At the same time, nearly half the people employed in agriculture left to find other kinds of work. Numbering almost 9 million in all, they moved into the many new jobs being created in the other two sectors. Most new opportunities were in manufacturing, which doubled employment from about 7 million to more than 13 million. The wholesale and retail trades, where employment grew from nearly 6 million to more than 11 million, added almost as many workers as manufacturing. Although expansion was greatest in these two fields, the service trades, construction, and transportation together added another 8.6 million jobs.

By 1974, agricultural employment had dropped to only 14 percent of the total. Manufacturing and construction employment had risen to 34 percent, and the tertiary sector provided the remaining 52 percent of the nation's jobs. In 1955 more than half the country's workers had been self-employed farmers, small shop owners, or poorly paid or unpaid family workers helping out on the farm or in the shop. Two decades later, fully 70 percent of the labor force was employed in paid positions with most of them drawing wages or salaries determined by market forces in a nationwide economy.

Among these income earners, the most emulated were white-collar workers drawing regular salaries and enjoying prospects of lifetime employment. They were known as *sararii-man,* or salaried workers, and they became the symbol of a new social category to which many now aspired. The sararii-man was a social type that had emerged during the prewar period in small numbers, consisting mainly of elite bureaucrats and corporate managers. The historical rarity of achieving such a position made it an object of desire for young company workers in the 1960s. So did the promise it offered of secure employment and a high income. Indeed the symbol of sararii-man status became so potent that many blue-collar workers took to wearing white shirts and ties while commuting to and from work, hoping that others would smile on their apparent good fortune.

Although millions of white-collar workers did win the status of sararii-man during this period, most people found work in lower-status positions. White-collar technicians and managers did increase considerably, more than doubling in number, but lower-paid, blue-collar workers laboring on factory lines were almost three times more numerous. Also numerous were modestly paid clerical workers and sales personnel. Rapid growth did create many high-paying, white-collar positions, and it did transform the occupational distribution of the nation's labor force. But most of the new jobs initially paid modest wages and salaries while exacting heavy physical demands from their occupants.

Finding a job during this period required workers to make at least one, and often more than one, move. This was especially true of those leaving farm villages to seek employment in cities or metropolitan regions. But it was also true of young school leavers taking their first job and of older workers moving from a poor job to a better one. The geographic mobility that ensued remade the demographic map of Japan.

Two features of this geographic mobility were especially important: the exodus from agriculture and the growth of metropolitan areas. In many years after 1955, almost one million people per year left rural villages. As a consequence, many regions experienced a net loss in population. These regions were in northeastern Japan, on the Japan Sea coast, and on the islands of Shikoku and Kyushu. Many prefectures in these areas suffered population declines into the early 1970s, as children finishing school and entire families departed to find work in the cities.

The metropolitan regions centered on Tokyo and Osaka attracted newcomers in greatest number. Tokyo with its surrounding prefectures of Kanagawa, Chiba, and Saitama was the strongest magnet. The population of these four prefectures almost doubled in two decades, rising from about 15 million to over 27 million. The region had attracted 25 percent of the nation's populace by 1975. Osaka and its neighboring prefectures of Kyoto, Nara, and Hyogo also marked sharp increases. Another 15 percent of the nation's population resided in these four prefectures by 1975. During the quarter century after 1950, the urban populace rose from 38 to 76 percent of the national total, and the customs of agrarian life receded quickly.

Other features of geographic mobility during this period warrant comment. People not only moved into the large cities in massive numbers; they left in large numbers, too. Referred to as the U-turn, these departures picked up momentum after the early 1960s. In some years, out-migrants were almost as numerous as in-migrants. Often people had compelling reasons for leaving Tokyo and Osaka to return to regional cities or farm villages, such as a job transfer or the obligation to take over a family farm. But many left the metropolitan regions because they preferred the larger housing, the shorter commutes, and the higher quality of life that small cities offered.

Industrial dispersion was another feature of geographic mobility. The Tokyo and Osaka regions attracted most of the new jobs in manufacturing, but some industrial enterprises located in small cities in rural areas, too. There was prewar precedent for this practice. Both the Hitachi enterprise and the Toyota enterprise had located their factories in small, rural cities to take advantage of cheap land and nearby labor. In the postwar era, many firms in the shipbuilding, petrochemical, electronics, and steel industries built plants in smaller cities. They sought locations outside the metropolitan regions owing to inducements from local governments, agreements among keiretsu firms, guidance from the central government, or a desire to reduce transportation costs. Whatever their reasons, all such firms created a singular circumstance for the cities where they located. Each community depended very heavily on the well-being of the single enterprise that dominated the local economy. That was not a problem for most communities during this period, but it proved to be later.

Japan's rapid industrial expansion and the geographic mobility it stimulated thus fostered several types of urban development. It led to the rapid growth of large cities such as Tokyo, Osaka, and Nagoya, the steady appearance of new suburbs on the periphery of those cities, and the explosive growth of regional industrial cities. Although each type of urban area had its own distinctive problems, all faced the same two challenges: providing adequate public services and housing.

The provision of public services was a serious challenge only partly met before 1974. The largest cities had foregone many public investments during the war, and they had all been badly damaged by wartime bombing. They had not fully recovered from those difficulties when high-speed growth began, so they were a little behind from the very beginning. Further complicating provision of public services was the speed at which cities grew in the fifties and sixties. So many people arrived in such a short time that it was nearly impossible to keep pace with current needs, much less compensate for past lapses. Planning for and controlling growth were also difficult, because governments lacked the powers and the inclination to do so. Much urban development was therefore chaotic at best. Finally, cities were strapped for cash during the early years of this period, and it took time for enough revenues to accumulate to meet the demand for services. Thus cities found it difficult to build roads, sidewalks, schools, and civic buildings fast enough. Traffic congestion, dangerous roads, antiquated libraries, and crowded schools were costs that new urban residents had to abide for many years.

The housing challenge was similar in many ways. Limited construction of housing after 1937 and destruction during the war had created a horrendous backlog of demand. Scarce capital was another constraint. Financial policy directed available funds to large industrial firms, not the mortgage market, and most families did not have the savings to purchase a home that required a down payment of nearly 40 percent. People did need a place to live, however, and most got something, even if it was not all they hoped for. Between the late 1950s and the early 1970s, Japan built more than 11 million new dwelling units, increasing its housing stock by about 65 percent. Private companies and public entities provided a small share of the total. The remainder was divided equally between owner-occupied single-family homes and small rental units built and operated by private parties.

Despite this gargantuan effort to house the growing urban populace, three problems persisted: cost, quality, and size. Burgeoning demand drove land prices up rapidly, especially in metropolitan areas where space was at a premium. High land prices, combined with the large down payments needed to qualify for a loan, made it difficult for many families to buy their own homes. Low quality continued to plague housing provision. Too much housing was built too hastily and too cheaply. Small rental units were thrown up overnight on plots of vacated paddy field, and poorly constructed, ferroconcrete buildings began to deteriorate almost immediately. Builders tried to address the matter of size, and the average housing unit grew by almost 50 percent during this period; yet, an average unit still provided only about 800 square feet of living space, and most city apartments were much smaller. These conditions caught the eye of a visiting European official, who described Japanese dwellings as "rabbit hutches." Japanese governments, architects, builders, and consumers have striven ever since to erase that humiliation.

**Interaction.** The nature of urban housing influenced the evolution of family life in the cities. In part because they were unable to find apartments or homes of a desired size, young families began having fewer children. Within two decades the average family size nationwide dropped from about five to about three and one-half persons. Many other factors affected this change, including a drop in demand for labor in rural areas, better knowledge of contraceptive techniques, and new attitudes toward education and social mobility. Young urban families began to stress the importance of high school and college educations. Saving for such expenditures, and preparing the children to be successful, dissuaded many families from having more than two children.

These considerations produced another social figure who emerged during this era, the *kyoiku-mama*, or education mother. She was, according to the ideal, the wife of a man who worked full time and brought home a salary adequate to the family's needs. In other words, she was the domestic counterpart of the sararii-man. His salary enabled her to avoid taking a job outside the home and to spend her time within the home, managing its daily affairs and its financial matters. Her other major responsibility was to rear the children, especially the males, to successfully pass the competitive tests needed to enter high school and college. These duties made her a kyoiku-mama, a gentle nag who kept her son at the books and ensured the good fortune of the family in the next generation. Although the kyoiku-mama was something of a stereotype, many women during the sixties found themselves forced into just such a role by both husbandly demands and societal expectations.

Such expectations imply that women's roles had not changed significantly. There is ample evidence to bear this out. Women were usually still taught as children to be subservient to the needs of their male siblings, and this subservience was reinforced in the educational system, where boys and girls were often separated and treated differently according to gender. Although, by the sixties, women found it easier to acquire more education, at the high school and even postsecondary level, they were still shunted into what most Japanese considered to be a more feminine curriculum. When they entered the labor force, they were obliged to take more menial positions as secretaries, shop clerks, production workers, or elementary teachers. Moreover, society expected them to leave work once they got married, to spend all their time rearing a family. They were essentially prevented from assuming full-time work in the lifetime employment system, and very few women entered the upper ranks of private firms or public organizations. In all of these ways, women continued to occupy a position subordinate to males and part of a heavily gendered division of labor.

The educational system continued to play a crucial role in reproducing differences between the genders. After the war, Japan's schools expanded with the growing populace, and Allied reforms made a middle school education compulsory under law. The earliest efforts at expansion thus strove to assure that everyone received schooling through the first nine grades. Instruction, especially at the elementary level, stressed a kind of mastery learning. It was assumed that all would be given an equal opportunity to acquire basic literary and quantitative skills, boys and girls alike. In the 1950s, the majority of students finished their formal education when they graduated from middle school.

By the 1960s, demand rose for more places in secondary and postsecondary institutions. Growing resources in both the public and private sectors made it possible to increase the number of spaces in both high schools and colleges. By the early 1970s, more than 80 percent of middle school graduates were going on to high school, and more than 30 percent of high school graduates were continuing on to further schooling. At higher levels, there was a sharp distinction between the sexes, however. Most men who pursued postsecondary education entered four-year colleges or the nation's most prestigious universities, public institutions such as Tokyo University (Todai) and Kyoto University (Kyodai). In contrast, the smaller proportion of women who advanced to postsecondary institutions usually attended two-year community colleges, vocational schools, or women's colleges, none of which prepared them to win top jobs in prestigious firms.

As in the prewar period, the level and prestige of one's educational qualifications determined the type of job one assumed on leaving school. A clear gradation of achievement emerged which coincided with an equally clear gradation of prestige in the world of work. The least prestigious jobs were those that required little education but made heavy physical demands: those in farming, construction, and small manufacturing concerns. Middle school graduates entered these jobs. Factory work at large industrial firms was the next step up in occupational prestige. Some middle school graduates entered such jobs, but the best firms preferred high school graduates. Society looked with more favor on white-collar positions calling for clerical and administrative skills. Medium-sized firms, big businesses, and the public sector all offered jobs like these; they went to male high school graduates and graduates of less prestigious colleges. Many young women with postsecondary degrees also found work with these kinds of employers. But owing to their training and to society's expectations for them, they nearly all worked for short tenures of five to six years under a thick glass ceiling, and they inevitably resigned when they married. The most prestigious positions were white-collar jobs in the national bureaucracy, large banks and insurance companies, major manufacturing concerns and trading companies, and universities. Men with college degrees and university diplomas competed for these jobs.

Having entered a career, most workers received incomes that were a function of their educational credentials, their age and length of service in the organization, and the size and stature of their employer. Young workers with modest educations working in a small firm with little stature earned the least. Those with university degrees and lengthy work experience in large, prestigious firms earned the most. Not only did the former receive lower regular wages; they also received smaller bonuses, which were extra payments given twice annually in amounts depending on the financial success of the employer. During this period, a good bonus at a large firm could increase a worker's regular annual salary by 50 percent, whereas workers in small firms received much less.

Under these circumstances, typical incomes in the mid-sixties (including bonuses, but before taxes) were as follows. A young factory worker in a small firm earned about ¥ 25,000 per month. A middle-aged, white-collar worker in a medium-sized firm earned about ¥ 40,000, and an older manager in a large firm earned about ¥ 70,000 per month. Thus, the best-paid workers earned about 2.8 times more than the lowest-paid workers. Government surveys of household budgets confirm these income patterns from a different perspective. They illustrate that the average monthly income of households in the top 20 percent was about 2.7 times greater than the average for households in the bottom 20 percent.

Two aspects of Japanese income distribution during this period warrant comment for their major effect on the character of Japanese society. First, the disparity between the highest salaries and the lowest

was quite small. An older, experienced worker in a prestigious corporation was likely to earn only about three times more than a young,
inexperienced worker in a minor firm. This narrow salary spectrum
produced a comparatively equal distribution of incomes. Second, for
most workers on salary, incomes rose with age and experience, which
meant they could count on increased earnings as they married, reared
families, bought houses, and sent children to college. By raising incomes
in step with increasing financial responsibilities, employers both eased
the economic anxieties of a worker's middle and later years and encouraged rational planning for savings and consumption.

Relatively equal incomes that rose with age strongly shaped patterns
of consumption during this era. Japanese families managed their incomes and expenditures with great care. They first brought their diets
up to a healthy level from the abysmal lows to which they had dropped
after the war. Then they purchased better clothing for everyone and a
sewing machine to mend it. They also made necessary repairs to housing. Only after these necessities were taken care of did families think
about spending on consumer goods. Even then, they purchased small
items that were almost like necessities, to make work at home easier.
Thus, consumers bought washing machines, refrigerators, and vacuum
cleaners when they had the money to do so beginning in the early
sixties.

By the mid-sixties, a hint of extravagance appeared as many families
began buying cameras. More discretionary purchases followed in the
seventies: stereos, cassette recorders, color television sets, cars, and
room air-conditioners. By the mid-seventies, nearly every urban household owned a washing machine, refrigerator, color television, and
vacuum cleaner. Only half owned stereos and casettes, and about one-
third owned a car. The diffusion of consumer goods was by no means
complete at that point, but many families enjoyed some material possessions that brought a little comfort to their lives.

Cultural critics have heaped abuse on Japanese consumers for their
allegedly mindless buying in this era. The critics see them as heedless
victims of big capital, mesmerized by the latest consumer gewgaws.
Although many consumers did buy the same goods at the same time,
they were not dupes. Their behavior marked the end of the long period
of material deprivation and was shaped by the relatively equal distribution of rising real incomes. Consumer behavior was also coupled with

**15. Shopping street, late 1960s.** *Small shops, owned and operated by a single family, such as the candy store and green grocer's on the left, have historically dominated retail commerce, as in this central Tokyo residential area.*

(Courtesy of Patricia S. Allinson.)

the restraint that produced increasingly higher savings rates throughout these two decades, yet modulated by the desire to reduce the burdens of daily life and attain small comforts. Sewing machines were a household investment that economized on clothing costs. Refrigerators and washing machines saved the time of busy mothers. Televisions and stereos brought enjoyment to people leading harried lives and residing in cramped quarters. When, after decades of going without, Japanese families had the opportunity to buy more things, they proceeded cautiously. They saved first, invested second, economized third, and only splurged when there was ample room in the budget to do so.

Consumption patterns, incomes, and educational attainments all became elements of a more complex set of status attributes during this era. The demise of the modern aristocracy immediately after the war had left Japan without an elite social stratum to which the most ambitious might aspire. The difficulties of reconstruction had deterred almost everyone from worrying about such matters until well into the 1950s. But as the economy boomed, incomes climbed, and fortunes rose, the natural conditions for social competition emerged again.

By the 1970s the criteria for status had become fluid and ambiguous. Educational attainment was important but not sufficient. A Todai degree did not lift a branch manager in a regional bank to a high social position nationally. Money, too, was important without being sufficient. Some of the richest people of this era were the hard-driving owners of small enterprises. Their money could buy them chauffeur-driven Cadillacs, but it could not purchase high social standing. Nor was political power an attribute sufficient to ensure high status. Tanaka Kakuei held cabinet posts and the prime ministership near the end of this period. He was one of the most influential figures in the country. But even before his downfall as a result of corruption, he attracted begrudging respect rather than envy and admiration.

As much as anything, occupational affiliation became a key measure of status among men. (Women, as we have seen, were obliged to derive their status from their husbands.) Men who held positions in the national bureaucracy, in large banks and insurance companies, in major corporations, and in the top universities were most likely to elicit society's esteem. Degrees from prestigious universities conferred status on these men to begin with and also enabled them to rise into the upper ranks of these organizations. At the top, they received some of the highest salaries in the country, and owing to the importance of economic affairs, they were also likely to exert influence over issues that mattered the most to Japanese society in this period. Bureaucrats, corporate executives, and university professors thus came to be regarded as society's most high-status persons.

**Dissent.** The very ambiguity and indeterminacy of status may have contributed to the phenomenon whose treatment closes this discussion of social processes. Extremely rapid rates of economic growth caused a wide array of environmental problems. Urban congestion, contaminated water, and a polluted atmosphere were three of the worst. Problems became so severe in some communities that people were forced to take action. The activists fell into two broad groups: pollution opponents and pollution victims.

Pollution opponents organized citizens' movements. Status ambiguity in Japanese society made it possible to draw together three groups of citizens who, in an earlier period, might never have been able to cooperate, much less join together: young housewives with progressive attitudes, older men tied to conservative political parties, and high school and university specialists in the sciences. In many communities, coalitions based on these groups strove to arrest the worst environmental abuses, either by bringing existing problems to public attention or by opposing further pollution-causing development. Citizens' movements enjoyed some successes in the short run. Even though they often disbanded once they achieved their objectives, their experiences provided valuable lessons in participation and organization for the members themselves and also for subsequent community activists.

Pollution victims were groups of persons forced into action by physical suffering and financial loss. They were residents of communities where industrial firms polluting the air, the water, or both caused numerous health problems, including death. These victims and their families often suffered for years, failing to win compensation from polluters while their health continued to deteriorate. Finally, they had no alternative but to take their cases to court.

Four major cases were heard during the late sixties and the early seventies, and all resulted in monetary awards to the plaintiffs. One of the most famous involved pollution victims in the Kyushu town of Minamata. Nippon Chisso, a chemical fertilizer enterprise, began poisoning waters in the local bay with mercury effluents in the early 1950s.

Local residents ate contaminated fish from the bay and contracted a devastating, often fatal, nervous disorder. The company and the national government refused for years to concede that Chisso was causing the problem. After exhausting all other forms of appeal, local residents finally brought suit and won monetary compensation for their losses. In this way, the Japanese court system was mobilized as a venue for redress of popular grievance, and a part of the citizenry gave warning that Japan needed to place some limits on unrestrained economic growth.

## PERFORMANCE

Japan put on a spectacular performance during the era of high-speed growth. Few nations had ever undergone such an extensive economic transformation in such a short period of time. England took almost a century to reduce its agricultural sector from 40 percent of the labor force to 15. Japan compressed this change into twenty short years. In two decades an agrarian nation with a few industrial centers became an urbanized society driven by an extensive industrial apparatus and supported by powerful commercial and financial organizations.

The dedicated effort to promote economic growth brought Japan into the front rank of nations, seemingly coming out of nowhere to surpass Canada, France, Great Britain, and West Germany. By the mid-1970s Japan's GNP was second only to that of the United States among the industrial democracies. Japan had gone a long way toward closing the gap between those two economies as well: the American GNP had been sixteen times the size of the Japanese in 1955; in 1974 it was only three times larger.

The disparity had narrowed on many fronts, especially in those industrial areas on which Japan had concentrated its efforts after 1955. The United States essentially abandoned the field of commercial shipbuilding after the war, in the face of competition from Great Britain, Japan, and other countries. As a result, Japan produced twenty-two times more commercial shipping tonnage in 1974 than the United States. Japan had almost closed the gap in raw steel production by building some of the most sophisticated and productive steel-making facilities in the world. Its output of raw steel in 1974 was equal to 89 percent of American production. In other industries, too, Japan had made rapid progress and was moving closer to parity with the United

**16. Olympic auditorium.** *Held in part on the former site of U.S. military housing in the Yoyogi district, the 1964 Tokyo Olympics symbolized the new Japan, especially in the architecture of the national auditorium designed by Tange Kenzo.* (Gary D. Allinson.)

States. Plastic production was 54 percent of the American level; synthetic fiber output, 50 percent; and vehicle production, 50 percent. Japan was also gaining ground rapidly in the production of television sets, stereo equipment, and cassette recorders.

Most of Japan's increasing output had first gone to satisfy demand in the domestic market. But in due course almost every industry turned to international markets for a portion of its sales. As a consequence, Japan's status as an international trader rose dramatically. Japan had been a minor participant in world trade for the first postwar decade; by the mid-seventies only the United States and West Germany sold exports that exceeded the value of Japan's (in U.S. dollars). Japan was also buying about 6 percent of the world's imports by then. This placed it well behind the United States and slightly behind West Germany but ahead of Great Britain, France, and the Soviet Union.

In two short decades Japan had become an urban nation, an industrial giant, and a major trading power. Dedicated effort and hard work by people in every walk of life had made these achievements possible. So had a salutary conjunction of international circumstances. As long as those salutary conditions persisted, Japan, and some other countries, too, did extremely well. But when key underpinnings of the international economy were shattered in the early 1970s, Japan's high-speed growth came to an abrupt halt.

# CHAPTER FOUR

# Affluence, 1974–1989

LIVING THROUGH THE ERA OF high-speed growth was like taking a fast drive up a pleasant slope. The course was clear. Changes occurred at a rapid pace. Good feelings abounded. Surviving the next fifteen years must have felt like stumbling down a hill in the dark. The course seemed unclear. The pace slowed dramatically. The path to the future produced as much anxiety as good feeling. Japan confronted a harsh, new international environment after the early 1970s and found itself obliged to carry out a series of economic adjustments whose effects were broad and penetrating. The slower rates of economic growth that ensued were beneficial in one way: they gave Japan time to assimilate the rapid changes of the preceding two decades. Social assimilation and economic adjustment required political adaptations, too. During this era, the ruling party encountered more opposition and faced greater instability than ever before, but it still clung tenaciously to power during a period when affluence was the keynote.

## ADJUSTMENT

Economic adjustments were forced on Japan by the demands of a radically different international environment. The foundations of bustling global commerce that sped development during the 1950s and 1960s eroded in the 1970s, leaving a less stable setting for international trade relations. Japan, like many other nations, was obliged to retrench economically. As politicians, bureaucrats, businessmen, union members, and the citizenry struggled to find solutions to the new challenges, change rippled through every sector of the Japanese economy. Some groups and industries suffered; others prospered and flourished. Despite setbacks, the economy managed to outperform its competitors abroad, and Japan grew accustomed to the pleasures and the problems associated with prosperity.

### International Conditions

There were four cornerstones supporting the expanding international economy of the fifties and sixties: secure access to relatively inexpensive raw materials, stable currency exchange rates, limited barriers to international trade, and high global demand. For nearly two decades, these four circumstances operated in fairly smooth combination to promote rapid growth, both in the advanced industrial democracies and in some later-developing countries as well. Owing in part to its very success, the system gradually began to collapse under its own weight. But changes beginning in the early 1970s fundamentally undermined the postwar system of international trade.

Among them, the most crucial for Japan was the first oil crisis, provoked by the Organization of Petroleum Exporting Countries (OPEC) in 1973 when it placed an embargo on oil exports, quickly driving up crude oil prices on international markets. Complex reasons arising from diplomatic, political, economic, and cultural considerations prompted OPEC's action. The effects however, were simple and straightforward. In one, quick stroke, OPEC shattered the premise of secure access to inexpensive raw materials. It also ignited a spate of new problems. Oil import bills rose sharply in Japan and other industrialized countries. High oil costs set off spiraling inflation, consumer anxieties, industrial cutbacks, and a global economic slowdown.

Even before the oil crisis, other changes had undermined the second cornerstone in the foundation of the trade system. In August 1971, the Nixon administration announced that the United States was unilaterally abandoning the gold standard, on which international monetary practices had been founded since the Bretton Woods agreements of 1944. The implications of this pronouncement were broad and significant. It signaled, most importantly, that a more flexible system of exchange rates would be necessary. Thereafter, currencies of individual nations would rise and fall in value, largely in conjunction with balance-of-payments surpluses and deficits. Successful exporting nations, such as Japan and Germany, were thus obliged to accept changes in the value of their currencies.

At a meeting held at the Smithsonian Institution in late 1971, ten leading industrial nations agreed to adopt a system of floating exchange rates linked to the dollar. As a result of this agreement, the value of the yen rose. Since the Dodge reforms of the late 1940s, the yen had traded on international markets at 360 to the dollar. After the Smithsonian accord, the value of the yen climbed to about 310 to the dollar. The appreciated yen had the effect of making Japanese exports more expensive to customers overseas, and that is one objective the Nixon administration sought. It wanted to complicate for Japan the capturing of foreign markets. But the American government, and others, failed to recognize that a stronger yen would also make imports less expensive in Japan. Thus Japan was able to continue selling goods at competitive prices in the international market because the costs of some imported raw materials remained low. The 1971 exchange-rate agreement thus produced crosscutting economic effects as it heightened tension between Japan and its trade partners.

International discussions aimed at constructing a different, more flexible system of monetary exchange continued after the Smithsonian meeting, taking on even greater urgency after the oil crisis. Eventually, countries adopted a system of exchange in which the dollar remained the de facto standard while the value of other currencies fluctuated against it. For Japan, one principal result of this system was an extended rise in the value of the yen. By the late 1980s, it had risen to around 130 to the dollar. Repeated fluctuations in the value of the yen produced many complex consequences. The most important were a much higher level of uncertainty for Japanese firms when planning for the future and constant pressure to keep the costs of production low.

The OPEC actions of 1973 and the monetary difficulties of the 1970s both bespoke change in the international environment affecting the third cornerstone of expanding trade. Competition from foreign producers made many countries more self-interested and protectionist. These anxieties were very strong in the United States, and they prompted American businessmen and politicians to devote unusual attention to Japan and its trade policies. Beginning in the late 1960s and continuing thereafter, the American government had adopted an in-

creasingly harsh and intransigent posture toward Japan. American officials gave especially close scrutiny to textiles, agricultural products,
steel, televisions, autos, semiconductors, and machine tools. Using its
influence as one of Japan's largest customers, the United States often
induced Japan to accept "voluntary" restraints on the export of Japanese goods. This kind of political intervention reduced the openness of
international markets and forced successful exporting nations, such as
Japan, to adopt a wide variety of economic changes in response.

After nearly two decades of booming international trade, by the
early seventies the domestic economies of the largest industrial democracies were nearly saturated with goods. Twenty years of rising incomes
and increasing consumption had provided many families most of the
things they wanted or could afford. Moreover, populations in
the wealthier countries began to grow more slowly. Thus, even in the
absence of the oil crisis, global demand was going to grow at slower
rates. When the crisis caused prices to shoot skyward, producers and
consumers both understood that the long international buying binge
was at an end. The fourth cornerstone had crumbled.

The conditions that emerged in the global economy by the early
1970s were thus deeply threatening to the salutary environment of the
1950s and 1960s. It became more difficult and more expensive to secure
energy sources. Prices fluctuated unpredictably. Nations grew contentious, so commerce flowed less smoothly. Buyers were more reserved
and squeamish about spending their money. Japan therefore had to
make some major adjustments in its domestic economy.

### Domestic Responses

Challenges posed by the international economy were difficult to address
in their own right. They were further complicated by conditions at
home in the 1970s. The opportunities of the 1950s had given way to the
dilemmas of success. Capital was more plentiful than ever, but firms
were hesitant to invest. Rapid technological advance was becoming
more difficult, because the backlog of available technology had been
well exploited. Consumers were slowing their purchases somewhat, and
the sharp inflation ignited by the oil crisis deterred them further. Costs
for everything were rising rapidly, creating serious problems for producers as well as consumers. Government debt was increasing. These
challenges called forth a new resolve and new reservoirs of ingenuity.

**Declining sectors.** Resolve was especially necessary to address one of the most difficult problems Japan faced during this period: the structural adjustment of declining industries. Of course industrial decline did not originate in the 1970s. Chapter 3 discussed the structural adjustment that coal mining underwent in the 1950s. In that case, the nation made a conscious decision to switch from coal to petroleum as its basic energy source, a decision that imposed severe costs on the mining industry, its workers, and their families in order for the economy as a whole to benefit from the ready availability of less expensive petroleum. Japan's cotton-spinning industry also went through a structural adjustment in the 1950s. Facing difficult competition from low-cost producers, spinning factories closed their doors and laid off thousands of workers. Some cotton-spinning firms transformed themselves and survived, however, by diversifying into the production of synthetic fibers and other products, such as cosmetics and plastic resins. In both these cases, the national economic effects of adjustment were limited because mining and textiles were relatively small industries whose declines were dwarfed by growth in newer, larger sectors.

Industrial decline in the 1970s was significantly different, for it struck at the core of the manufacturing sector and undercut the position of some of the nation's leading industries. Steel making and shipbuilding were both hard hit. Other declining industries were aluminum refining, paper making, synthetic fibers, chemical fertilizers, and petrochemicals. The sharp rise in oil prices was the principal cause of economic decline in most of these industries. Higher oil prices increased the cost of raw materials (in petrochemicals), or they increased the cost of energy supplies (as in the electricity-intensive aluminum industry), or they reduced demand for products (such as large oil tankers).

Japan addressed the problems of industrial decline by mobilizing all parties concerned: suppliers, producers, workers, consumers, politicians, and bureaucrats. The leaders in resolving problems differed, depending on the industry involved and the timing of the adjustments, but in all cases the private sector played an instrumental role from the outset. The process of adjustment was eventually facilitated by the passage of two laws, one in 1978, another in 1983. They spelled out the conditions under which industries could reorder themselves and the terms of government assistance. In contrast with earlier periods, the country generally avoided bureaucratically directed production cartels.

Both court rulings and Free Trade Commission directives after 1973 sharply reduced the ability of ministries to rely on *gyosei shido* (administrative guidance) and other types of informal authority. Instead, producers themselves played a major role in determining how their industries would adapt, and they implemented their own changes with some government supervision and assistance.

The shipbuilding industry offers one example of relatively successful structural adjustment. Japan's industry was the largest in the world when the oil crisis struck in 1973. It consisted of about sixty firms of three types: large firms operating five or more docks, medium-sized firms operating two or three docks, and small firms with only one dock. Together they were producing more than 50 percent of the world's commercial shipping tonnage. Large firms had the greatest capacity and produced most of the output. They were concentrating in the early 1970s on massive tankers that shipped petroleum around the world. When the oil crisis struck, global demand for petroleum plunged and the need for new supertankers almost vanished. Within three years, Japan's shipbuilders suffered a drastic drop in orders and found themselves with far too many docks and workers.

For several years, shipbuilders, ship owners, workers, foreign buyers, and bureaucrats engaged in discussions aimed at reorganizing the industry. In the late 1970s they agreed to scrap about 35 percent of the total capacity of the industry. Large firms scrapped the most (about 40 percent of their capacity), and small firms the least (about 25 percent of theirs). The large firms were often able to adjust by diversifying into other fields (such as the production of construction equipment or ocean-going drilling platforms) that took advantage of their engineering expertise. Smaller firms did not have the affiliations, capital, or skills to make such adjustments. They either consolidated or went out of business entirely. Many workers lost their jobs in their original firms, but some were reemployed by other firms in their keiretsu or by new firms created by their old employers. In addition, the government eased the transition of unemployed workers by providing wage subsidies, retraining allowances, and relocation expenses.

Structural adjustment in shipbuilding produced results similar to those in other industries. Most firms were able to survive as functioning entities, although in nearly every case they were smaller than before. Scrapping old docks reduced costs and made the surviving firms more productive, so they remained competitive on international markets. Workers were, for the most part, treated humanely. Firms made every effort to find work for those who wanted jobs, and the government cushioned some of the worst blows with its assistance programs. Nonetheless, many workers were driven into unemployment. Domestic consumers often benefited from the changes, because they were able to maintain ties with familiar suppliers who would be there to serve them in the future. Perhaps most important, the nation benefited by restoring major firms and large employers to profitability with only a small outlay of public funds.

Like some of Japan's industrial sectors, agriculture confronted continuing problems of decline during this era, too. On the surface, there were positive signs. Total agricultural income rose, although at slow rates. The incomes of farm households rose, too. They more than doubled between 1974 and 1989. For most of this period, the average farm household enjoyed a total income 20 to 25 percent higher than an average urban worker's household, and Japan's farmers continued to produce all the rice the nation consumed as well as more than 90 percent of its potatoes and vegetables.

These positive attributes masked, however, the sector's underlying decline. High incomes in farm households derived primarily from nonfarm work: agricultural income provided less than 20 percent of the average farm family's income by 1989. It was becoming more and more difficult to survive by farming alone, so the number of farm families continued to fall, dropping from about 5 million in 1974 to about 4 million in 1989. Among the families that remained on the farm, only 14 percent pursued agriculture as a full-time calling, and they concentrated on high-income endeavors: raising cattle and poultry, managing dairy herds, and producing fruits and vegetables. Many small farmers assumed heavy debts to buy the new equipment that enabled them to grow rice on a part-time basis. Despite widespread mechanization, however, agricultural productivity was only 25 percent that of the manufacturing sector.

Intentionally, and unintentionally, rising imports of soybeans, wheat, meat products, and even fruits and vegetables highlighted the nearly intractable problems of Japanese agriculture. Land laws, farm size, topography, and climate worked against competitiveness in agriculture. That sector's destiny paralleled the fate of some of the old industrial sectors. Most remaining farmers managed to prosper, but owing to the sacrifices of others and in the face of severe international competition.

**Expanding sectors.** Although many industries suffered decline during this period, others enjoyed dramatic growth. The two that prospered most were auto making and electrical manufacturing. By the late 1980s, fourteen of the twenty-five largest firms in Japan were in these two industries alone. Toyota and Nissan commanded the largest share of the auto market, followed by five smaller producers such as Honda and Mitsubishi. Between 1974 and 1989, production in Japan rose from about 7 million vehicles a year to more than 13 million. In 1980, in fact, Japanese vehicle production ranked first in the world. As domestic production increased, sales abroad rose, too. Consumers in the United States and Europe were eager to buy reliable, high-quality Japanese autos selling at a relatively low price. Less than 30 percent of domestic output was exported in 1974, but over 40 percent of Japan's trucks and cars were exported in 1989.

The popularity of Japanese automobiles abroad provoked serious trade problems, especially with the United States. Made anxious and angry by Japanese competition, American car manufacturers preferred political solutions to their economic problems. They persuaded the American government to negotiate voluntary restraints on the export of Japanese cars to the United States beginning in 1981. They tried or threatened other sanctions as well. Recognizing problems, Japanese auto makers began to build their own factories in the United States, where they could produce and sell cars that would not be subject to voluntary restraints, tariffs, or other formal and informal trade barriers. By building such plants, Japanese firms were also taking advantage of an increasingly stronger yen and the lower price of labor in the United States. A more protectionist trade environment thus promoted higher levels of Japanese investment in the United States and caused the interdependence of the two economies to strengthen in unexpected ways.

Japan's electrical manufacturing industry also prospered during this period. Two of the seven largest firms—Hitachi and Toshiba—were comprehensive electrical equipment makers patterned after GE and Westinghouse. They made large-scale electrical equipment, such as generating plants, as well as small appliances. The five other firms concentrated on smaller electrical products. The largest was Matsushita. Others were Fujitsu, NEC, Sony, and Mitsubishi Electric. All of these firms produced goods that responded to demand in the Japanese market, especially household appliances and office equipment. But after the 1970s, they moved quickly to manufacture such new products as videocassette recorders, computers, semiconductors, integrated circuits, and fax machines. The reorganization of Japanese firms drove demand for these items at home, so the domestic market provided a training ground in which to improve production processes and thus consistently reduce the prices of innovative, desirable new products. After securing a strong base at home, Japanese producers then launched into international markets. Like the auto makers, these corporations encountered trade problems abroad, and they, too, began investing heavily in production facilities overseas, especially in Europe, Asia, and North America.

The rapid growth of the auto and electrical industries after 1974 stimulated parallel expansion in the small and medium-sized enterprise sector. Continuing a trend that originated in the 1930s, if not before, final producers preferred to work with independent subcontractors who provided parts and components, instead of managing such production under a single corporate entity. This organizational preference nurtured literally thousands of profitable, small, parts manufacturers. At Toyota, for instance, more than two hundred firms belonged to an association of subcontractors who worked closely with the firm to provide components according to stringent guidelines and time tables. Matsushita, too, stimulated the evolution of a large number of parts producers and allied enterprises.

These developments created a new application for the term *keiretsu*, already in use to describe the diversified corporate groups, such as Mitsui and Mitsubishi, that were tied together by banking and other relationshps. In its new usage, keiretsu referred to the integrated production apparatus that emerged in the auto and electrical industries to serve the needs of final producers such as Toyota and Matsushita. These industrial keiretsu thus differed somewhat from the older, financially oriented keiretsu by being composed of manufacturing firms in a single industry. Nonetheless, by the 1980s the new keiretsu had become the most important enterprise groups in Japan's manufacturing sector. They had displaced the old zaibatsu-keiretsu firms, the vaunted steel companies, and the venerable textile makers in their rise to the top of the industrial prestige list.

Subcontractors were not the only small and medium-sized firms to flourish during this period. Many smaller firms arose to take advantage of opportunities offered by new products, new production processes, new technologies, and new demands. For example, the development of numerically controlled machine tools stimulated rapid expansion of small firms. Many of them built plants in specific regions, pooled resources, and worked cooperatively to create a whole that was more than the sum of its parts. Japanese entrepreneurs discovered that new scientific developments in such industries as ceramics and biotechnology could be pursued effectively through smaller organizations. Industrial robotics and office automation spurred the development of many small firms to meet the differing needs of a wide range of customers, too.

For all of these reasons, many new kinds of small enterprises incorporated during this era. Differing from their historical counterparts, with their limited technical capacities and unskilled laborers, these enterprises were technologically sophisticated concerns employing highly educated specialists. They were a timely and much-needed addition to the industrial scene, because they created many new jobs to compensate for those lost in the declining sectors. As a result, manufacturing employment actually rose slightly between 1974 and 1989.

Retail trade was another sector that experienced significant expansion during this period, owing principally to the introduction of new kinds of stores. For generations, Japanese consumers had shopped for daily necessities in small shops situated in commercial districts within easy walking distance of home. Such shops were labor intensive in the extreme. The owners of such stores, and the wives and children who assisted them, dealt individually with each customer, picking up the product, displaying and explaining its virtues, and tallying the sale. This pattern of commerce suited Japan well when labor was cheap and time plentiful, but it did not function nearly so well when workers were at a premium and shoppers were rushed for time. From another perspective, small stores also made poor use of expensive land, because their sales per square foot were low.

Responding to changing incentives and consumer behavior, a new breed of retailer appeared. As early as the 1960s, a quiet revolution in retail service began when more *serufu saabu* stores appeared. In this kind of store the customer her*self* could *serve* her needs by picking up desired merchandise from the shelves without consulting a clerk and carrying it to a register for checkout. During the 1970s and 1980s, more self-service stores accompanied the growth of new suburbs and the wider use of automobiles.

These stores took many forms. Some were small convenience stores selling mainly food products, developed on the Seven-Eleven model. Others were super-stores, three- or four-story structures containing a wide array of merchandise, including groceries, appliances, clothing, and furniture. New firms such as Seiyu, Ito Yokado, and Jusco quickly became dominant in this market. Finally, some of the additional stores were new branches of department stores, such as Mitsukoshi, Tokyu, and Takashimaya. They specialized in expensive, high-quality, consumer products, often goods imported from the United States and Europe. In just fifteen years after 1974, self-service stores tripled in number and department stores increased by about 50 percent. Even small retail establishments experienced a slight increase. Expansion created almost 2 million new retail jobs and led to a tripling in the value of retail sales.

Services formed the final sector in which pronounced expansion occurred during this period. A more affluent populace with more time on its hands and more money in its pockets stimulated demand in many ways. Banks, insurance companies, credit agencies, and brokerage houses expanded to serve the financial needs of individuals and firms. During the 1980s, Japan's financial institutions rose to dominate the lists of the world's largest. A desire for more leisure and entertainment stimulated the growth of publishing firms, television broadcasting, advertising, communications enterprises, amusement centers, and real estate companies developing resorts and second-home sites. Leasing organizations appeared for the first time, to serve the needs of new kinds of firms and new modes of business management. Independent research organizations, data management firms, and a range of new health providers expanded to meet other kinds of demand. A wide variety of private educational ventures developed to satisfy an almost insatiable craving for credentials, if not learning itself. Owing to these changes, the service sector grew to employ about 60 percent of Japan's labor force by the end of this period, when the value of the sector's output comprised almost 60 percent of GDP. These figures offer compelling signs that Japan had entered the ranks of the affluent, postindustrial democracies.

### Outcomes

Japan faced severe economic challenges in the decade and a half after 1974. It watched regretfully as the agricultural sector continued to shrink, but it acted resolutely when economic pressures forced cutbacks in many depressed industries. Amid these difficulties, the country found compensations in other areas. Auto making, electrical manufacturing, small enterprises, the retail sector, and the service trades flourished. Investment rates dropped from the high levels achieved during the era of high-speed growth, but they were still higher than investment levels in other industrial democracies.

So were growth rates. In the wake of the first oil crisis, the economy did not grow at all in 1974. Mixed performances by different sectors in subsequent years reduced the rates of growth that had prevailed earlier. Nonetheless, in the fifteen years after 1974, the GNP grew at rates between about 3 and 6 percent per annum, producing an average rate of about 4 percent a year. Low by previous standards, this rate was still about double the rate of growth in the United States, West Germany, and England during the same period. Japan's superior economic performance provoked the envy and resentment that lay behind some of the problems with its trading partners.

By eliminating unproductive capacity and by making current capacity even more productive, Japanese corporations continued to expand their international presence. The value of their exports increased five times during this period, and Japan retained its position as the third-largest exporter in the world. Imports grew more slowly. Their value increased 3.4 times, placing Japan consistently in the position of the world's third-largest importer. The gap between exports and imports began in the early 1980s to produce a consistently higher surplus on the current trade account for Japan, and as that surplus grew, so did Japan's conflicts with trading nations around the world. Trade surpluses and a stronger currency also provided the capital needed to invest abroad. Beginning in the mid-1980s, Japan began exporting capital in very substantial amounts, by building new factories, extending loans, purchasing bonds, buying equities, and snapping up prestigious properties around the world, especially in Europe and North America.

Many advanced industrial democracies encountered the same problems Japan did after 1971, but few dealt so effectively with them. Two problems were especially intractable in Europe and North America: high rates of unemployment and more jobs that paid low salaries. Japan avoided both these problems. Unemployment rose to about the 3 percent level, never reaching the double-digit level that became endemic in some European countries. Japanese employers deserve substantial credit for this outcome. They operated under a social contract that obligated them to find jobs for as many displaced workers as they could. Lingering memories of widespread unemployment in the 1940s, along with a commitment to full-employment policies, determined their responses. Japan also avoided the trap of creating mainly low-wage, dead-end jobs in the service sector, because many—although not all—the jobs in the expanding sectors offered good salaries. Real incomes did grow slowly during this period, but most workers enjoyed small annual raises that put more money in their pockets every year, producing a widespread sense of affluence during the 1980s.

## ASSIMILATION

Preceding chapters have illustrated how the Japanese citizenry suffered deprivation during the prewar, wartime, and early postwar periods, leaving most Japanese hungry for a better material life. The era of high-speed growth brought material rewards, but it seemed to many as if they had always to rush off to work without opportunity to enjoy their gains. The years after 1974 finally brought some respite from the frantic pace that rapid growth had stimulated, and people were at last able to take some time to chew on their rewards and swallow their gains. The chance to assimilate the benefits of a long period of steady growth fostered extensive changes in family and community life—indeed throughout Japanese society.

### *Family*

In a populace utterly preoccupied with economic growth, material conditions defined the character of family life. There were subjective, qualitative attributes that set families apart. These included a household's *kafu*, or family customs, and its *iegara*, or stature. Such attributes were a product of habit, long-standing residence, community relations and perceptions, and the personalities of family heads and their spouses. Kafu and iegara had counted for a great deal in the settled, rural society of prewar Japan, but in a mobile, urban society where anonymity was widespread and community bonds were weak, they were much less important. For most families, how much they earned, how they spent their money, and how they accumulated their savings were the real issues in defining their social standing. Household incomes, expenditures, and savings thus offer valuable perspectives on the family and how it changed during this period.

Steady economic growth brought visible affluence to most families in Japan after 1955. The average monthly income of urban workers' households increased more than sixteen times between 1955 and 1989. The greatest increases occurred during the period of high-speed growth, but even after the difficult years of the early seventies, incomes continued to rise. Most families, therefore, experienced some increase in the total amount of money available to spend and save each year.

Income differences persisted during this period. The difference between the average income for the top 20 percent of all households and the bottom 20 percent remained the same in 1989 as it had been in the 1960s; average incomes at the top were still 2.7 times more than those at the bottom. Salary differences also remained narrow. In 1989 a young worker in a small factory earned about ¥ 130,000 per month in base pay; a middle-aged, white-collar worker in a medium-sized enterprise earned about ¥ 350,000 per month; and an older man in a large firm earned about ¥ 500,000. On average, therefore, most people in the higher reaches of Japanese society earned about three to four times more than those in the lower.

Income differences did widen in some cases, however. Successful individuals who attained the highest positions in prestigious fields reaped increasingly more generous rewards. They included directors and branch managers of large corporations, physicians owning private clinics, university administrators, heads of research institutes, and ship's captains. Some writers, sports heroes, movie stars, television personalities, and owners of small companies also earned very high incomes. These highly paid individuals earned six times or more per year than a young factory worker. They formed a small portion of the total labor force, but they numbered in the tens of thousands. As much as anyone, it was these individuals who formed a nouveau riche class, whose conspicuous consumption set the tone for the late 1980s.

Most people had to make do, however, on much lower incomes, which they spent according to widespread and predictable patterns. Food, clothing, and shelter absorbed less than half of the total outlays for an average household by 1989—a far cry from the 1930s, when poor urban families had to spend 70 percent or more of their budgets on necessities. Food purchases accounted for 25 percent of all expenditures, housing and utilities costs for 10 percent, and clothing for 7 percent. The remaining 58 percent of expenditures were allocated to: medical costs (3), transportation and commuting (9), education (5), reading and recreation (9), father's spending money (9), social relations (9), and miscellaneous expenses (14). A closer look at spending for food, housing, education, and recreation reveals the character of Japanese family life in the late 1980s in more detail.

Food purchases had absorbed a steadily declining portion of a family's outlays since the early 1950s, when families often had to spend 60 to 70 percent of their incomes for food just to survive. As incomes rose in the fifties and sixties, families could spend more on food and still have money left to purchase other things, too. After 1974, the portion of all expenditures devoted to food continued to decline, although Japanese families consistently spent a little more of their incomes on food. As a result, people were consuming about twenty-six hundred calories a day per capita by the late eighties, almost double what they had been able to eat in 1946.

Food purchases differed in significant ways from a generation before. The consumption of rice and sugar dropped off, quite significantly in the case of rice. In contrast, people consumed more meat, fruit, milk, and dairy products. This shift in dietary preferences was especially pronounced among generations. Older people stuck with a diet based heavily on rice, vegetables, and fish. Younger people reduced carbohydrate consumption by eating less rice and increased protein intake by eating more meat and dairy products. As a consequence, adolescents in 1989 were on average four inches taller than their grandparents.

The most striking change in food purchases involved eating out. Dining at a restaurant had been a luxury few could afford in the fifties and sixties. Such a treat was usually confined to holidays or special occasions. In the seventies, greater discretionary income, increased leisure time, and more widespread use of automobiles made it possible for many families to go out to dinner once or twice a week. This demand was stimulated by the gradual appearance of family-oriented restaurants with adjacent parking lots. The Denny's chain from the United States was one of the first to tap this market, and its stores provided a model for many Japanese firms, such as Skylark and Lotteria, which followed in its wake. Together, they created new dining habits and new culinary tastes among younger Japanese.

Average outlays for housing create a deceptive sense of uniformity. On the surface, it appears that the average Japanese household spent a surprisingly small share of its income on shelter, and this was true of many families. Most families in rural areas and commercial districts inherited housing from their parental generation. Their housing costs were low because they were not paying rent or mortgages. Likewise, well-off, older families living in urban and suburban areas had often paid off their mortgages, so their housing costs were low, too. Many unmarried workers in their twenties lived in subsidized housing that kept their costs of shelter low as well. These groups were numerous, and their relatively low housing costs brought down the average for all households.

The families that spent most for housing were those headed by a married man in his thirties or forties with a child or two. Families like these were likely to be paying off large loans used to buy land and build their own homes. A single-family home in a Tokyo suburb often cost two or three hundred thousand U.S. dollars in the late eighties, and such a home was small by American standards. It would have had six rooms and about 1,000 square feet. But for a family that had recently rented a three-room apartment with only 250 square feet of living space, such a home was a dramatic improvement. A salary man in his forties paying off a loan for such a home might have been allocating 30 percent of the family's monthly outlays to housing costs. Therefore some groups—middle-aged, suburban home buyers, in particular—were likely to be paying far more than average for their housing. A substantial number of others—who had either inherited their homes or already paid off their mortgages—were paying much less.

**17. Urban neighborhood.** *A street fair attracts the middle-class residents of this typically mixed commercial and residential area in Tokyo, with its densely-built, low-rise, concrete structures.* (Courtesy of Patricia S. Allinson.)

One of the most rapidly rising expenditures for Japanese families in the seventies and eighties was education. Some of the increase went to pay for the direct costs of formal education: fees and expenses for children in public schools and tuition costs for children in private schools. Substantial educational outlays, however, went to underwrite the costs of tuition at *juku,* or academies. Juku were actually cram schools that prepared students to take competitive exams for entry into high school and college. They arose to meet a growing demand from parents who wanted to improve their children's chances of getting into a prestigious university. In high-status, urban neighborhoods, nearly every child of middle school age was obliged by the 1980s to attend two to three hours of juku sessions after an already long school day, either to satisfy parental demands or just to conform with peers in the neighborhood.

Families also spent substantially more on reading and recreational activities during the seventies and eighties. Some of their expenditures went to purchase books, magazines, color televisions, videocassette recorders, fine stereo equipment, videos, and compact disc players. Some money also bought tickets to museums and concerts, or even trips abroad. And some outlays purchased lessons. Women studied *ikebana* (flower arranging), foreign languages, pottery making, and so on. Men preferred *bonsai* (miniature plantings), sports, and singing lessons. Like dining out, these indulgences were also the product of more leisure time and discretionary income.

However much Japanese families spent, they also managed to save larger sums of money. The rate of savings fell somewhat during the eighties, in part because taxes took a slightly larger share of incomes than they had previously. But families continued to set aside on average as much as 15 percent of their disposable incomes, versus 5 percent for their American counterparts. Nearly everyone saved something, and older persons with higher incomes saved the most. Consequently, average household savings rose steadily, from about ¥ 3 million in 1974 to about ¥ 10 million in 1989 (equivalent to about $75,000 U.S.).

Patterns of savings behavior established during the period of high-speed growth persisted into the eighties. As before, families saved to pay for homes, educations, weddings, and retirement. Many also began saving for overseas travel. Japanese families remained conservative and averse to risk when managing their savings. They continued to place the largest share in secure accounts in banks and the postal savings system. They also invested heavily in life insurance. But they still shied away from securities; they used barely 10 percent of their savings to buy equities. Rather than gamble on the sporadic wins and losses endemic to the Japanese stock market, most families preferred slow, secure, steady gains.

The composite image of the Japanese family that emerges from the figures above resembles the behavior of families in earlier periods. Discipline and parsimony were still widespread. Careful management of basic expenditures and the still-strong inclination to save attested to these qualities. Conservative, risk-averse behavior persisted, especially in savings and investment decisions. These figures also reveal a sense of anxiety about family status, rooted in concerns about children, their educations, and their prospects for social mobility. Tuition payments and juku expenses were testimony to these anxieties. With the tension and the self-restraint, however, we detect by the late 1980s some signs of a more affluent, though not perhaps spendthrift, society. Families were clearly beginning to indulge themselves a bit: dining out more frequently, purchasing audio and visual equipment for the home, attending symphonies, visiting museums, taking cultural lessons, and even beginning to travel overseas in some numbers.

Again, however, the averages obscure significant differences among households. There were still many relatively poor families. A forty-year-old high school graduate employed by a small factory faced limited prospects for himself and his family. His salary might double, at best, by the time he reached his sixties, leaving him and his family in a small apartment for the rest of their lives. He would not have the discretionary income to indulge in many pleasures, and he might be unable to send his children to college. In addition, he and his spouse would face low incomes in retirement, owing to his inability to save very large sums of money.

In sharp contrast, the successful, highly paid individuals described above enjoyed radically different lifestyles. They were able to send their children to the best universities in Japan, or to prestigious institutions in the United States or Great Britain, for that matter. They flew first-class to San Francisco for a weekend of golf and shopping. They kept developers busy, in Japan and Hawaii, with their purchases of second homes. And they sat on savings accounts three or four times the average size, looking forward to a comfortable retirement in a luxurious setting.

The presence of such disparate households points to great diversity within Japanese society by the late eighties. The young factory hand above lived in a crowded, two-room rental apartment with no bathing facilities. Both father and mother worked to pay the rent, buy food, and defray other necessary expenses. They owned no car, and they walked to work to eliminate commuting costs. Such families seldom dined out. At home, they preferred a Japanese-style meal, adding a few cups of sake on special occasions. If they vacationed, they seized two or three days to make a quick trip to a nearby resort in a hot springs district.

Children from such families populated the nation's low-status, vocational high schools. Those schools struggled unsuccessfully to teach youth destined for dead-end jobs in small factories or restaurants. Constantly worried about making ends meet and setting a little money aside, families like these could give little thought to a leisured, comfortable retirement.

The arrivistes at the top of Japanese society could afford to build architect-designed mansions in exclusive suburbs and, ten years later, plunk down the cash to buy a retirement condominium on Maui. Necessities were of no concern to such families, and food absorbed less than 20 percent of their expenses. Dining out was common. Costly French, Indian, and Italian restaurants all had their appeal. Ski trips for the children, cello lessons for mother, golf memberships for father were all within easy reach. Mother did her shopping in a Mercedes sedan; father relished his BMW convertible. The children attended elite private schools and went on to the best universities. Leisurely visits to the capitals of Europe were common among families like these. Such trips familiarized them with the arts and antiques they would be buying, both for pleasure and for investment purposes. And retirement was a cause for pleasant reflection: the condo on Maui beckoned.

### Community

The emergence of such differing social groups and lifestyles inevitably affected the nature of community life. *Community*, a malleable term with rich connotations, is used here in two senses: in the residential sense, to refer to territorial and administrative units, such as villages, cities, and suburbs; and in the civic sense, to refer to social action and relationships in public spaces outside the environments of work and family life.

The character of social life in residential communities varied sharply during this period, reflecting economic differences between declining and expanding sectors. Many rural villages declined along with the retreat of agriculture, and many one-industry towns struggled when industries restructured. Remote, inaccessible villages were hardest hit, but any village with poor soils, short growing seasons, and meager economic prospects suffered the dilemmas of decline. Most young men and women left such villages to find better-paying, more secure work in the cities. Populations fell, leaving older adults and the elderly to oversee community affairs. The absence of younger families raising and educating children forced the closing of village schools, eliminating vital centers for community interaction. Tax bases shrank, further complicating the provision of public services. Elderly citizens missed the children and grandchildren who kept them vital and assisted them with their needs. The increasing proportion of elderly residents imposed further demands for health and welfare services on already hard-pressed public authorities.

One-industry towns devastated by the loss of the local industry were scattered throughout the country. Many were located in regions where the coal mining industry had once thrived, especially on the islands of Kyushu and Hokkaido. Others were situated on coastal shores and lost their economic bases when the steel industry closed mills and the shipbuilding industry scrapped docks. In all of these communities, despite the best efforts of the private sector and public authorities, unemployment rates shot up drastically. Younger workers were often able to take advantage of the government's retraining and relocation allowances, but that usually ensured their departure to other cities. Older workers who owned homes found retraining difficult or unappealing, and they resisted relocation. They stayed behind and filled the ranks of the unemployed. Household incomes dropped to dangerously low levels. Lower incomes meant sagging commerce and reduced property values. Combined with the loss of major employers, these changes caused tax bases to shrink. At the same time, demand for public services from an aging, unemployed populace increased. Local, prefectural, and national officials worked conscientiously to rectify the problems of communities like these, but their best efforts often ended in defeat.

Their problems were complicated by the very success of other communities. Given the slower pace of growth and the wider restraints on resources during this period, some one-industry towns benefited at the expense of others. Communities situated in the orbit of the auto industry and the electrical and electronics industries benefited handsomely during the seventies and eighties. Suburbs north of Osaka flourished as the Matsushita enterprise sold more National and Panasonic products. Cities such as Kariya, Toyota, and Okazaki in central Japan prospered with expansion at Toyota Motors, and the fortunes of Hitachi City rose with the well-being of the Hitachi enterprise. In all of these communities, young people flowed in to increase the population base, stimulate commerce, raise property values, spur services, and make educational demands. Good salaries produced average household incomes that far surpassed the national average. Booming industries increased the tax base, and an orgy of public spending ensued, as these cities built handsome civic centers and public libraries bursting with the latest technical gadgets.

Metropolitan areas also prospered as a result of these changes, none more so than Tokyo, which had become the hub of the Japanese economy after the war. As the nation's political capital and its educational and cultural center, it attracted investment and people in abundance. It also began to attract manufacturing concerns more rapidly than ever before. By the early seventies, it was literally choking on its success; atmospheric pollution, industrial congestion, residential concentration, and traffic paralysis were just some of its problems.

Beginning in the late sixties, the Tokyo prefectural government started to address some of these problems. Led by Governor Minobe Ryokichi, a progressive elected with the support of a left-center coalition, the prefecture turned its attention to improving the quality of life, directing special efforts to environmental problems and the provision of health and welfare services. At the same time, the national government sought to disperse industry away from concentrated areas around Tokyo and Osaka. The conjunction of these political and economic programs caused a gradual dispersion of industry away from Tokyo, reducing pollution problems and freeing up some industrial sites for civic, commercial, and residential development. Population also began to disperse as more young families found the money to buy homes in surrounding suburbs. The population of the center of the Tokyo metropolitan area actually began to fall. In place of small factory sites, crowded apartment zones, and two-storied commercial structures, the city witnessed a gradual expansion of high-rise commercial buildings. These gave the city a dramatically new and prosperous appearance, even though they signaled the end of an older way of urban life.

Agata Hikari beautifully conveys the social essence of such changes in her short story "A Family Party" focused on a new high-rise hotel recently completed in Shinjuku, a commercial district on the western edge of downtown Tokyo. The family gathering for the party used to live in the neighborhood over which the hotel now looms. Like many urban neighborhoods in midcentury Tokyo, this one had been a jumble of private homes, tiny factories, and small shops. Despite differences in wealth and status, the residents had carried out friendly, polite, and congenial—though distanced—lives among themselves. Selling their properties had brought fortunes to many. Some had moved to new suburban homes; others had stayed in the same area to lease new shops in the hotel. Nearly everyone had been changed by the forced move, whether old or young, male or female; how is driven home when the family gathers for its party in the slick, new, physically transformed setting of its old social context. With the mood of disoriented nostalgia she evokes, Agata makes us feel how this prosperous setting is actually the source of a new form of social poverty which undermines human attachment.

The family in Agata's story personifies the new suburbanites of contemporary Japan. More than any other kind of community, suburbs on the edge of the major metropolitan centers grew expansively during this period. Those around Tokyo and Osaka had begun to emerge in profusion in the 1920s and 1930s and continued to grow in the 1950s and 1960s. By the 1970s, new suburbs were mushrooming around the old ones. In the Tokyo area, many were situated at a distance of sixty to ninety minutes from downtown districts where commuting husbands worked. Some, such as Machida and Tama, were in the distant reaches of western Tokyo prefecture itself. Others, such as Kashiwa and Tokorozawa, were in the neighboring prefectures of Chiba and Saitama. Wherever they were located, these satellite suburbs attracted waves of newcomers. Beginning as little more than large towns in the sixties, suburbs like these often grew to embrace more than three hundred thousand residents by the late eighties.

Suburban growth was less chaotic and somewhat better controlled than it had been. This is not to say that new suburbs were well planned, smoothly functioning communities. Few were. Rather, people learned from some of the excesses of the rapid-growth period. City officials, urban planners, and residents, if not developers, were all eager to manage growth better. In many suburbs on the edge of Tokyo, voters elected to the mayoralty men who promised to enhance planning and direct more attention to the needs of residents, at the expense of developers and big business, if need be. Some of these men were

**18. Suburban skyline.** *Population densities of thirty-five thousand persons per square mile forced home owners and apartment dwellers to live cheek by jowl, even in this affluent Tokyo suburb.*                    (Gary D. Allinson.)

members of the progressive parties; others were conservatives who advocated socially and politically progressive policies. In both cases, these men spearheaded local legislation that gave cities more control over undisciplined commercial and residential development. They also devoted greater attention to civic needs, such as safer roads, adequate schools, public libraries, and social facilities for the elderly. New suburbs still faced many of the problems of their predecessors, but they also witnessed many improvements.

Behind some of these improvements were citizens with a heightened sense of civic consciousness. Many of them were young housewives who had recently moved into a new community. They resided in their own single-family homes in some cases, but they also lived in large-scale public housing projects (*danchi*) or in private rental apartments. They were provoked to action by inadequate public facilities, such as crowded schools, unsafe roads, stunted parks, and dilapidated libraries. Some of these women were undoubtedly taking cues from the successes of earlier citizens' movements and patterning their actions accordingly. They sometimes allied with progressive forces, such as labor unions and consumer groups, to promote their objectives. Others were driven to act out of necessity. By petitioning, lobbying, voting, and even running for office, members of these groups were able to achieve some improvements at the local level.

Did they succeed in creating a new civic community? It is almost impossible to answer this question with clarity and assurance. Many of these groups dissolved once they achieved their stated objectives, resembling, in this respect, not only the citizens' movements of the sixties and seventies but many other protest movements in Japan's modern history. Self-sustaining civic activism has been rare in modern Japan. There were exceptions in neighborhoods, cities, and suburbs where civic action groups did become institutionalized and where they continued to promote civic objectives. But in more cases than not, solving immediate,

**19. Public housing.** *This* danchi *(high-density residential development) is like many that have emerged since the 1960s to house the waves of families moving into the peripheries of Tokyo and other large cities. A nursery school and its play area appear in the foreground.*     (Gary D. Allinson.)

short-term problems inspired a kind of instrumental approach to citizen activism whose success promoted its quick disappearance.

The widespread preoccupation with economic matters, material conditions, children's educational needs, and father's occupational demands all militated against a stronger civic community. Long work weeks, five-and-a-half day school weeks, and still limited leisure time further obstructed civic participation. The fragility of social bonds in so many communities where most residents had only arrived in the last five or ten years also impeded civic affiliations. A weak history of voluntarism was a final impediment. This period thus witnessed the creation of many new residential communities, but few of them evolved into vibrant civic communities.

### Society

Demographic shifts played a major role in shaping social change during this period. One of these was a larger number of older persons living into their seventies and eighties. The elderly posed numerous problems in their own right; they also created new problems for families, especially for middle-aged women. Already pulled in many directions by conflicting demands, women came under still more pressure as caretakers for the elderly. This caused women to reflect more deeply on their identities, along with many others.

One major cause of demographic shifts was a decline in mortality rates. High rates of mortality before the early 1950s were attributable to large numbers of deaths in infancy and from tuberculosis. Nearly all babies then were born at home with the assistance of midwives. Routine births posed few problems, but difficult births entailed substantial risks. When people could not afford professional medical care or hospital visits, or when such care and facilities were simply not available in their town or village, risks of death at birth rose perceptibly. Infant lives were further threatened by the cold, drafty, unheated dwellings that so many lived in before the 1960s and by low incomes and poor diets.

After the late 1940s, most children were born in hospitals and private clinics with trained physicians, and this brought infant mortality rates down significantly. In 1947 the infant mortality rate was 77 per thousand. Within a decade, it was cut by half. By 1989, infant mortality had fallen to a modest 5 per thousand, one of the lowest rates in the world. Professional medical care available at low cost through a national health system had played a major role in this decline, but one must credit more education, higher incomes, improved housing, and better diets as well.

Tuberculosis had been one of the most dangerous epidemic diseases in prewar Japan. Young women toiling in hot, noisome textile mills were especially vulnerable to the disease. Returning to their native villages to recuperate, they would then infect others. The government began as early as the 1930s to provide vaccination, an effort that bore fruit in the early 1950s, when tuberculosis was essentially eliminated in Japan.

With the elimination of these two major causes of death, mortality rates dropped significantly. Nationwide mortality rates were about 15 per thousand in 1947, the first year after the war for which reliable figures are available. Within a decade they had dropped to about half that figure. During the eighties they stabilized at about 6 per thousand. And as mortality fell, longevity rose. The chaotic years of the 1940s had done nothing to improve average Japanese life expectancies in the upper forties. After the 1950s, however, longevity increased rapidly, with higher incomes, better housing, improved diets, and low-cost, professional medical care. By 1989, Japanese boys at birth could expect to live on average into their mid-seventies, and women, into their early eighties. These changes alone would have produced a society in which there were more elderly people, but the proportion of the elderly in the national populace increased rapidly for yet another reason.

The birth rate fell steadily after a sharp upward spike immediately following World War II. By the mid-fifties those high rates had tapered off considerably. Between 1955 and 1974, the rate of birth remained quite stable at about 18 to 19 per thousand. Thereafter, rates dropped steadily until they reached a level of only 10 per thousand in 1989, which was a level below that at which a society could replenish itself (without in-migration). Some older men, worried about the fate of the nation, blamed this dilemma on self-indulgent young women.

Young women did have a powerful influence on declining birth rates. Many variables went into the decisions they made annually which reduced the number of children carried to term. More young women were acquiring higher levels of education, and they were turning their credentials to advantage in the job market. They naturally sought to enjoy their careers and incomes by staying longer in the labor force.

Women's average age at marriage thus began creeping gradually upward. Postponing marriage until their late twenties or their early thirties reduced the likelihood of having large numbers of children. The high costs of housing and education lowered the likelihood even further. Once married, women used their improved knowledge of contraceptive techniques to reduce pregnancies, or they sought abortions when unwanted pregnancies occurred.

For all these reasons, the base of Japan's population pyramid began to shrink. By the late eighties, the population "pyramid" looked almost like a diamond: the bulge in the middle was created by large cohorts of people between twenty and sixty; a declining number of infants, toddlers, and adolescents produced a narrow base; and the relatively small cohorts of elderly people made up the comparably narrow peak. But, owing to the combined effects of longer life expectancies and a declining birth rate, the portion of the elderly in the total populace had risen significantly. Whereas people over sixty-five had constituted a steady 5 percent of Japan's population from the early 1880s into the early 1960s, their percentage of the population had increased thereafter: from 8 percent in 1975 to 12 percent by 1989.

Japan's elderly, or its Silver Citizens, posed a number of unprecedented problems. How could society profitably occupy so many older people? Where and how should they be housed? What kinds of health and welfare services did they need? And who would care for them? The debates began vigorously in the early 1970s. Many solutions were advocated, adopted, revised, rejected, and abandoned. But one tendency emerged clearly during the 1980s: government would provide some help, but families were expected to bear the larger burden. Government would address work and leisure activities and health and welfare provision. Housing and caring for the elderly fell primarily on families.

Owing to this approach to the needs of the elderly, an unusually high percentage of older people in Japan (60 percent or more) resided with family members or lived near them. Most of the burden of caring for older persons fell on the shoulders of women, daughters or daughters-in-law, in their forties, fifties, and even sixties. As long as older people were healthy and mobile, they were able to serve their own physical needs. As they aged, and as they deteriorated mentally and physically, however, they required more care. Ariyoshi Sawako offers a heart-rending depiction of one woman caring for a dying father-in-law in her famous novel *The Twilight Years*. An overnight best seller, it played a critical role in bringing the welfare of the elderly to national attention. Tending the needs of a bedridden parent requires skill, patience, endurance, and physical stamina. In many cases, women were forced to abandon their own interests and careers to provide necessary care.

Husbands expected their wives to manage the household and to raise the children. Children required constant attention, owing to anxieties about educational success and social mobility. Careers drew women in other directions. Some had jobs that provided essential income supplements for the family or the intangible satisfactions of an agreeable work life. Others would have liked to have jobs or to reenter a job abandoned a decade or two earlier. Avocational interests were yet another pull, at a time when better educations, higher incomes, and more leisure held out the possibility of hobbies, lessons, and travel not available before. But family duty, the needs of the elderly themselves, societal expectations, and governmental policies all put great pressure on women to devote themselves to the elderly when the need arose.

As much as any group in Japanese society during this period, therefore, women struggled to find a middle way between freedom and constraint. Their dilemmas stimulated an outpouring of creative literature by and about women. Ohba Minako created dreamlike fantasies exploring how Japanese women at home and abroad reflected on their roles as women, wives, and mothers. Tsushima Yuko wrote gritty stories about divorced and unmarried mothers and drew biting characterizations of the men in their lives. Takahashi Takako resorted to the indirect language favored by many male Japanese authors to examine relations between mothers and daughters. These writers and many others produced an abundance of provocative novels and short stories. Even when they set their tales in grotesque or fantastical contexts, they managed to preserve plausibility and to force women to think about their situations from every possible angle.

The tensions women faced between self-abnegation and self-indulgence affected other groups as well. Affluence offered many people a release from the confining regimentation that had previously characterized social behavior. People won the opportunity to pursue individual interests unrestrained by parents, work, and convention. Young people were more likely to venture onto unknown ground, and during the eighties they did. Rejecting the obsessive behavior of their workaholic fathers, some young men and women sought part-time work that paid ample sums in short periods of intense effort. Tired by their exertions, they quit their jobs and went on spending binges, buying designer clothing, eating at fancy restaurants, partying at trendy bars, and respecting no schedules. When the money ran out and they recovered, they sought new part-time jobs and began the cycle again. Older Japanese found such behavior incomprehensible. They referred to this younger set as *shinjinrui*, or the new species, as if they did not want even a biologic association with them. The shinjinrui acted to parody prevailing values in Japan, but they were also a parody of materialism in their own right. They carried self-indulgence to its ultimate extreme, and they pursued it with the same single-minded devotion that their fathers and mothers offered to job and family.

Eventually, the moral and emotional poverty of unconstrained materialism provoked concerns about the values of the nation itself. Two strains of thought emerged to address the problem. One fell under the capacious rubric of *Nihonjin-ron*, or the debate on Japanese identity. Those who engaged in this discussion drew on the gamut of possible ideas and produced an equally wide-ranging discourse. Much of their thinking was superficial, contradictory, and illogical. But most contributors to this discussion at least endorsed the virtue and importance of an essential Japaneseness rooted in their history as a uniquely homogeneous race organized into distinctive households and village settlements. The harmonious behavior, consensual politics, and cooperative labors of this people underlay Japan's worldly success as an economic superpower, according to the theory.

This kind of thinking bore a disconcerting resemblance to the chauvinistic, racialist rhetoric of prewar and wartime Japan. It is troubling that some distinguished academics in the nation's most prominent universities endorsed these claims. Many younger, well-educated Japanese found these ideas archaic and unappealing, but older people with conservative tendencies and even some younger men and women were attracted to them. For the latter groups, positive assertions about the uniqueness of the Japanese character provided a source of confidence and an anchor in an otherwise volatile world.

A second strain of thought also drew attention to the uniqueness of the Japanese people. Equally amorphous in its content and highly varied in form, this style of thinking invoked nostalgic memories of one's *furusato*, or native village. A mythical image of an idyllic rural village offered a touchstone of value in a rapidly changing environment. New suburbs invoked the term *furusato* as a model for encouraging civic cooperation. Suburban authorities hoped the imagery would help them to re-create the tranquil, harmonious relations of village Japan in their rapidly growing communities. The national railway conducted an advertising campaign around a furusato theme. It urged people to travel to pristine rural locales where they could get in touch with their roots and revivify spirits decayed by too much urban experience. The national government frequently invoked furusato imagery during the eighties, too. Conservative leaders saw the furusato as a device to impose a sense of order on a fractious polity. Some found these appeals enticing, but most either ignored them entirely or recognized how inapplicable they were to the complexities of life in an affluent society.

## ADAPTATION

Shifting economic fortunes and changing social mores complicated the lives of Japanese politicians. At the national and local level, the Liberal Democratic Party (LDP) continued to exercise predominant authority. Its command over the electorate became more shaky, however, and it faced challenges to its power on several fronts, especially at the local level. Rather than keen conflict that pitted one camp against another, politics during this period involved many participants acting on a volatile field of political action. Much political behavior actually led to a blurring of partisan identities which was subtly undermining support for the LDP and the Japan Socialist Party (JSP), too. Reorganization of the labor movement was one cause of this blurring, the characteristics of which were reflected in the policies adopted during the seventies and eighties.

### Partisan Change

The ruling party. The LDP maintained its dominance over Japanese politics between 1974 and mid-1989 in a context of deceptive stability. Every prime minister during this period rose from LDP ranks, and the

LDP formed every government. But its hold on the electorate slipped in many ways, and it confronted challenges to its authority at many levels. In addition, the party was riven by internal competition that was undermining its unity and integrity.

The five elections for the House of Representatives (HOR) during this period were held in 1976, 1979, 1980, 1983, and 1986. The LDP captured between 42 and 49 percent of the popular vote in these five contests. It managed to win a majority of seats in 1980 and 1986, but not in the other elections. In those three cases, the LDP had to cobble together a majority by aligning with an LDP splinter group called the New Liberal Club, or it had to invite into the party unaffiliated conservative candidates who had won seats on their own. Continued LDP dominance thus depended on a precarious hold over the electorate and sometimes tense coalitions of momentary convenience.

Prime ministers seemed to serve according to an apparently routine rotation. Of the seven LDP men who led the government between 1974 and mid-1989, six were prime minister for about two years each. They were Tanaka Kakuei (1972–1974), Miki Takeo (1974–1976), Fukuda Takeo (1976–1978), Ohira Masayoshi (1978–1980), Suzuki Zenko (1980–1982), and Takeshita Noboru (1987–1989). One man, Nakasone Yasuhiro, served a longer term of five year's duration, between 1982 and 1987. All these men were LDP faction leaders, and they won the prime ministership in part owing to an agreement to rotate the party presidency among the heads of the party's factions.

Factions, *habatsu* in Japanese, had been inherent features of the LDP's organization since its inception in 1955. They arose originally because two different political parties had merged to form the LDP, and members of those parties retained primary attachments to their former party colleagues. The factions persisted because they conducted essential party functions. They were vehicles for raising campaign funds, nurturing the careers of new members, sustaining the power of older members, determining party posts and parliamentary assignments, and identifying prospective cabinet ministers and prime ministers. The five factions in the LDP in the 1970s were headed by Tanaka, Miki, Fukuda, Ohira, and Nakasone. In the 1980s, Suzuki assumed leadership of the Ohira faction, and Takeshita of the Tanaka faction. Each faction operated as a somewhat separate fiefdom within the party to promote the interests of its members while also striving to promote the overall goals of the LDP.

Beginning in the early 1970s, the Tanaka faction became the cause of considerable intraparty conflict. Tanaka Kakuei had been forced from office in 1974 owing to revelations about corruption. Two years later he was indicted for bribery in a case involving the Lockheed Corporation of the United States. He fought his legal battles in court, and being an extraordinarily powerful and aggressive person, he fought them in the government as well. To ensure that the LDP would appoint justice ministers sympathetic to his cause, he began expanding the size of his faction by increasing the number of candidates he sponsored. This gave him more leverage for bargaining within the party and enabled him to play a key role in determining cabinet ministers and prime ministers. Tanaka's success at increasing the strength of his faction allowed him the casting vote over the selection of Ohira, Suzuki, and Nakasone. His powers declined rapidly in the mid-1980s, however, when he suffered a severe stroke. Most members of his faction eventually joined a new one led by Takeshita Noboru, who succeeded Nakasone in 1987. Therefore, Tanaka Kakuei himself, his successor as faction leader, and men deeply beholden to him together controlled the prime ministership for more than two-thirds of this period.

The unusual power exercised by the Tanaka faction influenced LDP conduct, shaped electoral support, and eroded public confidence in the LDP in particular and politicians in general. The apparently routine circulation of the prime ministership among faction leaders actually masked intense turmoil within the LDP. Factions competed against each other to elect members to the Diet. Faction leaders and faction members all jockeyed for position on public issues, in order to cast themselves in the best possible light. They did not hesitate to undercut or obstruct the efforts of other factions, and they were always eager to bargain for trade-offs that would advantage their cause. Disputes among faction leaders made it difficult to direct attention to pressing matters and to devise solutions quickly. These kinds of behavior drastically slowed the pace of action on major legislation and made politicians appear weak and venal.

The public's response to this behavior was ambivalent and ambiguous. Many public opinion polls indicated that a large majority of voters would prefer to have another party lead the government. Yet the same voters said they thought the best choice was still the LDP; few trusted the Socialists or Communists to do well. Ambivalence was especially pervasive among younger and middle-aged voters in urban and suburban areas. Their voting behavior produced an ambiguous set of signs during the seventies and eighties. Their party attachments weakened, and many of them began to think of themselves as independents tied to no single party. They switched votes frequently from one election to the next, sometimes voting for LDP candidates, sometimes for those of other parties. Collectively, their voting choices undermined the position of the LDP in urban constituencies.

In rural areas, however, the LDP retained its overwhelming strength in HOR contests. Voters in rural areas seemed content to accept public projects that the LDP claimed to be directing to their villages and regions. They also seemed willing to accept the inducements—coming in the form of trips, presents, and cash "gifts"—that the party used during election campaigns in rural districts. The LDP's already strong rural base was further expanded by nationwide misapportionment; in comparison with urban districts, most rural ones had more representatives than their populations warranted.

Election campaigns were costly. Candidates needed money to pay campaign staffs, rent advertising trucks, print materials, and provide the requisite "gifts" for loyal supporters. They also needed large sums of money to underwrite the costs of personnel and office space in their districts, where their assistants carried out countless constituency services. The national government provided funds only for a tiny staff in Tokyo, so individual legislators had to underwrite further service at their own expense. Politicians thus had constantly to raise large sums of money, both to win and to retain their offices.

This need for money left politicians highly vulnerable to rich firms or persons perfectly willing to use their assets to "buy" politicians. This they did with outright cash contributions, excessive honorarium payments, inflated entrance fees to cocktail parties, and grants of stock in newly listed firms. Illegal and quasi-legal fund-raising, always a problem for Japanese politicians, in the seventies and eighties became far more serious. The sums of money involved now were huge by the standards of a typical Japanese family; for they ran into millions of dollars. Compounding the fund-raising problem was its higher visibility. Newspapers and prestigious magazines conducted a more vigorous form of investigative journalism. They sensationalized and exposed to public view the sometimes seedy persons, groups, and corporations providing political contributions and the benefits they reaped in return. The Tanaka faction was not alone in provoking public dismay over political financing; but its problems and conduct drew persistent attention to the widespread corruption afflicting Japanese politics, with its corrosive effect on voters, thus undermining support for all political parties, especially the LDP.

**The opposition.** Corruption and factional bickering in the LDP offered the opposition parties a promising opportunity to promote their cause at the expense of the ruling party, but one at which they were only partly successful. The opposition seemed especially ineffective at the national level, where progressive and centrist parties failed to capitalize on the problems of the LDP. The largest party in the progressive opposition, the JSP, saw its support dwindle steadily in HOR elections. It attracted 21 percent of the vote in 1976 but only 17 percent by 1986. Factional conflicts within the party, the inability to present attractive policies to a diverse electorate, and a damaging attachment to one wing of the union movement all hampered its cause. The Japan Communist Party also suffered a drop in electoral support, from 10 percent in 1976 to 6 percent in 1986. Ever more affluent voters found its programs increasingly archaic.

The parties of the center fared no better. The moderate Democratic Socialist Party (DSP) clung to a steady 6 to 7 percent of the vote, and the Clean Government Party (CGP) to another 9 to 11 percent. Both parties were hampered by their close identity with their major supporters, private-sector union members in the case of the DSP and Soka Gakkai members in the case of the CGP. Had the opposition parties all been able to work together in coalition, they might have been able to unseat the LDP, but differing policies, personalities, and constituencies made that impossible.

At the prefectural and local levels, the opposition enjoyed slightly more success. Governor Minobe Ryokichi of Tokyo had inaugurated an era of progressive local government in the late 1960s. The 1970s marked the heyday of this movement. Men aligned with the progressive and centrist parties won office as governors in the most populous urban prefectures, and many Socialists took office as mayors in cities and suburbs. At its peak, the progressive movement embraced about one-fourth of all city mayors. Unified under the League of Progressive Mayors, these one hundred or so officials promoted policies that appealed to the civic needs of the new urban and suburban residents. Some dedicated their efforts to special projects, as did the mayor who made sewer service to the entire city his top priority. Others devoted their attention to civic centers, parks, or new public libraries. Most worked to correct the costs of overly rapid development in the sixties. Many were quite popular, and they often won reelection three or four times. It seemed, for a moment, as if the progressive opposition were going to ride a groundswell of local support into national office.

Unfortunately, some elements of the progressive coalition exploited the movement in a way that tainted its achievements and dimmed its prospects. During the seventies, unions of local government employees affiliated with the national federation called Jichiro' (see Chapter 2 above) exploited their political ties with local executives to win lucrative wage contracts. In some prefectures and large cities, unions were so successful that their most senior officials earned salaries higher than those of national civil servants, rankling officials in the central government, especially those in what had been called the Agency of Local Autonomy. That body had eventually been elevated to ministry status, and in the early 1960s it changed its official English title to the Ministry of Home Affairs. This action both celebrated its prewar ancestry and notified the public that descendants of the old Home Ministry were intent on regaining their authority.

For their purposes, officials in local governments drawing high salaries and generous retirement bonuses were the perfect target. Most Japanese citizens thought that prestigious national bureaucrats should be paid more than a public servant in city government. They were also delighted to think that lower salaries might reduce their taxes. National bureaucrats, LDP politicians, and conservative politicians on the local level all joined to conduct a counterattack against the high compensation Jichiro had won for its members. This political offensive had broader objectives as well, directed at all public-sector labor unions and the progressive movement.

By the late seventies, conservative efforts were beginning to bear fruit. When Tokyo's Governor Minobe retired from office in 1979, Suzuki Shun'ichi succeeded him. Suzuki was not merely an elderly conservative identified with the LDP; he was also a former high-ranking official in the Ministry of Home Affairs. He exemplified almost everything the progressive movement was fighting against: a bureaucratic style of politics, LDP policies and practices, and intrusion in local affairs by the state bureaucracy. Suzuki's victory administered to the progressive movement a symbolic blow from which it never recovered.

In its stead, there emerged a new mode of local governance which was characterized by its suprapartisan qualities. Instead of avowing an LDP or JSP tie, candidates for prefectural governor or city mayor declared no affiliation and ran on fusion tickets. Thus a candidate once allied with the local JSP might persuade the DSP, the CGP, and some progressive groups within the local LDP to endorse his candidacy and to support his administration. Or a known conservative politician might run for office with endorsements from the DSP and the JSP and pursue progressive policies with slightly different partisan support. These trends blurred partisan identities. Local residents seemed primarily interested in effective management of local government which responded to their highest priorities. If all or most of the political parties in a prefecture, city, or suburb could agree on those priorities, so much the better. Results mattered most, not partisan rhetoric. Gradually, the policies and achievements of politicians took on greater import than their partisan attachments.

In addition to public employee unions in local government, other public-sector unions also played a role in undermining support for the progressive movement. Chapter 2 explained why unions of government employees were antagonized in the late 1940s when the Japanese government, acting under pressure from the office of the Supreme Commander for the Allied Powers, retracted the right to strike granted in 1945. Public employees in such national government enterprises as the Japan Tobacco Monopoly and the Japan National Railways had long struggled to retrieve that right.

During the 1970s, government unions conducted collective actions to win back their rights. Often called "right-to-strike strikes," their actions were usually work-to-rule protests. When they worked to the rules on the commuter trains, they ensured delays at crowded urban stations because hundreds of people piled up when trains moved at the "legal" pace during rush hour. These actions ultimately backfired on the workers conducting them. The strikes infuriated commuters, mobilized popular sentiment against public employees, and reinforced the conservative counterattack already underway. Public-sector workers affiliated with Sohyo, in local and national unions alike, thus jeopardized their economic status at the same time they fostered public aversion to the JSP and its programs.

Private-sector labor unions affiliated with Domei pursued a much different tack in the seventies and eighties. They did not adopt the political, adversarial approaches that Sohyo and its public-sector employees used. Rather, Domei and its workers turned to low-key, cooperative modes of behavior conducted within the confines of individual enterprises. Cues offered by unions abroad and the imperatives of industrial adjustment were two powerful forces persuading private-sector workers to adopt their approach. They were intent on preserving firms and protecting wage increases, even if it meant working closely with management and accepting some layoffs.

Steel workers in large firms often took the lead in demonstrating the new mode of consultative, cooperative behavior. Affiliated with the International Metal Federation, they patterned their behavior on that of steel workers in such countries as West Germany, where labor-management consultation was institutionalized under law. Japan's steel unions cooperated with management to achieve productivity gains, and they sought to benefit accordingly in their wage negotiations. Because they often concluded their negotiations earlier than other unions, the steel workers set a target for other unions to shoot at. After about a decade during which this kind of moderate behavior became more widespread, unions in the private sector established in the mid-1980s a national forum to promote a single umbrella organization for labor in Japan.

Along with their moderating economic behavior, private-sector workers began moderating their political behavior, too. Some union workers had always voted for LDP candidates; more began to do so after the mid-1970s. During the 1980s, private-sector union leaders showed a willingness to lobby and consult with members of the Nakasone government. For his part, Nakasone strove to court them. He was trying to reorient the LDP away from its rural base, and affluent union members living in urban areas would be a promising addition to his new LDP constituency.

With their behavior after the early seventies, private-sector unions contributed further to the blurring of partisan identities. No longer did the JSP contest the LDP across a stark divide. Rather, key groups in Japanese society bargained directly across almost the full spectrum of partisan allegiances. And when the members of those groups cast their ballots, they felt free to pick and choose among partisan alternatives. Party loyalty diminished and political independence and volatility increased. Thus, after returning the LDP with a resounding majority in the lower-house election of 1986, voters turned on the party and sent it to defeat in an upper-house election just three years later. By the late 1980s, LDP stability was both deceptive and fragile.

### Policy Change

Policies toward depressed industries (discussed in the first part of this chapter) were among the most important adopted during this period. Four other policy initiatives were undertaken to address issues raised by social changes. Two dealt with medical care for the elderly and employment opportunity for women. The other two bore directly on the pocketbooks of Japanese consumers; they dealt with administrative reform in the central government and a national consumption tax.

Some of the earliest laws dealing with matters of concern to the elderly were actually implemented a year or two before this period began. The most important of these was a bill passed in 1972 providing free medical care for persons over seventy. This national bill was inspired by the success of a similar policy first initiated in the Tokyo Metropolitan Prefecture during Governor Minobe's tenure. It was thus an LDP achievement stimulated by progressive political pressure. Beneficiaries of free medical care used it lavishly, and health care costs for the elderly began to rise rapidly, so that LDP politicians and bureaucrats in the Ministry of Health and Welfare (MHW) and the Ministry of Finance (MOF) soon grew concerned about these heavy burdens on the public purse.

Throughout the 1970s and into the early 1980s, politicians, bureaucrats, physicians, and the public carried on a struggle to achieve a balance between the health needs of the elderly and the financial capacities of the government. Physicians organized in the Japan Medical Association had for years supported policies that encouraged frequent visits to physicians, long hospital stays, and heavy use of prescribed medicines. Bureaucrats in both MHW and MOF wanted to resist abuse of this system and curtail its costs. They sought to implement patient fees that would reduce costs and deter overuse. The public opposed fees but was not well organized to articulate its interests in competition with the other parties. After years of debate, the government finally, in 1982, passed legislation that eliminated free medical care for the elderly by introducing a small monthly charge and nominal fees for service. Bureaucrats in MHW and MOF and politicians in the LDP took the lead in pushing this legislation through, against the opposition of the Japan Medical Association and the wishes of many in the Japanese public.

The desire to cut government expenditure was the motivation behind the administrative reform movement of the 1980s, too. Conservative politicians and MOF officials all worried about the heavy reliance on bonded indebtedness to fund government expenditures, which had grown since 1975. Conservative politicians also wanted to reduce the political and economic powers of public-sector unions, especially in the national railway and the national telecommunications monopoly. To achieve these objectives, the Suzuki government established in 1981 the Second Provisional Commission on Administrative Reform. Consisting of nine members drawn from many walks of life, the commission issued its recommendations in 1983. As a result of its work, the government passed laws to privatize the railways and the telecommunications monopoly, reduce government outlays, simplify government regulations, and reorganize the prime minister's office.

The administrative reform movement was Japan's version of the conservative, antigovernment programs so apparent in Great Britain and the United States in the 1980s. It was driven by antiunionism and by the desire to reduce government's role in the economy. Although Japanese government expenditures had never reached the high levels common in Europe, or even the more moderate levels of the United States, they had begun to rise. As a consequence, families found themselves slightly more pinched by taxes, especially families headed by salaried workers in urban areas. Their taxes were withheld at the source, so they were not evading taxation in the same way that many farmers and small proprietors were. Prime Minister Nakasone wanted to draw more urban, white-collar workers into the LDP, and his strong support of the administrative reform movement rested on his desire to appeal to such voters.

The second pocketbook issue that commanded attention during this period was politically more complicated. For many years, bureaucrats in the MOF had wanted to introduce a tax on consumption modeled on those levied in many European countries. Recognizing that private consumption by individuals accounted for the largest single share of the national economy, the bureaucrats were acting rationally to tap a logical source of increased revenue. But a consumption tax that required a buyer to pay an additional 3 to 5 percent for every item purchased was highly regressive. It would impose far higher proportional costs on low-income than on high-income families. Therefore, the JSP and other opposition parties opposed this tax vociferously. To make a consumption tax more palatable, the LDP first reduced the income tax slightly, to appeal to middle-income, white-collar families of the sort Nakasone was trying to draw into the party.

Nonetheless, the consumption tax itself remained unacceptable to the public. Whenever the government introduced tax legislation in the Diet, the electorate responded with a stinging rebuke to the LDP at the next opportunity. After more than a decade of debate and opposition, the Takeshita government finally succeeded in passing a bill, and a 3 percent tax on all consumption went into effect in early 1989. This was a victory for conservatives and bureaucrats, but it was costly to the LDP in the long run, as events described in Chapter 5 illustrate.

The one other major bill passed during this period was the Equal Employment Opportunity Act (EEOA) of 1985. With more women possessing higher qualifications entering the labor force in the sixties and seventies, female workers increasingly challenged the job discrimination they faced. Customary practices, not labor law, obliged them to leave work after marriage and to stay out of the labor force until children were grown. Some younger women wanted to pursue uninterrupted careers, but they encountered many obstructions. The most frustrated among them took their cases to court, causing expense and embarrassment to private firms, which eventually signaled a willingness to support legislation to offer lifelong careers to women. The EEOA resulted from this concession by management, pressure from working women, and action by conservative and progressive legislators. Unfortunately, the EEOA makes weak provision for redress of grievance. In part for that reason, its passage has done relatively little to reduce job discrimination and to improve women's chances of winning top jobs in prestigious firms. In fact in some ways the law may actually have undermined their cause.

Policy change in Japan during the eighties was driven by many participants addressing complex social and economic issues. In contrast with earlier periods, the participants in policy discussions were more numerous. Politicians and bureaucrats had always played a role in devising policies, owing to their strategic positions in the government and legislature. Large corporations had also participated when issues bore directly on them, as the problems of employment opportunity and industrial restructuring did. Public-sector unions at the national and local levels and private-sector unions in industries and enterprises had always played their roles in shaping policies. But other groups not previously involved were also significant participants during this period: the elderly and their representatives, women, suburban residents, consumer groups, and citizens acting as taxpayers. The expansion of participation attested to a growth of citizenship in the Japanese polity. A more affluent society had conferred greater resources on many groups, both requiring and enabling them to engage politically in new ways. By organizing, lobbying, bargaining, suing, and voting, many—though not all—used their citizenship to challenge the long-standing dominance of bureaucrats and LDP politicians.

Thus economic adjustment, social assimilation, and political adaptation all fostered the emergence of a qualitatively different society by the late 1980s, one. fraught with contradictory and crosscutting tendencies. Some industries expanded and prospered; others withered and declined. Almost everyone grew more affluent, but wider gaps appeared between those at the bottom and those at the top. Politicians and bureaucrats had to confront more political participants, and the solutions they devised produced mixed results. Japan had become a highly fragmented society. The uneasiness, anxieties, and contention that appeared in the 1970s and 1980s were a by-product of this increasing dividedness, if not divisiveness. Individuals, families, business firms, interest groups, and others seemed preoccupied with their own concerns. They pursued their interests on a broader ground of political competition which gave rise to constantly shifting coalitions of actors. A more dissenting, self-centered atmosphere promoted greater flux, less cohesion, and diverging goals.

The hypothetical families discussed earlier in this chapter exemplify these changes. The factory hand was consigned to a life of moderate material comfort, lived largely in the confines of an industrial district. He represented a nativist element in Japanese society. He dined on rice, fish, and sake, relaxed with Japanese television programs, and traveled within the country. He was likely to vote for LDP candidates in local and national elections. Men like him probably found appeals to Japanese essentialism, the furusato, and tax cutting highly congenial.

The rich family differed on almost every count. Its members were cosmopolitans. They enjoyed ethnic foods, listened to foreign music, traveled overseas, and bought Western art. They were probably independents politically, if they voted at all. They could measure claims about Japanese uniqueness against their friends and associates in the United States and Europe. They probably found furusato appeals bemusing, and they might have ignored debates over welfare laws and administrative reform.

The material and psychological differences in these two families were repeated millions of times over by the 1980s. No two Japanese families were exactly alike, so all responded in a different manner to the political, economic, and social demands they faced. Their differences, and the diversity they nourished, make it extremely difficult to generalize about the character of Japan in 1989, save to note that it had acquired a level of dynamic tension unprecedented in the postwar era.

# CHAPTER FIVE

# Immobility, 1989–

DURING THE YEARS FOLLOWING 1989, Japan experienced a number of extraordinary events. Two domestic events occurred within a short time of each other in early 1995. The first was a major earthquake centered south of the port city of Kobe. The quake killed and injured many, devastated Kobe's port facilities, leveled superhighways, and destroyed thousands of homes, apartments, and businesses. The costs of revival and rebuilding were a major setback for the Japanese economy. A few months later, members of an extremist religious sect called Aum Shinrikyo dropped bags containing a deadly sarin gas at several subway stations in Tokyo, killing a dozen people and injuring many others. (For one intriguing reference, see Murakami Haruki's *Underground*.) The effects of this incident were short-lived, but while it remained in the public eye, it caused many Japanese to reflect nervously on what kind of society was breeding such fanatics.

Foreign incidents also buffeted Japan, injecting tensions arising in more distant parts of the globe into the minds and affairs of its residents. A war in Kuwait, initiated by an Iraqi invasion and ended by the United States and its allies, caused Japan embarrassing difficulties. Japan was constrained from participation in the war by Article 9 of the postwar constitution, which explicitly prevents the use—indeed, the very existence—of an offensive military capability. Nonetheless, Japan had to underscore its support of the United States and its allies by "contributing" (under considerable duress) a billion dollars to allay the costs of anti-Iraq forces. This incident exposed Japan's diplomatic and defense policies to critical international scrutiny and seems to have diminished Japan's stature in the eyes of many nations.

Much closer to home, Japan had to deal in the late 1990s and the early 2000s with the sporadic and unpredictable behavior of its neighbor North Korea. Especially after Kim Jong Il inherited leadership from his father, North Korea engaged in saber-rattling activities, such as sending missiles across the Japanese islands, to prove that North Koreans could deliver a destructive warhead if they wanted. North Korea also continued to make threatening claims about developing nuclear weaponry. Other nations essentially left Japan to its own devices where solving its relations with North Korea were concerned, and the Japanese public seems to have dealt with these threats by ignoring them.

Another blow to Japan's economic well-being struck in 1997, when many nations in East and Southeast Asia suffered a financial crisis brought on by excessive borrowing and deflating currencies. Japanese banks suffered untold losses when borrowers in those regions failed to repay loans, and Japanese exporters saw their sales decline sharply. Coming at a time when the economy seemed on its way to revival, this crisis further prolonged the economic slump that Japan had already been facing for nearly a decade.

These events and others contributed to what many commentators eventually dubbed "the lost decade." Japan did not witness much progress during the 1990s, but neither did it suffer obvious regression. Rather, the entire society seemed to sink into a puzzling immobility on nearly every front. Deflation—in a variety of forms—became a fact of life for the economy. Discord was the keynote of the era politically, as fractious political parties and a confused electorate tried to resolve intractable problems. And detachment characterized Japan socially. People seemed to turn their backs against the many problems society faced, absorbed as they were with personal and family issues. Problems arose for many reasons, but one powerful force shaping the domestic difficulties that Japan confronted during the 1990s was the demography of an aging society.

## DEMOGRAPHY

Aging was just one crucial aspect of demographic trends in Japan during the 1990s. People over the age of sixty-five had increased, to constitute an ever larger share of the nation's populace. They had been about 5 percent of the population as recently as 1960. By the turn of the millennium, they constituted over 17 percent of the total, a portion that would continue to rise steadily in the future. At the same time, young people under the age of fifteen declined in number to comprise a smaller percentage of the population. They shrank from nearly 30 percent of the total in 1960 to about 15 percent in 2000. Thus, what had once been a population pyramid (with large numbers of young people forming the base, a sizable contingent of middle-aged people forming the middle, and a small group of elderly at the top) reshaped itself into a population diamond (with small numbers of young and elderly at the base and the top, respectively, and a large contingent of middle-aged adults in the middle). This recomposition of age groups in the national populace had extensive social, political, and economic implications.

Smaller cohorts of young Japanese had notable social effects on two core institutions: families and schools. Families that had only one child in 2000 were able to economize and save in a way that families with two or three children could not. Small families often built expensive new homes for themselves, with lavishly appointed study centers for the child. They could afford to hire private tutors or to pay tuition at after-school prep academies, to enhance their child's ability to pass entrance exams to selective higher-level schools. And they were better able to afford the costly tuition fees at elite private high schools that virtually guaranteed admission to desirable colleges and universities. Families like this became intensely focused on the academic success of their only child, whether male or female, with the stay-at-home mom playing the dominant role in nurturing academic success in the next generation. Many couples like these consciously chose to have fewer children in order to maximize the returns on scarce material and psychological resources and to confer as many advantages as possible on their child in the competitive game of educational attainment.

Other families opted to have fewer children in order to maximize the freedoms of the mother. Having witnessed the burdens that their own mothers suffered in the 1970s when they were being brought up, some young wives of the 1990s and after vowed not to becomes slaves to their children and to the status of the household in the same way that their mothers had been. These younger wives pursued a life course that maximized their options to pursue personal—in contrast with purely familial—ends and interests. Having only one child to care for markedly increased the possibility that young wives in such families could take a job, develop a hobby, or join a civic group. Women like this, dressed in stylish clothing but trotting around at a frantic pace, crowded the subways and byways of upscale neighborhoods in the Tokyo area at the turn of the millennium.

Fewer children of school age had significant effects on the national system of education. After a sharp upward spike in birth rates in the first four to five years after the war ended in 1945, the number of children born fell almost without exception in every year thereafter. There was a slight echo in the 1970s of the baby boom of the early postwar years, but thereafter births dropped perceptibly on an annual and a per capita basis. By the 1990s, Japanese women were giving birth each year to just enough babies to maintain the population at a stable level. With fewer children entering the schools each year, however, educational demands declined. Fewer schools and teachers were needed, and fewer school supplies and subcontractors, too. In the 1990s, many elementary, middle, and higher schools were closed; the numbers of active teachers fell; and school suppliers found their markets contracting. Subtly, changes like these provoked the sense of psychological and economic malaise that permeated the 1990s.

In contrast, the growing numbers of elderly persons caused far more obvious problems. In part, this was attributable to the sheer scope of the matter. Some 25 to 35 percent of all Japanese households housed one or more persons over the age of sixty-five during the 1990s. Consequently, many people of all ages were directly conscious of the demands and costs of elder care. Extensive coverage in the print and visual media also raised public consciousness, because health and medical-care issues were constantly at the forefront of the national political agenda. Add to this the need for income maintenance in retirement and the impact such welfare policies had on the working population, and nearly everyone in Japanese society quickly understood why having more elders affected almost everyone to some degree.

The growth of an aging society had an insidious effect on economic conditions in Japan during the 1990s. Few Japanese over the age of sixty-five stayed gainfully employed. Instead, they began accepting pensions from various public or private plans, or they drew down the savings they had so conscientiously been accumulating for decades. Some retirees were able to live much as before from the pensions and savings they now received, but many—in fact, a large majority—suffered a sharp drop in annual income once they retired completely. To compensate, they spent less. When millions of the elderly entered full retirement in the 1990s, consumption demand therefore dropped sharply. This is only one of many reasons, but nonetheless an important reason, why the Japanese economy as a whole slipped into the doldrums during the decade. Quite simply, the consumption outlays of a notable share of the populace fell sharply as more people entered full retirement.

Furthermore, the composition of expenditures among the elderly shifted perceptibly. When literally millions of people no longer went off to work five or six days a week, the need for fashionable clothing, dry cleaning, commuter transport, and midday meals at restaurants all declined. Men who had once stopped off for drinks and snacks on their way home from work no longer made such expenditures regularly, so some leisure and entertainment outlays fell. These kinds of cutbacks affected department stores, small shops, and bars and restaurants; and they contributed significantly to the downturns in these segments of the Japanese economy in the 1990s.

At the same time, retirees over sixty-five found outlays of other kinds growing dramatically. Health needs became a paramount concern, and spending on pharmaceutical products and medical care rose sharply. Often trapped in the home by physical disabilities, the very elderly (people in their late seventies and over) created new demands for in-home health care. If they were fortunate, they could rely on enlightened municipalities to provide such services, but more often than not, they had to pay private providers or subsidize the costs of public providers. Either way, the elderly eventually had to devote more cash outlays to medical and welfare expenditures. This was a boon to the service sector of the Japanese economy, but it came at some expense to the once-proud manufacturing sector.

A large and growing population of elderly people imposed expenses in other ways. Budgets of the national and local governments came under stress, because more nonworking elderly reduced revenues and expanded outlays simultaneously. People who were fully retired continued to pay income and real-estate taxes, but income taxes dropped sharply once a person stopped working and relied on savings to survive. At the same time, these people placed more demands on the public purse, because they increased the use of public facilities and services. The fiscal dilemmas of the national government in the 1990s—and of many prefectural and local governments, too—were in part a product of the changing demography of Japanese society.

People sandwiched between the smaller numbers of young Japanese and the increasing numbers of the elderly—that is, those in their early twenties to early sixties—found themselves under increased and complicated pressures. They felt obliged to devote ever more attention to their children, and some of them at least felt guilty when they did not. They also felt obligated to reciprocate the care given them while young by their own parents, so they struggled to deal conscientiously with the needs of aging mothers and fathers. The middle-aged cohorts were also expected to devote themselves without stint to their employers, especially if they worked at a private firm. Given such pressures, the social stress, the political discord, and the economic dilemmas detectable within Japan in the 1990s are easier to understand, as later comments illustrate.

Demographic change was not the sole explanation for Japan's unusual period of immobility after 1989. Nonetheless, shifting demographic patterns had deep and pervasive, though sometimes hidden and subtle, effects on the nation's destiny at the turn of the millennium. We thus need to bear demographic trends in mind as we examine more closely social, political, and economic changes in the 1990s and later.

## DETACHMENT

In the late 1980s, a young author with a distinctive voice published the novella *Kitchen*. Still in her early twenties at the time, the writer's family name was Yoshimoto. Her pen name, Banana, signified her unconventionality. Banana Yoshimoto, as she came to be known in the West, immediately attracted a huge following in Japan. Her novella was reprinted numerous times and sold millions of copies. We can assume, therefore, that she stirred the emotions and captured the imaginations of many in Japan and that her work offers an index to Japanese social perceptions during this period.

There are three principal characters in *Kitchen* and five minor figures. The central personality is Sakurai Mikage, a college-aged woman who is dealing with the recent death of her grandmother when the story opens. Mikage is peculiarly subject to personal loss. Her parents and her grandfather all died when she was still young, so the death of her grandmother leaves her completely bereft. Feeling her anguish, Tanabe Yuichi befriends her. A college student also, Yuichi had sometimes assisted Mikage's grandmother when she bought flowers at the shop where he worked. The third main character in the novella is Eriko, Yuichi's "mother," whom Mikage meets for the first time when she visits Yuichi's home. Five other figures who appear only briefly in the story are Mikage's former boyfriend, her three associates at her new job, and a transvestite who works at Eriko's bar.

Mikage's first meeting with Eriko nearly sweeps her off her feet. She is astonished by Eriko's perfect features, her exotic beauty, and her undemanding cheerfulness. Yuichi quickly reveals, however, that appearance is not everything. Eriko is actually Yuichi's father, Yuji, who underwent plastic surgery and a sex-change operation after the death of the woman who was Yuichi's mother and Yuji's wife. In Mikage's open, magnanimous way, she ponders this information for a moment and easily accepts it. When Yuichi and Eriko/Yuji extend a heartfelt invitation for her to stay with them temporarily, Mikage decides to move in. She is entranced by the two of them, by their contemporary sofa, and by their kitchen, whose stolid utility is her momentary anchor in the world.

As the story progresses, it evolves into a romance. Mikage stays with the Tanabes for several months. Personal obligations keep all of them very busy, and they see little of one another. Eventually, Mikage moves into an apartment of her own and ties are cut off entirely. Some time later, out of the blue, Yuichi phones Mikage to inform her that Eriko is dead. She has been killed by an enraged suitor at her own bar, but not before she clubbed her attacker to death with a dumbbell. Yuichi is obviously at wit's end, now every bit as alone in the world as Mikage herself.

In an effort to comfort someone who stood by her in a time of difficulty, Mikage goes to Yuichi's home to spend the night with him. Job duties force her to leave the next day and to stay away for several days after that. But during her travels, Mikage finally realizes that she loves Yuichi. On a sudden impulse, she takes a long, expensive taxi ride from the resort where she is working to a mountain inn where he is recuperating. Their brief encounter both revives Yuichi's flagging spirits and reveals his love for Mikage. Despite having spent many nights together, Mikage and Yuichi have never been sexually intimate. Nor are they sexually intimate on this occasion. They part company, and readers are left to assume that they will come together eventually as man and wife.

The artful treatment of this pure romance may be what attracted legions of young (overwhelmingly female) readers in Japan and elsewhere. Although the romantic story line does have a powerful narrative attraction, it is other features of the work that lend it value as a commentary on contemporary society. The manner in which Yoshimoto depicts social institutions, relationships, and psychology offers an intriguing vision that warrants closer scrutiny.

One of the most striking aspects of Yoshimoto's world is the almost complete absence of the social institutions ordinarily associated with postwar Japan: the family, the workplace, and the schools. Not one functional nuclear family appears in the book. There are no direct descriptions of a workplace, although we are told about the flower shop, the cooking school, and the bar. Even though Mikage, her boyfriend, and Yuichi are all college students, no one ever sets foot in a classroom. There is some parody involved in these omissions, but the omissions are also intentional. Yoshimoto is suggesting that the real lessons of life are not taught by parents, colleagues, teachers, or classmates. They are learned in chance encounters through the ups and downs of daily life.

In a more subtle way, Yoshimoto has written a searing indictment of Japanese families. She suggests that families impede loving relationships. We discover nothing about the relationship between Mikage's own mother and father and very little about that between Yuichi's father and mother. We do learn from Eriko that his relationship with his wife (Yuichi's mother) was strong and devoted. Their relationship throve, however, only because Yuji (later Eriko) eloped with Yuichi's mother, and they never again saw the parents who raised them. Yuichi and Eriko/Yuji have a pragmatic, mutual respect for each other, but one can hardly call them a happy family in the conventional sense. Finally, in the case of Mikage and Yuichi, only when all of their relations have died is it possible for them to acknowledge their love for each other.

Social bonds, love, and intimacy are obstructed in Yoshimoto's world by the family and by the plight of the individual. Loneliness is everyone's burden. The figures in her story are utterly preoccupied with themselves. They are completely absorbed with their own problems and are easy prey to a spontaneous materialism. No one conducts serious conversations about human relationships; they can impart their views only through argument or sarcasm. When Mikage and Yuichi finally come together, they do so through intuition, silence, and serendipity. Of course, Japanese value silence and intuition under these circumstances, and serendipity heightens the romantic tension in the story. These matters aside, the novel implicitly denounces bonds that knit society together while depicting autonomous individuals for whom freedom really means loneliness.

Like the *shinjinrui*, the participants in the debate on Japanese identity, and the promoters of *furusato* imagery (all discussed in Chapter 4), Banana Yoshimoto was also exploring identity, self, and society in writing *Kitchen*. She offers a far deeper and more engaging source for reflection, one that found a large audience among younger Japanese. Whether they embraced her vision or not, the very appeal of her book suggests a willingness on the part of many to contemplate a society far different from that of their parents and grandparents.

In a laconic way, one of the social features of contemporary Japan toward which Yoshimoto points in *Kitchen* is the growing phenomenon of social detachment, which is especially conspicuous between generations. *Kitchen* thus foreshadows some of the generational differences that became so manifest during the 1990s.

Although Japanese under the age of twenty were not the largest social group in the country in the 1990s, they were in many ways the most conspicuous and the strongest trendsetters. A stroll through any of the "hot spots" in Tokyo during the late 1990s—especially Shibuya and Harajuku—exposed the curious traveler to flocks of young men and women strolling about and fiddling with the symbol of their age: the cell phone. They were a sharp contrast to middle-aged sararii-men, usually walking alone, no cell phone in sight, head bent, faces wrapped in an expression of genial anxiety, or pairs of young suburban mothers chatting amiably in their expensive designer clothes, laden with recent purchases, rushing off to the next emporium. Finally making contact, the young men and women would brighten up and, ear bent to phone, engage momentarily with a distant friend before reconnecting with their strolling companions and diving into the closest McDonald's.

These fleeting signs symbolized core features of the younger set. Even though they spent a lot of time in schools, education was not the issue foremost on their minds. Keeping up with their peers was exceedingly important, and that meant having a lot of the right stuff: cell phones, designer leisure wear, and a bedroom filled with the latest electronic gadgets. All of this required money, and that was another reason why many younger, married couples were having only one child. The material costs of raising a youngster in Japan during the 1990s were high. In the big cities, weekly allowances for a middle-schooler equivalent to $100 (U.S.) were not uncommon. The consumption that such support nourished was conspicuous, in the stores and on the street.

From the time they were born, these youngest cohorts were surrounded by material goods. They also enjoyed the private space in which to store and display such goods. Unlike their parents and grandparents, they lived in apartments or homes large enough to provide them with their own rooms from an early age. When they were infants, their rooms were crowded with stuffed animals. As they grew older, the obligatory supports of formal education crowded out the animals; Teddy gave way to desks and bookshelves. Then came audio and video equipment as well as expanding wardrobes. By the time such children were ready to leave home for college, there was virtually no space in their "space."

However, crowding did not deter many younger Japanese from cocooning themselves in their rooms and shutting themselves off from others in the family. The fathers of many of them were seldom at home during the week under any circumstances; and mothers, too, were often out of the home. Even if they did not have a part-time job outside, mothers of such children were frequently away from home, engaged in the pursuit of hobbies or civic activities. A large population of "latchkey children," youngsters who let themselves into locked apartments or homes not occupied by parents or siblings, emerged who were, of necessity, self-reliant in some ways but oddly dependent on cell phones, play stations, and TV, in other ways.

Whether the members of this youngest cohort in Japanese society in the 1990s were strolling the streets with their friends or enmeshed in an electronic cocoon at home, they were detached from their parents and their grandparents. Their social obligations and their leisure diversions enmeshed them in a youth culture all their own, alien in most ways to the two previous generations. Those older generations had often grown up in rural areas or in small business communities where the informal demands of agricultural and commercial life had brought all generations together through the need for cooperative labor on the farm or in the shop. But fathers holding white-collar jobs at big companies did not call on their sons to drop by and lend a hand, and dwellings that were empty when children arrived home after school weakened the ties between mothers and children. Left to their own devices and thrown together principally with others of their own age, members of the youngest generation in contemporary Japan developed their own distinctive world and worldview.

Just as youth had to adapt to a changing social environment, so also did older cohorts in Japan during the 1990s, especially the elderly. They had to find their way through an often new world for which the past provided few prescriptions. By 2000, many elderly were living into their seventies and eighties as a matter of course. As recently as 1950, many people had seen their lives end at forty-five or fifty—in other words, well before their children had a chance to complete college or to get married. In 2000, many of the elderly—sometimes well before their lives ended—could expect to see their *grand*children complete college and get married.

Both from the perspective of the elderly themselves and from the more general perspective of Japanese society, providing meaningful activities for millions of new elderly citizens became a major challenge. Individuals and families were primarily responsible for addressing this challenge. Therefore, well before they reached retirement age, many Japanese developed avocational interests that they could carry into and through their final years. Others developed hobbies after retiring. Flower arranging attracted older Japanese women, and caring for miniature plants (bonsai) and lawn bowling attracted older Japanese men. Many local governments tried to provide activities that appealed to older Japanese, alleviating some of the burden on individuals and families. In addition to sports activities and some instructional services, local governments also arranged lectures, managed sight-seeing activities, and provided additional services that absorbed the time and interests of older citizens.

An even more pressing challenge was to provide adequate physical and medical care for rapidly increasing numbers of the elderly. The national government consciously resisted this challenge by working to shift as many burdens as possible onto families, relying on Confucian rhetoric and indigenous social values to limit public expenditure. Eventually, however, the burdens of privatizing—or familizing, to coin a phrase—elder care proved overwhelming for families, and especially for the middle-aged or elderly women on whom the burden fell most heavily. As a consequence, near the turn of the millennium the government passed legislation crafted to relieve some of the burdens of family care for the elderly. Called the Long-term Care Insurance Program, this undertaking aimed to provide assistance to housewives caring for the elderly in the home. The legislation underwrote with government funds the costs of in-home, partly professional care-givers who relieved housewives of some of their burdens.

However well-intentioned this program was, it was also beset with problems. Even though it was going to require enormous sums to finance (through a tax on people between the ages of forty and sixty-four), the program was going to provide only a small share of the services actually needed. (In effect, it would offer a few hours respite per week to housewives burdened with virtually round-the-clock care for an elderly father or mother-in-law living in the home.) The quality of care-givers (who could be certified with only two weeks of training) and the private-sector firms employing them was entirely open to question. The management of the program, which was delegated to municipal governments, was going to put heavy strains on organizations poorly equipped to handle them. In short, this program was conscientiously conceived to address serious needs, but it embodied the potential for widespread mishaps, misdeeds, and misfortune.

In the meantime, the primary responsibility of caring for the elderly would rest where it always had in Japanese society: on the family. In practice, this meant that the already heavily burdened middle cohorts in contemporary Japan would have to shoulder the heaviest responsibilities for both care and financing of the elderly, at the same time they had to deal with the needs and demands of the young, not to mention their own lives and careers. These sandwich-cohorts, aged from their mid-twenties to their mid-sixties, thus confronted highly taxing social demands at the very time they were striving to secure their own fortunes. The following section suggests how these conditions helped to shape the volatile world of Japanese politics during the 1990s.

But let us close this section on social features of Japanese life during "the lost decade" with a brief analysis of a short story by another popular author. Murakami Haruki was somewhat unusual among twentieth-century Japanese writers. After completing college he spent a number of years operating small bars, usually night-time drinking establishments. Working at night freed him to write during the day, and he produced a number of novels and short stories that brought him widespread attention. Growing weary of the demands on his time, he left Japan in the 1980s to live abroad for several years. He continued writing, and his reputation grew. In the late 1990s, he returned to Japan. The sarin gas attacks on subways in Tokyo, carried out in early 1995 by Aum Shinrikyo, provoked his interest in analyzing Japanese—as opposed to global, contemporary—society, and his focus shifted to put Japan at its center.

His story "The Folklore of Our Times" appeared originally in English in *The New Yorker* of June 9, 2003. The content of the story (and its title, too) may well have found inspiration in Banana Yoshimoto's novella discussed above. The tale bears some resemblance to her work, with its small cast of characters and a preoccupation with what we might call "romance." Only three figures appear in the story: the narrator, who is a thinly disguised version of Murakami himself, and two former high school classmates of the narrator from Kobe, Mr. Clean, who is never referred to by name, and Mrs. Clean, who was Fujisawa Yoshiko before she married. (Yoshiko, by the way, is a homonym for "good" girl.)

There is surprisingly little action in the story, which consists mostly of a one-sided dialogue between Mr. Clean and the narrator. Mr. Clean provides the bulk of the information and the narrator chips in occasionally with what are called *aizuchi* in Japanese, short utterances meant to indicate that the listener is still alive *and* awake. Some of these utterances are vintage Murakami, and they invest the story with a bit of low-key hilarity—if you catch all the cues.

Mr. Clean's lengthy story details his relationship with Mrs. Clean, while in high school and later. When they were high school students, the two of them were inseparable, largely because they seemed to have had so much in common. Both were top students and good athletes, and many students doted on them, although not the "cool" Narrator/Murakami. It turns out that Mr. and Mrs. Clean were romantically attached during their high school years, but, like Mikage and Yuichi in *Kitchen*, they never physically consummated their relationship. They did engage in what the story calls heavy "petting," but Mrs. Clean insisted that they should not have sex until after *she* was married. And she made it clear while they were still in high school that, however much she loved Mr. Clean, she knew that he and she would never marry—largely, it seems, because they were the same age and that was just not the done thing. Men married younger women and women married older men, or, as she liked to put social truths, "this was this, and that was that."

True to her assertions, Mrs. Clean/Yoshiko did marry another man, a television director four years her senior. After the passage of perhaps twenty years, out of the blue she called Mr. Clean and offered to make good on her earlier promise. Mr. Clean, who did not realize that he lived close to her in Tokyo, beat a hasty path to the door of her shiny new condo. Still unmarried himself, and still besotted with Yoshiko over two decades after they had broken up, he was at last able again to spend a private hour with her. They passed the time "petting," just as they had decades ago. When they said goodbye that night, both understood that they would never see each other again, although Narrator/Murakami makes clear that she will always be there—in Mr. Clean's mind.

Once again, we seem to have before us another chaste romance. Boy meets girl; they share interests and inclinations; boy and girl fall in love, but not into bed. End of story. Nonetheless, however adolescent the story seems on the surface, there is more here than meets the eye. Given what has been said so far, a reader might imagine the conversation in the story between the narrator and Mr. Clean taking place over chicken on skewers with a cold beer in a back-alley dive in Tokyo. But that is not the case at all. Narrator/Murakami and Mr. Clean meet quite by accident sometime in the late 1980s in an exclusive restaurant in the countryside near Lucca, Italy. Narrator/Murakami is by then a wealthy, internationally renowned author, and Mr. Clean is a rich businessman who runs a furniture import enterprise in Japan. Both are sophisticated cosmopolitans, equally comfortable in Japan and in Europe, and they spend the evening carefully selecting epicurean dishes and vintage wines, possibly even ordering in Italian. These are no provincial rubes, as the narrator would have you believe. They are men of the world, like so many successful Japanese authors, academics, and other professionals were by 2003.

Yet the powerful message of this story dwells not on their cosmopolitan sophistication (which functions largely as a comic foil) but on their arrested development (an especially apt metaphor for Japan itself in 2003, when the story appeared). Here they are, dining over expensive food and drink in an exclusive restaurant in Italy when they are nearly forty years of age, and they spend their time dwelling on events that absorbed them when they were teenagers in the 1960s. Of course, many people in their forties do reminisce over dinner about their high school years, because they still seem formative, somehow. But Murakami and Mr. Clean are engaged in more than reminiscence. The latter's relationship with Mrs. Clean in high school has arrested his social development—he is still unmarried, after all— and it has obviously done something to arrest his psychological development, too. As the author of this story, Murakami seems to be suggesting that the Japanese people have been able to slip on the external garb of materialist consumers, as he and Mr. Clean do at the Lucca restaurant, but they have yet to internalize comfortably the meaning of affluence and to reconcile it fully with their lives, either individually or collectively.

## DISCORD

Murakami and Yoshimoto ponder how to reconcile affluence and individuality for the characters in their imaginative worlds. In the real world, Japanese politicians had to deal with the preservation of affluence and its collective consequences throughout some very difficult years after 1989. They were not entirely flawless in their conduct or solutions, so the 1990s witnessed what can only be called some rather messy political developments. The most messy involved party conflict and electoral competition on the national level, but conflict continued to be a persisting feature of politics at lower levels of the system, too.

And all the while, the Japanese citizenry seemed to grow ever more disenchanted with political life, for good reasons.

### Contention in National Politics

The volatility and the rate of turnover among national leaders in the years after 1989 were the highest in Japan's parliamentary history, even higher than during the tumultuous 1930s. When Koizumi Jun'ichiro assumed the post of prime minister in early 2001, he was the eleventh man to hold the position in thirteen years. No one during that interval held the prime minister's post for even three years, and one man held it for as little as two months. There are many reasons for such volatility. The quality of the men running for and holding the post of prime minister was a critical reason. Partisan conflict was another, because disputes within the Liberal Democratic Party (LDP) were common, and conflicts between the LDP and other parties were endemic. Instability created by a major reform to the electoral system in the mid-1990s was yet another reason. Policy dilemmas and the ineffectual political response to them further contributed to volatility, not to mention political discord and disengagement.

Some of the men who became prime minister after 1989 had the experience, stature, and ability to discharge the duties of the post properly. Others did not. Those lacking in experience, stature, and ability included Uno Sosuke (who had to step down after only two months, when the media revealed that he had paid off a geisha to keep quiet about his relationship with her), Mori Yoshiro (who seemed to give finishing a round of golf higher priority that national crises; he lasted one year in office), and Koizumi Jun'ichiro (who was more devoted to style than substance).

Men who endured a bit longer and who were able to win credit for some accomplishments included Takeshita Noboru, Hashimoto Ryutaro, and Obuchi Keizo. It is no coincidence that all three of these men were originally members of the Tanaka faction. They had won their spurs in a highly competitive setting; they had major ministerial experience before becoming prime minister; and they were decisive, energetic leaders.

A third group of prime ministers consisted of individuals who were thrown into office largely by accident. They found themselves in the right place at the right time, and the prime minister's post fell to them by default. This group included Kaifu Toshiki, Hosokawa Morihiro, Hata Tsutomu, and Murayama Tomiichi. All were transitional figures who had short tenures over which they had almost no control.

Before examining these leaders and their administrations more closely, we need to emphasize that amid volatility there was at least one source of continuity: the LDP. Although there was a period of about eighteen months when the prime minister did not govern as an LDP party member, in one degree or another the LDP remained the dominant party in the country after 1989. It is important to note, however, that the shrinking national support given to the LDP after the early 1970s became fully manifest by the early 1990s, to such a degree that the party was actually dislodged from its ruling heights for a short time.

Takeshita Noboru, a high-ranking figure from the Tanaka faction, was prime minister for about two years at the end of the 1980s. It fell to him, as a legacy from Nakasone Yasuhiro, to preside over the legislative approval of a 3 percent consumption tax. This tax was like a VAT (value-added tax) levy of the European variety, as opposed to a sales tax of the American kind. Japan's consumption tax was initially very unpopular, and it cost Takeshita his job in short order. The infamous Uno Sosuke succeeded him for a short two months. Desperate to find someone with a clean, noncontroversial reputation, the party turned to Kaifu Toshiki. Kaifu was a member of a minor faction within the LDP, and he had only limited cabinet experience in a politically weak ministry, Education. But his faction had a "clean" image and he himself had a reputation for being youthful and articulate in public (because he contrasted so visibly with the many mumbling, elderly figures in the LDP). He won the job, presided over a successful lower-house election contest, and essentially kept the LDP ship afloat until Miyazawa Kiichi replaced him in 1991.

Miyazawa was one of the senior statesmen of the LDP. He had entered the Diet shortly after the end of World War II, following a career in the Ministry of Finance. He had been a private secretary to a former star of the ministry, Ikeda Hayato. Miyazawa had also served as minister of finance and minister of international trade and industry; he was perhaps as well known outside Japan as he was within. As a member of the Ikeda-Ohira factional line, he was a senior party figure whose pragmatic political influence within Japan had always been considerable, although he had never developed a reputation for ruthless political maneuvering in the way that Tanaka and some others had. Therefore, he found it difficult to impose his will on contending factions within the party. Ultimately, it was contention within a faction that brought him down.

For decades, the largest faction within the LDP was the one that Tanaka Kakuei had formed and controlled. Its strength rested on the membership of a large number of highly talented and very ambitious parliamentarians. Such talent and ambition were also a source of weakness for the faction and of danger for the party. To put it simply, there were more talented, ambitious men in the Tanaka faction than there were valued places for them. In the late 1960s, Tanaka had brought into the faction many new members, some of them sons of former Diet members. These hereditary parliamentarians were well educated, smart, adept, and well connected. They won ministerial positions and high-ranking party positions in the 1970s and the 1980s, and they were ready for top government and party posts by the 1990s—but there were not enough posts of the right kind for all of them. Some began to chafe visibly. When these ambitious dissidents within the Tanaka faction lost an intra-faction leadership battle in the summer of 1993, they broke off from the former Tanaka faction to form their own subgroup within the party. Soon after that, they refused to support Prime Minister Miyazawa in a vote of confidence, obliging him to call a lower-house election. This apostasy forced the subgroup to leave the LDP entirely. It re-formed as a new party, one of three that appeared in 1992 and 1993, and began to campaign for the upcoming House of Representatives election.

That election, held in July 1993, was one of the most unusual in recent history. Not only did the LDP, two centrist, and two leftist parties sponsor candidates. Three new "reform" parties led by former LDP Diet members, a few tiny splinter parties of the left and center, and a variety of individual candidates all ran, too. The outcome was muddled, but one thing was clear: the LDP failed to win a majority. It might have returned to office by forming a coalition with one of the breakaway parties, but it was unable to do so. Consequently, after nearly a month of negotiations, a coalition of non-LDP parties (as the Japanese press described them) formed a new government that took office in August 1993.

At the head of this unwieldy coalition of seven parties stood Hosokawa Morihiro, because as founder of the recently established Japan New Party he held the casting vote. If he had thrown his party's weight behind the LDP, then the LDP would have been able to return to office. By aligning himself with the LDP's opponents, Hosokawa insured that LDP rule would end, at least temporarily, and that he would become prime minister. He was not shy about this possibility, because he was in many ways born to rule. Hosokawa's distant ancestors had been *daimyo* (regional lords) governing a large domain in central Kyushu and a grandfather, a member of the prewar aristocracy named Konoe Fumimaro (see Chapter 1), had been prime minister in the 1930s.

Hosokawa was a man of dashing appearance who contrasted sharply with the elder figures then leading the LDP. In a society caught up in youth trends, he struck the right chords, and he entered office with high approval ratings. He used his political capital to push through a significant reform in the electoral laws (discussed below), but he shortly ran aground and was gone from office within eight months. The many parties in the ruling coalition simply could not devise a policy program that would keep them united, nor did Hosokawa display the leadership abilities needed to govern effectively. When a scandal arose, over loans he accepted from a firm already enmeshed in political controversy, he quickly resigned as prime minister.

Hata Tsutomu followed him. Once a powerful figure in the Tanaka faction, Hata was among the cohort of ambitious politicians who left that faction in 1993. He was no more effective than Hosokawa in keeping together the fractious non-LDP coalition that was trying to govern, and he lasted barely two months in office.

Confirming just how fractious the non-LDP coalition had been, the next government was formed by two of its former member parties in alliance with the LDP. One of the two was the Japan Socialist Party (JSP), a sworn opponent of the LDP and its conservative predecessors throughout the postwar era. This about-face on the part of the JSP severely undermined public confidence and trust in the party and its leaders. Within a few years, it had essentially disappeared as a viable element on the partisan spectrum, first because it joined with the LDP in a coalition government, and second because it reversed many of its oldest, trademark policies.

To return to power, the LDP had to allow the JSP party president to assume the prime minister's post. He was a former union official and local government worker named Murayama Tomiichi, and he had made barely a mark on national affairs during his years in the Diet. Already in his seventies when he became prime minister, Murayama made a valiant effort to lead the government, but he did not have the energy, the experience, the contacts, or the political support necessary for success. The devastating earthquake that struck the western city of Kobe in early 1995 may have been his undoing. It caused a major setback economically. But more importantly, a slow and somewhat inept government response brought criticism of Murayama and the JSP. Some Japanese newspapers reported that LDP members at all levels of government intentionally dragged their feet in responding to the earthquake in order to embarrass the ruling JSP. We may never know the truth about these matters, but we do know that within a year of the Kobe tragedy, Murayama had resigned as prime minister.

Murayama's departure opened the way for the LDP's return to center stage. In early 1996 Hashimoto Ryutaro became the new prime minister, now leading an LDP-directed coalition government. With the government facing critical financial problems owing to a slumping economy, a weak banking sector, and the costs of welfare and medical care, Hashimoto had to devote much of his time and political capital to the unpleasant task of raising the consumption tax from 3 to 5 percent. This did little to increase his popularity or that of the LDP. Moreover, politicians were preoccupied with fighting an election that had to be held before late 1997 under the entirely new conditions created by the electoral reforms of 1993. Few were very engaged in the policymaking process and the country drifted. When the election was finally held in late 1996, it produced an ambiguous outcome. The LDP did not win an outright majority in the lower house, but it did win enough seats to form a coalition and continue to govern. Hashimoto was able to hang on for another year, but in late July 1998, he stepped down following a poor showing by the LDP in an upper-house election. He had served for over two and a half years, the longest tenure in the decade, but he left on a sour note.

Hashimoto's successor was yet another member of the former Tanaka faction, Obuchi Keizo. Known as a congenial, behind-the-scenes operator, Obuchi ascended onto center stage to little fanfare. Most people thought of him as a caretaker, standing in to right a faltering ship of state. However, he surprised people with his energy. He took charge quickly in an attempt to alleviate the banking problems that were thwarting economic recovery. He also worked diligently to bring LDP breakaway parties into a governing coalition, in order to secure firm majorities for the LDP in both houses of the Diet. At this task he was successful, but the effort may have killed him. Early in 2000, Obuchi suffered a debilitating stroke that soon proved fatal. The stroke occurred shortly after Obuchi had engaged in highly acrimonious negotiations with Ozawa Ichiro, the leader of one of the LDP's breakaway parties, about the terms of the coalition, and at a time when Obuchi was exhausted from his leadership efforts.

Mori Yoshiro became prime minister under questionable circumstances while Obuchi was still in hospital. A college rugby player known as a good guy among his LDP colleagues, Mori was a long-serving, loyal foot soldier in the party. He had paid his dues and held some ministerial posts. He thus won the prime minister's position to a large extent by default. This proved to be poor grounds for selection, because Mori immediately got himself in hot water with some ill-considered decisions and a lot of oafish behavior. In less than a year, his popularity ratings had plunged to postwar lows, and the party grew eager to remove him.

Displaying a bare minimum of etiquette and personal consideration, party members forced Mori to step down after a mere twelve months in office. The new prime minister came from the same rank of LDP backbenchers as Mori. He was a man in his late fifties who had held two low-status ministerial positions. Returned from a district near the naval base in Yokosuka, he had inherited a constituency that his father had represented. Taking a page from Hosokawa Morihiro, the new prime minister, Koizumi Jun'ichiro, also worked hard on his hair. No combed-over bald spot for him. He cultivated a great shock of hair, lightly curled, swept out confidently on the sides. His coiffure ceded nothing to George W. Bush's fast-graying mane when they played catch together at one of the president's retreats.

When Koizumi assumed office, the Japanese people thought they had swept in a savior who spoke the language of reform, and they gave him strong support. His approval ratings began near 80 percent, because he made a few initial gestures that implied he might actually be a reformer. One of these was the appointment as minister of foreign affairs of the daughter of Tanaka Kakuei. Tanaka Makiko was a colorful character in her own right, a strong-willed and outspoken woman who sailed into the ministry on the winds of change. Members of the ministry, however, saw her will and candor as ineptitude and incompetence. Despite her popularity, Tanaka Makiko never won over the well-entrenched bureaucracy; and some of her actions became embarrassing for Japan itself. Koizumi finally forced her out of office, and immediately his approval ratings fell by almost half. He had during the interim been almost completely unable to muster support for his reform visions, and the economy continued to stagnate while the banking problems persisted, despite many cosmetic efforts to resolve them. Nonetheless, Koizumi won reappointment in 2002 and 2003 by arguing that his reforms were on track and that time would be needed to carry them through.

After securing the post of prime minister for at least one more year, Koizumi called for a quick lower house election in late 2003. He did this both to strengthen his position within the LDP and to enhance the LDP majority in the Diet. Events betrayed him on both counts. The LDP lost ten seats (falling to 237 out of 480) and the three-party coalition that Koizumi led lost twelve seats in total. The LDP thus fell below a clear majority in its own right, but the coalition won enough seats to form a government and to continue to lead the country. The Democratic Party, in contrast, increased its seat count from 137 to 177, making it a more tenable opponent. Weakened but not dislodged, Koizumi and the LDP remained under keen pressure to pursue more effective policies, amid a skeptical and not very supportive citizenry in a nation where only six in ten voters had bothered to cast ballots.

This account of short-term prime ministers bespeaks the general volatility of Japanese politics in the 1990s. Some of that volatility was a product of the qualities and aptitudes of the prime ministers themselves, but some was also directly attributable to the major electoral

reform passed in late 1993 under the "reformist," non-LDP government led by Hosokawa Morihiro. Reform had been a clarion call
among political intellectuals (journalists and academics) in Japan for
years before 1993. Their main objectives were to reduce the influence
of money on national politics, to diminish if not erase the corruption
in electoral competitions, and to create an environment in which rea-
soned, informed political debate might take place. The reformers also
wanted to devise an election system that would produce two-party,
rather than multiparty, contests, so that policy debate would be more
sharply defined and the prospects for exchanges in party control of the
government would be more likely. These were well-intentioned objectives, but the laws eventually passed to achieve them failed on nearly
every count.

Preceding chapters illustrate the unusual features of Japan's
medium-sized, multi-member, single-vote system of electing HOR members that traced its origins to the 1920s. (In recent years, political scientists have taken to calling this the SNTV, or single, non-transferable
vote system, but that acronym is both misleading and incomplete.) The
previous system had its shortcomings, which were exacerbated
by failure to reapportion in a fair and timely manner. Nonetheless,
Japanese voters and political candidates alike at least understood the
system and had grown accustomed to it. Reforming it completely, as
the Diet voted to do in 1993, promised to open a Pandora's box filled
with uncertainty.

One of the many reasons why Japanese politics seemed to drift into
a period of immobility and stasis in the mid-1990s had precisely to do
with the uncertainties that the new electoral system fomented. Those
uncertainties forced sitting legislators to spend an inordinate amount
of their time and energies on the electoral side of the political equation,
and not the legislative or bureaucratic sides. If they hoped to survive
the next election, they had to expend tremendous effort in gauging the
effects of reform on their constituencies, on reconstructing their campaign organizations, and on reconstituting their electoral bases.

The electoral reform, when finally passed, abolished the former
multi-member districts and replaced them with two new and different
election venues. The new law established a lower house with five
hundred seats. Of these, fully three hundred would be filled with the
victors of contests held in small districts where one person with the

most votes was returned. These districts spanned the nation, and their boundaries were drawn according to the number of voters in the district. In this way, some of the worst malapportionment of seats that had crept steadily into the election system since the 1950s was rectified, and urban areas won a fairer share of representation in the Diet. The remaining two hundred seats were filled on the basis of a second ballot to be cast at the same time by each voter, indicating a preference for a party and not an individual. The country was divided into geographical districts. Each district was given a number of seats roughly in proportion to its population. Party lists were posted, indicating which individuals in a given order would represent a given party in that district. Voters cast a ballot for the party they preferred, with lesser attention paid to an individual on the lists. The more votes a party received, the more candidates it returned to the Diet. This part of the election mechanism thus functioned in a manner similar to PR (proportional representation) systems in Europe.

The single-member, small district element within this system was designed, in theory, to promote two-party electoral competition based, again in theory, on clear policy alternatives. In fact, this aspect of the reform essentially ensured the continued dominance of the LDP in the lower house. No other party enjoyed the financial capabilities, the organizational scope, and the campaign skills that the LDP did. Therefore, no other single party could compete with the LDP across the country. The other two hundred seats arose as a political compromise with the smaller parties serving in opposition to the LDP before 1993. Supporters of those parties were often concentrated in relatively small geographic areas, usually in well-populated metropolitan regions. Some observers realized that, if reforms created a system in which all five hundred HOR seats were filled from single-member, small districts, small parties—especially the Komeito and the Democratic Socialists—might be eliminated entirely.

Opposition party leaders thus insisted on having the PR districts integrated into the new electoral order. They were certainly right to do so, because once the new system went into effect, some of the small parties won almost no seats in the single-member districts; they survived only by taking seats in the regional districts. Conversely, the LDP took the lion's share of the small districts and inevitably had to yield to its opponents in the regional contests, especially in the metropolitan regions of Tokyo, Osaka, and Kyoto. More than ever, the LDP came to represent voters in rural areas, while its opponents drew their support from voters living in the largest cities and their immediate suburbs.

### Conflicts Over Issues and in Local Politics

Voters disturbed by this turn of events took out their frustrations more in local elections than in Diet elections, it appears. Previous chapters illustrate how voters casting ballots in prefectural and municipal contests came to display a higher level of autonomous, if not actually obstreperous, behavior as early as the 1970s. The 1990s witnessed substantial reinforcement of this tendency, especially in metropolitan prefectures.

Justified discontent with the behavior of elected politicians, especially at the national level, was certainly one force underlying electoral choices in prefectural and municipal contests. But more fundamental changes, associated with the demographic transition discussed at the opening of this chapter, were also at work. After the early 1970s, the demographic structure of Japan's electorate underwent a significant change as literally millions of elderly voters who had long been loyal supporters of the LDP passed away. At the same time, an influx of younger voters who had been born, reared, and educated in the postwar era entered the lists. These new voters were very different from their elders. They did not live in small face-to-face communities, and they were often residents of cities or large, anonymous metropolitan regions. They had weak attachments to political parties, and they were moved more by images than by policies. Most of them were independents; few were loyal supporters of the LDP—or of other parties, for that matter. It was voters like these who ignored the LDP in the 1993 HOR election and who abandoned the JSP while they turned to the JNP, Hosokawa's party. Their collective behavior in the Tokyo area and in many suburban districts was instrumental in unseating the LDP, in devastating the JSP, and in giving the new opposition parties a chance.

Voters continued to signal their independent behavior in subsequent prefectural elections. In 1995, both Tokyo and Osaka held elections to replace long-serving governors. In Tokyo, the LDP and the JSP along with the Komeito endorsed a worthy successor to Suzuki Shun'ichi. He was another former bureaucrat from the Ministry of Home Affairs who

**20. Contemporary Tokyo.** *In the secondary city center of Shinjuku, the twin towers housing the offices of the Tokyo Metropolitan Government (center left) form a striking symbol of the civic and material prosperity of Japan in the 1990s.*

(Courtesy of Irving I. Gottesman.)

had had a long, distinguished career in government service. He also enjoyed the experience needed to administer the prefecture as well as the multi-partisan appeal that had become so necessary for success in prefectural elections. A clutch of fresh faces heralding progressive reform ran against him, along with a former comedian then serving in the upper house of the national Diet. The comedian won. The list of competitors in Osaka was somewhat different; but in Osaka, too, an entertainer with no executive experience in local government won office. Whether voters were being contrary or independent, the outcome of these elections reaffirmed how unpredictable Japanese politics had become.

A similar unpredictability arose when these men stood for re-election in 1999. The comedian who had been governing Tokyo drew a list of formidable competitors, including one Ishihara Shintaro. Ishihara was a graduate of Tokyo University who had first made a name for himself in the 1950s as a popular novelist just out of college. He parlayed this fame into a fortune and later into a political career, by winning a seat in the Diet from a Tokyo district, on the LDP ticket. He made some minor waves while in office and even managed to hold a ministerial position for a short time. But he won greatest attention when he co-authored, with the head of Sony, Morita Akio, a short tract titled "The Japan That Can Say No." This was a blunt, nationalistic diatribe focusing its ire on the United States, while engaging in some chest-beating brought on by Japan's economic gains in the 1980s. Ishihara used the governorship of Tokyo mainly as a bully pulpit for his neo-nationalist ideas.

Meanwhile, in Osaka, the former entertainer who had served four years as governor, "Knock" Yokoyama, managed to win re-election after a largely inconsequential term in office. Shortly after, however, he was arrested and tried for his sexual harassment of a young campaign aide. The court found him guilty, and he was forced to pay her a substantial monetary judgment and to resign from office. The victor in the election held to replace him was an independent running for office for the first time, a woman named Ota Fusae. When she assumed the post of governor in February 2000, Ota became the first female ever to serve as a prefectural governor in Japan's modern history.

The occasionally bizarre outcomes chronicled above bespoke a growing disenchantment with politics among the citizenry of Japan. At the national level, the turnout for Diet elections dropped by more than 10 percent in the 1990s, from about 75 percent in the early part of the decade to about 60 percent at the end. In local elections, interest was much lower. Prefectural elections had attracted fewer voters than national elections for much of the postwar period. But by the 1990s, they often brought out less than half of the electorate. Young voters ignored them at very high rates, the elderly often forswore the effort to get to the ballot box, and many more middle-aged voters than ever before wrote off such contests. The retreat from electoral politics was confirmed in opinion surveys that revealed a sharp rise in unaffiliated voters who felt an attachment to no political party; they often made up 40 percent or more of some samples. In some surveys, barely one in five voters was willing to declare him- or herself a supporter of the LDP, and the new breakaway parties rarely won support from even 10 percent of the respondents. To put it in the vernacular, many Japanese voters were turning off and tuning out in the 1990s.

This was an understandable response, as much of the foregoing analysis suggests. Beginning in 1993 with the implosion of the Tanaka faction and the reform of the electoral system, individual politicians engaged in often shameless behavior as they struggled for power and place in a very unstable political environment. They often shifted from one party to another in the blink of an eye, some of them changing parties more than once in just a year or two. The strength of personal ties to voters and the efficacy of a politician's support group enabled, and perhaps emboldened, them to make these shifts. But eventually even loyal supporters lost patience and trust, and some previously secure politicians suffered the ultimate cost: electoral defeat. Amidst this tumult, legislators as a group performed rather poorly.

One of the main pieces of social legislation passed during this period was the bill establishing long-term care for the elderly discussed above. Legislators tried also to address some of the most pressing economic problems facing the nation, especially the banking crisis. Between 1992 and 1999, the Diet passed eight bills to deal with financial and other economic matters. These bills included provisions for (at different times, and in different amounts) tax reduction, public investment, land purchases, housing, and assistance for financial institutions. The sums involved were enormous; they totaled over ¥100 trillion (or about $1 trillion U.S.). Fully one-half of the bills involved expenditures worth 3 percent or more of Japan's gross domestic product. Yet, in effect, many of these bills seemed to be a case of throwing good money after bad. At the end of this period, Japan's banks were still carrying bad loans in huge amounts, the exact amount unknown owing to weak disclosure provisions. Consequently, all of the time, effort, and resources expended on the nation's financial institutions had barely halted the deterioration in their financial positions. The nation's economy was still just stumbling along, and the future seemed precarious. It is no wonder that many felt deflated.

## DEFLATION

Japan's economy hit the skids in the 1990s. The 1980s had not been an exceptionally good time, but the economy had continued to grow, and in the late 1980s, a kind of boom arose, marked by rapidly rising land prices and a speculative stock market. When the Bank of Japan began to put the brakes on over-speculation, land prices and equity values plunged quickly, driving the economy into a precarious state. Growth rates fell into the low single digits in most years during the 1990s, and in a few years the economy actually shrank. This kind of decline had been rare in the postwar period, so the country was not well prepared to find effective solutions. In fact, several years into the new millennium, Japan was still striving to emerge from its economic malaise.

Foreign observers, especially those writing in the American press, pointed their fingers at the banks and their bad loans as the primary causes of Japan's economic problems. Although bad loans and weak financial institutions were significant contributors to economic dilemmas during the 1990s, they were by no means the only factors. There were other difficulties as well. Some were a result of the shifting demography of Japanese society. Other difficulties arose because changing global competitors made inroads in sectors where Japan had once been dominant. Still other difficulties appeared as a consequence of Japan's earlier successes. This discussion of Japan's economic standing in the years after 1989, out of necessity, dwells on its economic problems more than its achievements.

The bad-loan problem for Japanese financial institutions appeared when prices for assets (especially real estate and equities) began to fall at the very end of the 1980s. The speculative booms in both land and equities that arose in the mid- to late 1980s had been fueled in many cases by bank loans. Firms and individuals won loans from banks by using inflated land values or stock holdings as collateral. Banks, in turn, were careless in assessing the financial well-being of their loan customers, and the true value of their assets, in particular. When the land price bubble burst about 1990, customers found it difficult to make interest payments. As real-estate values continued to plunge, some customers stopped paying interest and principal charges entirely. Some financial institutions were left holding empty commercial structures valued at a tiny share of their original cost, and thus a small share of the loans extended to build them. Bank profits plunged, and many banks fell into the red.

At the same time, a collapse in the stock market weakened the financial standing of banks. Like banks in most countries, Japanese banks had to possess their own intrinsically valued assets in order to meet regulatory standards. Japanese banks had relied heavily on shares they owned in customer firms (often in manufacturing, commerce, real estate, and so on) to satisfy such requirements. Under the circumstances of the 1990s, however, shares in such firms were plunging in value, undermining the very security of the banks themselves.

Rather than call in bad loans to get them off their books, it appears that Japanese banks often extended more loans, backed with even weaker security than the original ones, thereby deepening their problems. They were able to do this because only one government agency, the Ministry of Finance, was responsible for overseeing their behavior. The ministry faced a direct conflict of interest, because it was required both to supervise and to regulate the banks, and it seems to have opted for lax supervision rather than rigorous regulation. This pattern of dubious relationships in the financial sector explains why the Diet found itself during the decade of the 1990s repeatedly passing legislation aimed at bailing out the nation's banks. Not until the late 1990s were laws passed to establish an independent bank regulatory agency, and by then it may have been too late to rectify the errors of the past.

Eventually, banks became unwilling or unable to make loans. This outcome did not affect very many large corporations. They had been able to raise funds needed to carry on business either by floating loans with major banks overseas or by issuing stock abroad. The firms that suffered most were small establishments and medium-sized firms that needed loans to finance expansion, or just to get started. In the 1990s, as in the 1960s, these smaller firms were the backbone of the Japanese economy. They still constituted over 99 percent of all firms, and the value of their output was consistently over half of the total in many sectors. When these smaller firms could not win the financing they needed from Japanese banks, many went bankrupt. How many never got started in business owing to lack of capital, we will never know. But it is certain that capital scarcity in the small and medium-sized enterprise sector helped to deflate this essential segment of the Japanese economy in the 1990s. As a result, fewer new firms were started, and many established firms either had to tread water or went under. As this happened, job opportunities either stabilized or shrank.

The demographic shift that Japanese society was undergoing in the 1990s was a second significant factor affecting the Japanese economy. A rapidly aging population had two principal effects on expenditures. First, they fell in the aggregate; and second, the composition of expenditures changed. National data on household budgets indicate that retired workers in their late sixties often spent about half as much on a monthly basis as employed workers in their fifties. This reduction in outlays was a rational response by households to the economic facts of life. No longer enjoying the kinds of incomes they received when working, retirees naturally cut their expenditures. But when millions of households adopted such behavior on an annual basis across more than a decade, the aggregate effect was to reduce sharply consumption expenditures on the national level. A rapidly aging retired populace thus contributed to the shortfalls in consumption outlays that had once driven high rates of growth in the Japanese economy.

This same populace contributed in another way to the economic dilemmas Japan confronted in the 1990s. Older retirees were obliged to shift their outlays from the purchase of goods produced by Japan's manufacturing sector to the purchase of services provided by the tertiary sector. Instead of new cars, new homes and appliances, and more and better clothing, the elderly were far more likely to want, or need, health providers or leisure activities. Such a shift in preferences and outlays promoted changes in the composition of economic activity in the national economy. On the whole, such changes undermined the well-being of large manufacturing firms paying high salaries to full-time male workers, while promoting the expansion of service-sector firms paying lower wages to female workers who were often employed part-time. What had once been stable firms employing a well-compensated, secure labor force found themselves subtly undermined, with more small, ephemeral, service-oriented firms paying low salaries to a volatile labor force emerging to fill the gap.

International competition was another factor undermining the large, stable firms paying good wages to secure workers. As previous chapters note, international competitors had begun to challenge some of Japan's major industrial sectors well before the 1990s. Its iron and steel industry had come under competition decades earlier from lower-cost, new producers around the globe. Their appearance undermined Japan's export markets and forced cutbacks at many of Japan's domestic steel mills. The oil embargoes of the 1970s had been a disaster for Japan's shipbuilding industry and resulted in cancelled orders as docks were closed across the country. The decline in the iron and steel and the shipbuilding industries contributed to dire economic conditions in what had once been thriving cities and regions across the country. Closed mills and docks, and eliminated jobs, contributed to further declines in aggregate output as well as reductions in consumer outlays.

Beginning in the late 1980s, Japan's frontline industries—autos and consumer electronics—also came under competition from lower-cost producers in Asia and Eastern Europe and from reinvigorated producers in Europe. Some individual firms continued to thrive (such as Toyota in the auto industry and Sony in consumer electronics), but others (such as Nissan in the auto industry) fell on hard times. Eventually, a French auto firm took over Nissan, and its fortunes appeared to be reviving in 2003. Poor management, acrimonious labor relations, and strategic miscues contributed to the problems in some firms, but all firms in Japan faced one set of generic difficulties in the international arena: high costs, and thus high prices.

High costs were in part a product of Japanese economic success. Throughout the 1960s, 1970s, and 1980s, wages for Japanese workers rose steadily. Rising incomes were one of the benefits that Japan's economic miracle bestowed on its workers. However, high wages in Japan—as in Germany, also—eventually became an economic liability, because the steadily rising prices of Japan's manufactured goods even-

tually drove consumers to lower-priced competitors. This tendency had
set in during the 1980s, but it became especially conspicuous during
the 1990s, as lower-cost producers from Asia and elsewhere grew able
to provide cheaper electronic equipment and other consumer goods on
a wide scale. They threatened the status of some of Japan's main firms
and contributed further to the economic dilemmas the domestic economy faced during the 1990s.

Paradoxically, Japan itself exacerbated problems like these. As labor
and land costs rose in Japan during the 1980s, more and more small
and mid-sized firms in Japan decided to move their production facilities overseas. The reasons for doing this were numerous and varied.
Some did so to take advantage of cheap land readily available, and
often partly developed by countries eager to lure foreign investment.
Other firms moved their production overseas to take advantage of
lower labor costs. Some did so to escape environmental regulation and
penalties they might face if they remained in Japan, especially dirty
industries such as papermaking. Some firms moved overseas at the
behest of final producers (in the auto industry, for example), which
wanted their suppliers in geographic proximity. These were all rational
reasons for transferring production overseas, but they had two perverse
effects: they sent more and more production facilities out of Japan, and
they created jobs—not for Japanese nationals living, working, and consuming domestically—but for foreign nationals living in their own
countries. Overseas investments thus contributed in significant ways to
the general downturn in the Japanese economy, because by the turn of
the millennium, about 15 percent of the value of Japanese-owned manufacturing output was produced outside the home country.

One way to illustrate the significance of the changes that struck the
Japanese economy during the 1990s is to examine the rankings of firms
(according to declared income) at the very top of Japan's corporate
hierarchy, and how they shifted during that decade. At the beginning
of the decade, fourteen manufacturing firms and twelve financial institutions dominated the fifty highest-ranking firms. Six electric power
companies and six construction firms followed, with firms in services,
insurance, international trade, transportation, and the retail trades
completing the list.

During the 1990s, penetrating changes reshaped corporate Japan
and the list of top firms changed visibly. The banking crisis discussed

above removed ten of the twelve banks from the list, because the continuing fall in real-estate and equity values worsened the bad-loan problem and reduced their profits. These dilemmas depressed new real-estate development and construction, too, so that all six of the construction firms disappeared from the list by the end of the decade.

By that time, the industrial sector was represented by twenty firms, an increase of six over the early 1990s. But here, too, significant change had occurred. Firms making heavy industrial products and industrial chemicals, along with firms making autos, auto components, and consumer electrical appliances, made up the top industrial entries in the early 1990s. By the early 2000s, firms in the former categories (industrial products, industrial chemicals) had fallen from the list, while firms in the latter three categories had strengthened their positions. They had been joined by firms manufacturing for an affluent consumer market, where cosmetics, home products, video games, pharmaceuticals, and food and beer were in high demand.

Reflecting and embodying a clear trend in the Japanese economy by the turn of the millennium, service-sector firms rose to prominence among Japan's top enterprises. Leasing companies and consumer finance organizations leapt suddenly to high positions. So, too, did convenience stores and discount retailers. Insurance firms staged a comeback. The changing composition of Japan's most successful firms thus bespoke the country's retreat as a producer of heavy industrial goods, as well as the growing anxieties of its domestic households (which preferred leasing to buying; buying at discount; saving through insurance purchase, not equity investing; and so on).

We might also read out of the composition of this list of top fifty firms the now evident existence of an affluent, consumer-oriented society, and previous remarks offer ample evidence to underscore this claim. Despite the nation's economic problems, many Japanese were now quite affluent by historical standards, and they were also avid consumers. However, most Japanese households retained a conservative orientation to consumption in general and to savings in particular, as the placement of household assets illustrates very clearly.

At the end of this period, families invested nearly one-half of household assets in certificates of deposit (CDs) offered by banks or the postal savings system. They held a substantial portion of their savings in demand deposit accounts—most in the postal savings system, the rest at private banks. Life insurance was a highly desirable savings vehicle; it ranked second only to CDs in popularity. What is so striking about these preferences is not so much that they all are quite conservative, in emphasizing preservation of principal, but that they all provided unusually low returns. Interest paid on most savings vehicles like these in the 1990s approached barely 1 percent per annum. Of course, that was a far higher return than that offered by a stock market that plunged over 70 percent in the 1990s.

Having long avoided equity investment as a form of savings, the Japanese public was further dissuaded from doing so by the events of the late 1980s and after. Household savers had just begun to dabble in equity investing when the bottom dropped out of the Japanese market, and many either pulled back or pulled out entirely. These experiences explain why, on average, Japanese households placed only 11 percent of their savings in equities at the turn of the millennium. These facts also explain why Japanese firms continued to be so dependent on bank loans for their financing, and why financially weak banks contributed so much to the economic immobility of the 1990s.

High rates of savings by households, and the preference to invest savings in conservative (principal-preserving) vehicles, bespeak yet another anxiety hanging over the Japanese economy in the 1990s: worries over job security. People of all ages and all walks of life faced either difficulty finding work or the possibility of losing a job. Young people found it especially difficult to break into the labor force with a good entry-level job. To keep labor costs low, many large, once-prestigious employers chose not to hire new workers and began to rely more on temporary workers. Some were provided by incorporated temp agencies, where informal agreements among workers, agency, and employer(s) provided a measure of job security, although poor to non-existent benefits. In other cases, individuals took it upon themselves to find work, usually for short duration with no promise of long-term job security. Such workers came to be known as *friita* (a Japanese-language shorthand for the German term *frei arbeiter*, or free worker). Some estimates contended that perhaps 10 percent of the Japanese labor force held such positions around 2000.

Members of the core labor force, those between their mid-twenties and early sixties holding a regular job, had worries of other kinds. Firms were constantly searching for economies in the stalled economy of the 1990s, and cutting labor costs was an obvious solution. There-fore, many businesses reduced the amount of compensated overtime they offered (while often demanding more unpaid overtime work), and they also cut bonus payments. Most firms regarded outright layoffs as their last option, so they would sometimes reassign workers to smaller firms within a corporate group. This saved the initial employer money, of course, but it also resulted in pay reductions for workers reassigned (because smaller firms consistently paid lower salaries than larger firms did). However, as the 1990s wore on, some firms simply had to fire workers, and the unemployment rate rose from the strikingly low level of 1 percent that had obtained from the late 1950s through the early 1980s to reach 6 percent during the 1990s. Thus, outright unemploy-ment along with intermittent employment of *friita* were other factors reducing consumer purchasing power and contributing to the defla-tionary economic environment of the 1990s.

Part-time workers, who were usually women between their early thirties and their late fifties but sometimes elderly males, too, faced dif-ficulties in the slumping economy. Firms felt that they owed their strongest loyalties to regular, full-time workers, so staff reductions com-monly struck part-timers before regulars. When a fifty-five-year-old mother of two lost her part-time job, or when a sixty-year-old house-hold head in semi-retirement lost his, it had a devastating effect on a household's economy. Over time, these kinds of losses multiplied, and they gradually reduced the aggregate purchasing power of the Japanese populace. Other tendencies identified above—the emergence of *friita*, job reassignments, and the reduction of full- and part-time job opportunities—all reduced purchasing power. Even price reductions, offered by everyone from the flashiest department stores to the drabbest local grocer, often failed to attract customers, so that deflation became a pervasive, insidious fact of economic life.

Before drawing this gloomy portrait of the Japanese economy after 1989 to a close, it is important to situate Japan in a broader interna-tional context. Although many sectors of the Japanese economy failed to perform in the 1990s at the exceptional levels of the "high-growth" era between 1955 and 1974, or even at the levels of the more subdued 1980s, Japan continued to maintain a high standing internationally. Its gross national product (GNP) at the turn of the millennium was second only to that of the United States, and still well above Germany, Great

Britain, and France. Its GNP on a per capita basis was in many years
the highest in the world. Its annual output of raw steel, automobiles,
and some other commodities ranked Japan at the very top or among
the top three in the world. Life expectancies for males (in the high seventies) and females (in the mid-eighties) were consistently among the
longest in the world, testifying to the overall levels of affluence and
welfare in the country. Japan was no longer racing ahead of its competitors in the world economy, but it was able nonetheless to preserve
and slowly build on the dramatic economic achievements of earlier
decades, while sustaining a very high standard of living for most of its
citizenry.

We obtain a more immediate understanding of features of economic life
in Japan after 1989 by looking closely at four people in a hypothetical
household three years after the turn of the millennium. This portrait
does not depict an actual household. Rather, it is a figurative norm
drawn from statistical data on demographic, social, economic, and
political attributes of Japanese households in the early years of the
twenty-first century and from newspaper accounts and personal
observation.

     The four members of our figurative twenty-first century household
are Nakagane Heinosuke, a forty-year-old sararii-man; his wife
Yoshiko, aged thirty-eight; their daughter, Noriko, who is ten; and
Heinosuke's seventy-year-old mother, Junko. The members of this
"household" actually reside in two dwellings. One is a modern home
recently built in a suburban community located almost two hours by
train from Heinosuke's place of work. The other is a tiny, dank room
covering eighty-one square feet, situated in a row of small rental apartments located ten minutes by foot from Heinosuke's office in downtown Tokyo. He sleeps there four or five nights of the week and travels
to the new suburban home on weekends. He tried the two-hour daily
commute to work when they first moved into the new home, but he
inevitably got to work late or had to leave work early and miss the
essential socializing that went on when his buddies stopped off for a
beer or a meal on their way home. By living in the apartment near
work, he can get extra sleep and still arrive at work on time (usually,
anyway), and he is able to take part in the after-work socializing that
burnishes his chances for promotions and raises.

**21. Contemporary home interior, 1992.** *A mother and her daughter make dinner in a new kitchen equipped with an electric frying pan and a rice cooker (on the table), an electric oven (right rear), a built-in storage and sink area (rear), and an American-style refrigerator (left).*

(Courtesy of Patricia S. Allinson.)

Heinosuke has grown far more conscious than before of these informal features of employment in a Japanese firm ever since he lost his first job after college, four years ago. Having been a close friend of the leader of his music club while still at university, Heinosuke had relied on that friend to smooth his entry into one of Japan's largest and most prestigious recording companies. Heinosuke had done all right from the beginning, but he had never stood out in his recruiting class, and he had made only a modest impression on his older colleagues. When the firm fell on especially hard times and had to cut its work force and its salary bill, Heinosuke became one of the victims. The company cut him loose, but only after it found him a position in a related firm that

identified, evaluated, and managed new musical talent. His new salary
was just 80 percent of his old one, exclusive of bonuses; and this was
a financial blow, especially because he had taken out a huge mortgage
to pay off the costs of a new home, which was completed just three
months after Heinosuke started at his new job. He was hopeful,
however, that the prospects for improved earnings at the new firm
might result in larger bonuses that would compensate for the lower
salary. Now, four years later, he is still clinging to that hope, despite
the economic slowdown, while feeling utterly pressed to meet the mortgage payments each month and to come up with the rent for his city
apartment as well.

Yoshiko, meanwhile, feels wholly distraught because she is the one
who had pressed so hard to build the new home. She knew they would
need the space for Heinosuke's mother, because she could no longer live
alone in the dilapidated family home after her husband died. The home
was worth little financially, but it was located in a highly desirable outer
city district well served by subway and rail lines. The value of the
land was worth five times the value of the house, so the mother-in-law
made a good deal of money from the sale. She invested most of that
sum in CDs, whose interest payments supplement her modest pension
income, and gave the balance to Heinosuke to invest in the new home.
Without her assistance, they could never have bought the land and built
the new structure. Of course, her assistance came with a string attached:
Junko would be living with them in their new home. She has her separate wing on the ground floor, but she takes most of her meals with
the family.

All of the imponderables involved in these gifts and obligations are
just one source of Yoshiko's anxieties. She also feels guilty because she
gave up a part-time position that she really enjoyed in order to move
to the new home and, in effect, begin to care for Junko. She did not
make a lot of money in that job, but what she made would come in
very handy now, especially with Heinosuke's income so uncertain.
Moreover, Noriko will be off to college in just eight years and they have
set aside hardly any money for her tuition. Where will that money come
from if Yoshiko does not earn it?

Even Noriko is growing a bit concerned about her family's life.
When she was very young and living with her parents in a tiny apartment in Tokyo, she remembers seeing her father very little. She does

remember his staggering in late at night, often drunk after eating out with his cronies after work, and his racing off in the morning, usually late for work. But she also remembers weekend strolls around the lake at the nearby park and leisurely dinners on Sunday nights. Now she almost never sees or even hears her father, except when she stumbles over him in the living room while he naps in front of the television on Sunday afternoons. Mom is around a lot, but she seems oddly detached, constantly preoccupied, and a little difficult to engage with. Having Gram at home fills some of the void, but it is not the same thing. Gram takes only a polite interest in the TV shows and music groups that Noriko likes, and she is so busy with her own friends that the two of them can talk only about the food they eat and the chores they share. Otherwise, they inhabit different worlds.

Different worlds, indeed. Heinosuke is of necessity chained to his job. By its very nature, Heinosuke's work often requires late nights out and frequent weekend work. He dare not call in sick or casually take a day off, because he might miss a key concert or fail to corner a hot promoter. Yoshiko is tied to the home, neighborhood, and community, and to Noriko and Junko. Interminable sports days and speech contests at Noriko's school seem to take up inordinate amounts of time, and the school personnel are very strict in their expectations: they want Yoshiko there every time Noriko performs. Junko is still surprisingly energetic and self-reliant, but Yoshiko has begun to see hints of worse days to come. Junko seems more forgetful all the time, and she is having more difficulty using the somewhat unreliable local bus system. If she cannot get out on her own to pursue hobbies and visit temples with her age mates, how will Yoshiko keep her entertained at home?

Junko feels quite content with her new situation. She has managed to make a lot of good new friends through the Senior Center that the municipal government operates. Many are aging widows like her, who share common experiences and face similar dilemmas. They reminisce about their lives growing up under a military government, coming of age after the war, and raising families during the boom years. In comparison, the present seems easy: they have an abundant, varied diet; they live in spacious, comfortable homes; and they can buy nice, new clothes whenever they feel like it. It is odd that Heinosuke and Yoshiko see so little of each other, she thinks, and Noriko seems to live such a solitary existence. None of them seems entirely unhappy, but they are all quite anxious. Like me, Junko assumes, they make do and soldier on.

Much like the Nakagane family, Japan as a nation seemed to soldier on during the 1990s. The frenzy of the high-growth years was now a thing of the past. The country had adapted to affluence during the 1980s, only to see the benefits of wealth seemingly freeze in the 1990s. Japan was still affluent by the standards of any international comparison, and certainly by comparison with its own recent past. But following more than a decade of immobility, many Japanese harbored justifiable doubts about just what the future might hold. Like the lives of individuals in the Nakagane household, the collective life of the nation seemed suspended in time and shrouded with anxiety.

# Sources and Suggested Readings

## SOURCES

Published scholarly monographs on postwar Japan written in English are still few in number, most of them written by political scientists, anthropologists, sociologists, and economists, not historians. They rely mostly on surveys, interview data, and secondary sources rather than original documentation. Much official documentation on the postwar era is still unavailable to scholars in any case. Therefore, in order to present an accurate and authoritative history of the years between 1945 and 2003, I have relied on the most reputable sources published in Japanese to confirm dates, facts, and statistics.

The principal source for dates has been the second edition of *Kindai Nihon sogo nenpyo* (A comprehensive chronology of modern Japanese history), published in 1984 by Iwanami Shoten. For later years, I have relied on the *Asahi nenkan*, a yearbook published by the *Asahi Shinbun*, one of Japan's largest comprehensive daily newspapers.

For factual data on events, individuals, and institutions, I have used two major references. The first is *Nihon kingendaishi jiten* (A dictionary of modern and contemporary Japanese history), edited by a committee of scholars drawn heavily from professors at Kyoto University and published by the Toyo Keizai Shinposha in 1978. The second is *Sengoshi daijiten* (Encyclopedia of Postwar Japan, 1945–1990). Published by Sanseido in 1991, it is edited by a group of scholars associated primarily with Tokyo University.

The *Nihon tokei nenkan* (Japan statistical yearbook), published annually by the Office of the Prime Minister, has served as the primary source for statistical data. It is similar to the Statistical Abstracts of the United States in its content and coverage. A second useful digest on which I have sometimes relied is *Suji de miru Nihon no hyaku-nen* (One hundred years of Japan through numbers), published in revised form in 1991 by the Yano Tsuneta Kinen Kai. Finally, an especially valuable source of statistical data for the immediate postwar period is *Kindai Nihon keizaishi yoran* (A guide to modern Japanese economic history), edited by Ando Yoshio and published in 1978 by the University of Tokyo Press.

## SUGGESTED READINGS

### General Works

Allinson, Gary D. *The Columbia Guide to Modern Japanese History.* New York: Columbia University Press, 1999.

Committee for the Compilation of Materials on Damage Caused by the Atomic Bombs in Hiroshima and Nagasaki. *Hiroshima and Nagasaki: The Physical, Medical, and Social Effects of the Atomic Bombings.* New York: Basic Books, 1981.

Cook, Haruko Taya, and Theodore F. Cook. *Japan at War: An Oral History.* New York: New Press, 1992.

Davis, Winston B. *Japanese Religion and Society: Paradigms of Structure and Change.* Albany: State University of New York Press, 1992.

Dore, Ronald P. *Land Reform in Japan.* London: Oxford University Press, 1959.

Dower, John W. *Empire and Aftermath: Yoshida Shigeru and the Japanese Experience, 1878–1954.* Cambridge, Mass.: Harvard University, Council on East Asian Studies, 1979.

——. *War without Mercy: Race and Power in the Pacific War.* New York: Pantheon Books, 1986.

Gluck, Carol, and Stephen R. Graubard, eds. *Showa: The Japan of Hirohito.* New York: W. W. Norton, 1992.

Gordon, Andrew, ed. *Postwar Japan as History.* Berkeley: University of California Press, 1993.

Kawai, Kazuo. *Japan's American Interlude.* Chicago: University of Chicago Press, 1960.

Murakami, Haruki. *Underground: The Tokyo Gas Attack and the Japanese Psyche.* New York: Vintage International, 2000.

Reader, Ian. *Religion in Contemporary Japan.* Basingstoke, England: Macmillan Press, 1991.

### Politics

Allinson, Gary D., and Yasunori Sone, eds. *Political Dynamics in Contemporary Japan.* Ithaca: Cornell University Press, 1993.

Calder, Kent C. *Crisis and Compensation: Public Policy and Political Stability in Japan.* Princeton: Princeton University Press, 1988.

Campbell, John Creighton. *How Policies Change: The Japanese Government and the Aging Society.* Princeton: Princeton University Press, 1992.

Flanagan, Scott C., et al. *The Japanese Voter.* New Haven: Yale University Press, 1991.

Fukui, Haruhiro. *Party in Power: The Japanese Liberal-Democrats and Policy-Making.* Berkeley: University of California Press, 1970.

Garon, Sheldon. *The State and Labor in Modern Japan.* Berkeley: University of California Press, 1987.

Haley, John Owen. *Authority without Power: Law and the Japanese Paradox.* New York: Oxford University Press, 1991.

Hayao, Kenji. *The Japanese Prime Minister and Public Policy.* Pittsburgh: University of Pittsburgh Press, 1993.

Ishida, Takeshi, and Ellis S. Krauss, eds. *Democracy in Japan.* Pittsburgh: University of Pittsburgh Press, 1989.

Koschmann, J. Victor. *Authority and the Individual in Japan: Citizen Protest in Historical Perspective.* Tokyo: University of Tokyo Press, 1978.

Kubota, Akira. *Higher Civil Servants in Postwar Japan.* Princeton: Princeton University Press, 1969.

Maclachlan, Patricia L. *Consumer Politics in Postwar Japan: The Institutional Boundaries of Citizen Activism.* New York: Columbia University Press, 2002.

McKean, Margaret A. *Environmental Protest and Citizen Politics in Japan.* Berkeley: University of California Press, 1981.

Packard, George R. *Protest in Tokyo: The Security Treaty Crisis of 1960.* Princeton: Princeton University Press, 1966.

Pempel, T. J. *Uncommon Democracies: The One-Party Dominant Regimes.* Ithaca: Cornell University Press, 1990.

Pharr, Susan. *Political Women in Japan.* Berkeley: University of California Press, 1981.

Rosenbluth, Frances McCall. *Financial Politics in Contemporary Japan.* Ithaca: Cornell University Press, 1989.

Samuels, Richard J. *The Politics of Regional Policy in Japan: Localities Incorporated?* Princeton: Princeton University Press, 1983.

Steiner, Kurt. *Local Government in Japan.* Stanford: Stanford University Press, 1965.

Steiner, Kurt, Ellis S. Krauss, and Scott C. Flanagan, eds. *Political Opposition and Local Politics in Japan.* Princeton: Princeton University Press, 1980.

Stockwin, J. A. A., et al., eds. *Dynamic and Immobilist Politics in Japan.* Honolulu: University of Hawaii Press, 1988.

White, James W. *The Sokagakkai and Mass Society.* Stanford: Stanford University Press, 1970.

## Economics

Allen, G. C. *A Short Economic History of Modern Japan.* 4th ed. New York: St. Martin's Press, 1981.

Allinson, Gary D. *Japanese Urbanism: Industry and Politics in Kariya, 1872–1972.* Berkeley: University of California Press, 1975.

Clark, Rodney. *The Japanese Company.* New Haven: Yale University Press, 1979.

Cohen, Jerome B. *Japan's Economy in War and Reconstruction.* Minneapolis: University of Minnesota Press, 1949.

Cole, Robert E. *Japanese Blue Collar: The Changing Tradition.* Berkeley: University of California Press, 1971.

Cusumano, Michael A. *The Japanese Automobile Industry: Technology and Management at Nissan and Toyota.* Cambridge, Mass.: Harvard University, Council on East Asian Studies, 1985.

Dore, Ronald P. *British Factory—Japanese Factory: The Origins of National Diversity in Industrial Relations.* Berkeley: University of California Press, 1973.

Fruin, W. Mark. *The Japanese Enterprise System: Competitive Strategies and Comparative Structures.* Oxford: Clarendon Press, 1994.

Gerlach, Michael. *Alliance Capitalism: The Social Organization of Japanese Business.* Berkeley: University of California Press, 1992.

Gordon, Andrew. *The Evolution of Labor Relations in Japan: Heavy Industry, 1853–1955.* Cambridge, Mass.: Harvard University, Council on East Asian Studies, 1985.

Hadley, Eleanor M. *Antitrust in Japan.* Princeton: Princeton University Press, 1970.

Havens, Thomas R. H. *Architects of Affluence: The Tsutsumi Family and the Seibu-Saison Enterprises in Twentieth-Century Japan.* Cambridge, Mass.: Harvard University, Council on East Asian Studies, 1994.

Hein, Laura. *Fueling Growth: The Energy Revolution and Economic Policy in Postwar Japan.* Cambridge, Mass.: Harvard University, Council on East Asian Studies, 1990.

Johnson, Chalmers. *MITI and the Japanese Miracle: The Growth of Industrial Policy, 1925–1975.* Stanford: Stanford University Press, 1982.

Lincoln, Edward J. *Arthritic Japan: The Slow Pace of Economic Reform.* Washington, D.C.: Brookings Institution Press, 2001.

———. *Japan: Facing Economic Maturity.* Washington, D.C.: Brookings Institution, 1988.

Ohkawa, Kazushi, and Henry Rosovsky. *Japanese Economic Growth: Trend Acceleration in the Twentieth Century.* Stanford: Stanford University Press, 1973.

Okimoto, Daniel I. *Between MITI and the Market: Japanese Industrial Policy for High Technology.* Stanford: Stanford University Press, 1989.

Patrick, Hugh, and Henry Rosovsky, eds. *Asia's New Giant.* Washington, D.C.: Brookings Institution, 1976.

Samuels, Richard J. *The Business of the Japanese State: Energy Markets in Comparative and Historical Perspective.* Ithaca: Cornell University Press, 1987.

Yoshino, Michael Y., and Thomas B. Lifson. *The Invisible Link: Japan's Sogo Shosha and the Organization of Trade.* Cambridge, Mass.: MIT Press, 1986.

## Society

Allinson, Gary D. *Suburban Tokyo: A Comparative Study in Politics and Social Change.* Berkeley: University of California Press, 1979.

Beardsley, Richard K., John W. Hall, and Robert E. Ward. *Village Japan.* Chicago: University of Chicago Press, 1959.

Ben-Ari, Eyal. *Changing Japanese Suburbia: A Study of Two Present-Day Localities.* London: Kegan Paul International, 1991.

Bernstein, Gail. *Haruko's World: A Japanese Farm Woman and Her Community.* Stanford: Stanford University Press, 1983.

Bestor, Theodore C. *Neighborhood Tokyo.* Stanford: Stanford University Press, 1989.

Brinton, Mary C. *Women and the Economic Miracle: Gender and Work in Postwar Japan.* Berkeley: University of California Press, 1993.

Cummings, William. *Education and Equality in Japan.* Princeton: Princeton University Press, 1980.

Dore, Ronald P. *City Life in Japan: A Study of a Tokyo Ward.* Berkeley: University of California Press, 1959.

Imamura, Anne. *Urban Japanese Housewives: At Home and in the Community.* Honolulu: University of Hawaii Press, 1987.

Kondo, Dorrine. *Crafting Selves: Power, Gender, and Discourses of Identity in a Japanese Workplace.* Chicago: University of Chicago Press, 1990.

Lebra, Takie. *Above the Clouds: Status Culture of the Modern Japanese Nobility.* Berkeley: University of California Press, 1992.

Long, Susan O. ed. *Lives in Motion: Composing Circles of Self and Community in Japan.* Ithaca, N.Y.: East Asia Program, Cornell University, 1999.

Plath, David. *Long Engagements: Maturity in Modern Japan.* Stanford: Stanford University Press, 1980.

Rohlen, Thomas. *Japan's High Schools.* Berkeley: University of California Press, 1983.

Smith, Robert J. *Kurusu: The Price of Progress in a Japanese Village, 1951–1975.* Stanford: Stanford University Press, 1978.

———. *Japanese Society: Tradition, Self, and the Social Order.* Cambridge: Cambridge University Press, 1983.

Smith, Robert J., and Ella L. Wiswell. *The Women of Suye Mura.* Chicago: University of Chicago Press, 1982.

Tobin, Joseph J., ed. *Re-Made in Japan: Everyday Life and Consumer Taste in a Changing Society.* New Haven: Yale University Press, 1992.

Upham, Frank. *Law and Social Change in Postwar Japan.* Cambridge, Mass.: Harvard University Press, 1987.

Vogel, Ezra F. *Japan's New Middle Class: The Salary Man and His Family.* Berkeley: University of California Press, 1967.

Wagatsuma, Hiroshi, and George DeVos, eds. *Japan's Invisible Race: Caste in Culture and Personality.* Berkeley: University of California Press, 1966.

## Literature

Abe, Kobo. *The Woman in the Dunes.* Trans. E. Dale Saunders. New York: Alfred A. Knopf, 1964.

Agata, Hikari. "The Family Party." In *Unmapped Territories: New Women's Fiction from Japan,* ed. Yukiko Tanaka, pp. 84–119. Seattle: Women in Translation, 1991.

Ariyoshi, Sawako. *The Twilight Years.* Trans. Mildred Tahara. London: Peter Owens, 1984.

Gessel, Van. *The Sting of Life: Four Contemporary Japanese Novelists.* New York: Columbia University Press, 1989.

Gessel, Van, and Tomone Matsumoto, eds. *The Showa Anthology: Modern Japanese Short Stories.* 2 vols. Tokyo: Kodansha, 1985.

Ito, Ken K. *Visions of Desire: Tanizaki's Fictional Worlds.* Stanford: Stanford University Press, 1991.

Kawabata, Yasunari. *Snow Country.* Trans. Edward G. Seidensticker. New York: Alfred A. Knopf, 1956.

Lyons, Phyllis I. *The Saga of Dazai Osamu: A Critical Study with Translations.* Stanford: Stanford University Press, 1985.

Mishima, Yukio. *Acts of Worship: Seven Stories.* Trans. John Bester. Tokyo: Kodansha, 1989.

Mitsios, Helen, ed. *New Japanese Voices: The Best Contemporary Fiction from Japan.* New York: Atlantic Monthly Press, 1991.

Nagai, Kafu. "The Scavengers." In Edward G. Seidensticker, *Kafu the Scribbler: The Life and Writings of Nagai Kafu, 1879–1959,* pp. 339–344. Stanford: Stanfrod University Press, 1965.

Nagatsuka, Takashi. *The Soil: A Portrait of Rural Life in Meiji Japan.* Trans. Ann Waswo. Berekeley: University of California Press, 1993.

Oe, Kenzaburo. *A Personal Matter.* Trans. John Bester. New York: Grove Press, 1968.

Rubin, Jay. *Haruki Murakami and the Music of Words.* London: Harvill, 2002.

Shono, Junzo. *Still Life and Other Stories.* Trans. Wayne P. Lammers. Berkeley: Stone Bridge Press, 1992.

Tanaka, Yukiko, and Elizabeth Hanson, eds. *This Kind of Woman: Ten Stories by Japanese Women Writers, 1960–1976.* Ann Arbor: University of Michigan, Center for Japanese Studies, 1995.

Tanizaki, Jun'ichiro. *The Makioka Sisters.* Trans. Edward G. Seidensticker. New York: Perigee Books, 1981.

Tomioka, Taeko. "Facing the Hills They Stand." In *Japanese Women Writers: Twentieth Century Short Fiction*, ed. Noriko M. Lippit and Kyoko I. Selden, pp. 138–167. Armonk, N.Y.: M. E. Sharpe, 1991.

Treat, John Whittier. *Writing Ground Zero: Japanese Literature and the Atomic Bomb.* Chicago: University of Chicago Press, 1995.

Yasuoka, Shotaro. *A View by the Sea.* Trans. Karen Wigen. New York: Columbia University Press, 1984.

Yoshimoto, Banana. *Kitchen.* Trans. Megan Backus. New York: Simon & Schuster, Pocket Books, Washington Square Press, 1994.

# Postwar Prime Ministers

| PRIME MINISTER | PERIOD IN OFFICE |
| --- | --- |
| Prince Higashikuni | 8/1945–10/1945 |
| Shidehara Kijuro | 10/1945–5/1946 |
| Yoshida Shigeru | 5/1946–5/1947 |
| Katayama Tetsu | 5/1947–3/1948 |
| Ashida Hitoshi | 3/1948–10/1948 |
| Yoshida Shigeru | 10/1948–12/1954 |
| Hatoyama Ichiro | 12/1954–12/1956 |
| Ishibashi Tanzan | 12/1956–2/1957 |
| Kishi Nobusuke | 2/1957–7/1960 |
| Ikeda Hayato | 7/1960–11/1964 |
| Sato Eisaku | 11/1964–7/1972 |
| Tanaka Kakuei | 7/1972–12/1974 |
| Miki Takeo | 12/1974–12/1976 |
| Fukuda Takeo | 12/1976–12/1978 |
| Ohira Masayoshi | 12/1978–7/1980 |
| Suzuki Zenko | 7/1980–11/1982 |
| Nakasone Yasuhiro | 11/1982–11/1987 |
| Takeshita Noboru | 11/1987–6/1989 |
| Uno Sosuke | 6/1989–8/1989 |
| Kaifu Toshiki | 8/1989–8/1991 |

| | |
|---|---|
| Miyazawa Kiichi | 8/1991–8/1993 |
| Hosokawa Morihiro | 8/1993–4/1994 |
| Hata Tsutomu | 4/1994–6/1994 |
| Murayama Tomiichi | 6/1994–1/1996 |
| Hashimoto Ryutaro | 1/1996–7/1998 |
| Obuchi Keizo | 7/1998–4/2000 |
| Mori Yoshiro | 4/2000–4/2001 |
| Koizumi Jun'ichiro | 4/2001– |

# Index

CPSIA information can be obtained
at www.ICGtesting.com
Printed in the USA
LVHW031616271218
601926LV000028/181/P